Improvements
in the quality of working life
in three Japanese industries

Improvements in the quality
of working life
in three Japanese industries

S. Takezawa et al.

International Labour Office   Geneva

ISBN 92-2-103051-2

First published 1982

658.31422
T 136 i Kz.

916236

Printed by the International Labour Office, Geneva, Switzerland

TABLE OF CONTENTS

ACKNOWLEDGEMENTS

This monograph is a product of the two ILO research contracts entitled "Improvements in the Quality of Working Life in Selected Japanese Industries", both entered in 1976. One contract went to the Japan Institute of Labour for the technical assistance, while the other came to the author as co-ordinator of the project. The present author assumes the total responsibility for writing this report.

The author acknowledges with deep appreciation the continuous support and encouragement rendered by Mr. Georges Spyropoulos, Chief, Working Conditions and Environment Department, ILO, who was Chief, Conditions of Work and Life Branch at the time of the initial contact. The author also would like to thank Mr. Joseph Thurman and Miss F.J. Dy who, working closely with Mr. Spyropoulos, kindly helped develop this project from its very infant stage.

In Japan, the Japan Institute of Labour assumed the institutional responsibility for the preparation of industry reports. For this, the present author is particularly grateful to its former president, the late Dr. Ichino Nakayama. The Institute provided research facilities and took care of all the secretarial work. Especially, many thanks are due to Mr. Osamu Hirota, currently Chief, Research and Study Department, without whose warm assistance this project could not have been completed smoothly.

The principal actors in industry report preparation, however, are those labour union leaders and corporate executives who so enthusiastically contributed their time and wisdom to the success of their respective study committees. The names of participating representatives are listed with their affiliations on the page immediately following the acknowledgements. The author is very grateful to the chairmen and members of the committees for their contribution of case reports and for their final comments on the respective industry reports.

Each of the three industry reports was drafted by the present author and submitted to the committee for a final review and approval. Comments and corrections were invited and incorporated in the final version. Unless requested specifically by the members who initially gave the case reports, no alterations have been made in the facts or figures included in each industry report, even to update the data.

The two chapters, Chapters 1 and 5, are written by the author and he is solely responsible for their contents. There has been a delay in the preparation of these chapters, but it is hoped that much of the time gap thus caused since the completion of industry reports is made up by the new materials incorporated in the first and the last chapters.

Mr. Thomas J. Nevins translated the three industry reports from their Japanese originals into English. No doubt his mastery of the two languages and his knowledge of industrial relations in Japan have helped make the three chapters highly readable. The author wishes to thank him warmly for his professional service.

The author's students at Rikkyo University, Tokyo, Japan, helped him at several stages of the project's progress. Especially, many thanks are due to Misses Harumi, Iwanami, Keiko Sato and Eiko Sumi, and Mr. Kazukoshi Matsuse.

Last but not least, much appreciation is due to Miss Keiko Ishikawa for her hard work and devotion in undertaking the secretarial work required for the project.

Shin-ichi Takazawa.

STUDY COMMITTEES

Shipbuilding industry

Chairman	Nobuo Asazawa, Ishikawajima-Harima Heavy Industries Co. Ltd.
Vice-Chairman	Tadavoshi Hisatomi, Zosen Juki Roren (Japan Confederation of Shipbuilding and Engineering Workers' Unions)
Members	Tetsuo Kanazawa, Nippon Kokan Shipbuilding and Heavy Industries Workers' Union
	Yoshimichi Kimura, Sumitomo Shipbuilding and Machinery Co. Ltd.
	Nobukazu Koosaka, Mitsui Shipbuilding and Engineering Co. Ltd.
	Fusao Maruyama, Ishikawajima-Harima Heavy Industries Workers' Union
	Susumu Nagahara, Mitsubishi Heavy Industries Workers' Union
	Hidehiro Nishizawa, Mitsui Engineering and Shipbuilding Workers' Union
	Tadayoshi Satou, Sumitomo Heavy Industries Workers' Union
	Ikuo Shinohara, Nippon Kokan Kabushiki Kaisha
	Mitsuo Suzuki, Mitsubishi Heavy Industries Ltd.
Technical Experts	Tsuyoshi Inagami, Hosei University
	Tsuneo Ono, Japan Institute of Labour

Electrical machinery industry

Chairman	Kiyoshi Imazato, Mitsubishi Electric Corporation
Vice-Chairman	Masaru Fujino, Denki Roren (All-Japan Federation of Electric Machine Workers' Union)

Members	Yukuo Ajima, Mitsubishi Electrical Workers' Union
	Takeshi Fukaya, Labour Union of Hitachi Workers
	Ikuo Hirai, Matsushita Electric Industrial Workers' Union
	Hideto Kinoshita, Hitachi Ltd.
	Seiichi Kume, Nippon Electric Co. Ltd.
	Sokichi Kurihara, Oki Electric Workers' Union
	Akira Ose, Oki Electric Industry Co. Ltd.
	Judoh Shibata, Matsushita Electric Industrial Co. Ltd.
	Isao Yorimitsu, Nippon Electric Workers' Union
Technical Experts	Tsuyoshi Inagami, Hosei University
	Tsuneo Ono, Japan Institute of Labour
	Shunichiro Umetani, Tokyo Gakugei University

Automobile industry

Chairman	Futoshi Fjuii, Nissan Motor Co. Ltd.
Vice-Chairman	Yoshio Enomoto, Confederation of Japan Automobile Workers' Unions
Members	Yasuhiko Fukatsu, Toyota Motor Workers' Union
	Kunitake Goshima, Toyota Auto Body Co. Ltd.
	Kazuyuki Hayashi, Toyota Auto Body Workers' Union
	Hiromi Kosaka, Federation of Japan Automobile Workers' Unions

Takesi Ogata,
Isuzu Motors Workers' Union

Yasuo Ooike,
Toyota Motor Co. Ltd.

Sanshiro Ono,
Isuzu Motors Ltd.

Tadashi Sato,
Toyota Motor Co. Ltd.

Michiaki Shinkai,
Honda Motor Co. Ltd.

Kazuaki Takashima,
Honda Motor Workers' Union

Isao Taniguchi,
Confederation of Japan Automobile Workers'
  Unions

Technical Experts   Tsuyoshi Inagami,
Hosei University

Kazutoshi Koshiro,
Yokohama National University

Tsuneo Ono,
Josai University

Shunichiro Umetani,
Tokyo Gakugei University

Co-ordinator for all the committees

Shin-ichi Takezawa,
Rikkyo University

INTRODUCTION

This concise report gives an account of a study on the changing
patterns of the quality of working life in three major industries in
Japan.   These three industries selected are shipbuilding, electrical
machinery and automobile manufacturing, each of which plays an important role in the Japanese economy, as well as in the present-day
world market.   The period under investigation varies slightly among
industries but generally covers a decade from the late 1960s until
the latter half of the 1970s, a period when active improvements were
made in the quality of working life.

A typical thesis on the working life in Japan begins (and often
ends) with a description of career employment, seniority-based wages
and promotions, enterprise-based unionism, and consensual decision
making.   This report does not deny the significance of such "pillars"
as they apply to the "work ways" of regular male employees in most
large firms.   One can easily argue that even the oil crisis has made
few long-lasting impacts if the focal point of analysis centres
around these features.

Such "comparative" approaches have two pitfalls which could lead
to critical mistakes in understanding the industrial relations process
in Japan.   First, comparative views are bound to be static and tend
to give a picture which grossly ignores change aspects.   As can be
easily inferred from the enormous pace of economic change, Japanese
industrial relations have continued to experience dynamic changes
over the last generation.   Industrial relations in Japan can be
understood best only if the successive accommodations to the changing
environment made continuously by labour, management and governments
are placed in a proper perspective.

Secondly, comparative descriptions tend to give an erroneous
impression that Japanese industrial relations lack universal features
by focusing attention on differences by the very nature of the approach.
Differences thus found may then be accounted for by reference to
mystical cultural origins, thus preventing a serious understanding and
learning for practical ends.   Japanese workers, for example, may be
described as having a peculiar set of needs and aspirations, just as
Japanese management does.

The present study describes the dynamic changes in the working
life as they have occurred in Japanese industry.   An emphasis is
placed on a variety of improvements made in the three industries
during the period when changes took place most actively in relevant
union, management and government programmes.   The study also reveals
that the changes installed in the workplace, mostly through the joint
efforts of unions and management, represent largely the universalistic
values held by industrial workers throughout the world.   Workers'
changing needs and aspirations embodied in the unfolding improvements
in conditions of work will be found by no means peculiar to only
Japanese workers.

This monograph consists of the following five chapters.
Chapter I gives a bird's-eye view of Japan's recent socio-economic
transformation which is essential to understand properly the nature
and scope of changes in the working life in Japan.   The chapter

begins with the early years after the Second World War when, in the state of turmoil, foundations were laid for the forthcoming economic growth and union-management co-operation.   But a major emphasis is placed on the last two decades when the economy and the working life improved much in parallel in Japan.

Chapters II to V respectively deal with the improvements made in the last decade or so in the quality of working life in the ship-building, electrical machinery and automobile industries.   Readers will note in these chapters that the concept of quality of working life is being used broadly, referring to every aspect of the working life where significant improvements have been made from the workers' viewpoints.   This broad interpretation comes from the union management study committee set up for each industry, which at the very beginning of deliberation was given the task of defining the area of exploration under the theme of quality of working life.   Each committee was asked to select whatever areas it regarded as being significant to the improvement of quality of working life in the particular industry.

When the term "quality of working life" was first coined in countries where English was the predominant language, a top priority was frequently given to work organisation and job contents, and improvements in such areas were accepted as improvements in the quality of working life.   Yves Delamotte and Kenneth F. Walker further add a bit of European tinge when they state that the quality of working life draws attention particularly to the "workers' need for meaningful and satisfying work and for participation in decisions that affect their work situation".[1]   Such problem areas produced new issues for management, labour and governments in Europe and North America in the 1960s and early 1970s.

But these definitions may be too narrow in a broader inter-national perspective.   In a wider usage, the quality of working life may embrace all the possible aspects of work-related life, including wages and hours, work environment, benefits and services, career out-look, human relations, etc. that are relevant to worker satisfaction and motivation.[2]   In fact, in its broadest and most abstract usage, the quality of working life means the total aggregation of "values", both material and non-material, derived by a worker through his/her life as a wage or salary earner.   What becomes a critical problem in a particular country at a given time is determined through the acti-vated needs of workers and the prevailing conditions relevant to their need satisfaction.

---

[1] Yves Delamotte and Kenneth F. Walker, "Humanisation of Work and the Quality of Working Life - Trends and Issues", International Institute for Labour Studies Bulletin, No. 11, 1974, p. 4.

[2] Also in English-speaking industrialised nations, the quality of working life is frequently defined broadly.   See, for example, Richard E. Walton, "Criteria for Quality of Working Life" in Louis E. Davis and Albert B. Cherns, The Quality of Working Life, Vol. 1 (New York, The Free Press, 1975), pp. 91-104;   Herbert C. Merton, "A Look at Factors Affecting the Quality of Working Life", Monthly Labour Review,   Vol. 100, No. 10, Oct. 1977, p. 64; Jerome M. Rosow, "Quality of Working Life Developments in the United States", mimeographed, 1981, 28+v pp.

   The approach used in this study has made it possible for both
union and management representatives to choose freely the areas of
working life where, in their joint opinion, the most significant
improvements were made during the previous decade.   It was not
difficult for each committee to reach a consensus on the topics to
be discussed, since they were, in most cases, the areas where both
unions and management had been working together to bring about
improvements within the limits of available resources.   A short
explanation of the developments in other countries known as the
quality of working life, amelioration of conditions of work, industrial democracy, or humanisation of work was given by the present
author when he briefed on the nature of study prior to discussions.

   The topical areas adopted by the three industry committees for
discussions are listed in table 1.   It is clear that the three
industry groups, while sharing some common problems, also had certain
interest areas which were only specific to the respective industries.

   Chapter V summarises the findings from the three industry reports.
Here the priorities given and developments made in the three industries are reviewed in relation to those found in the rest of the
national scene.   When applicable, supplementary facts are provided
in order to update the contents of industry papers.   Finally,
policy implications of the findings will be discussed with special
attention paid to international audience.

Table 1: Major topical areas for study

Shipbuilding industry	Electrical machinery industry	Automobile industry
1. Wages and wage systems	1. Wages and bonuses	1. Wages and wage systems
2. Retirement allowance and pension	2. Retirement system and retirement allowance	2. Retirement system and payments
3. Working hours and holidays	3. Working hours	3. Working hours
4. Employee benefits and services	4. Employee benefits and services	4. Employee benefits and services
5. Safety and health	5. Employment of handi-capped workers	5. Employee education and training
6. Work restructuring schemes	6. Reorganisation of work	6. Humanisation of work
7. Small group activities	7. Small group activities	7. Small group activities and-self management
	8. Worker participation in management	

Note: Order of appearance and wording are not necessarily the same as used in the respective industry reports.

CHAPTER I

THE CHANGING ENVIRONMENT OF WORKING LIFE IN JAPAN

This chapter is written to give the reader some basic understanding of the developments in Japan's industrial relations and
working life during the 1960s and 1970s in order to provide a
proper background against which specific changes in the three
industries may be viewed. The over-all economic and social ends
achieved during the period generally gave Japanese workers a sense
of deep satisfaction and continuous progress, even though business
recessions hit Japan too in 1957-58, 1962, 1964-65, 1970-71 and
1974-75. The last recession, triggered by the oil embargo of 1973,
left the most serious impact. None the less, most Japanese will
admit their pride in the nation's over-all performance, because in
the days of extreme poverty and hunger experienced after the Second
World War, they as youths held really few hopes for the future.

1. Early postwar developments

It took Japan about ten years before the reconstruction from
war destruction became fairly visible. The year 1945 was a
particularly bad year for food supply, with the rice crop only at
45 per cent of a normal year's harvest. There were no imports of
foods under the military occupation, and many civilian and military
repatriates were further crowding the population. Japan was no
exception to the rule that a sudden contraction of resource supply
would inevitably split a society into opposing interest groups.
Psychologically, Japan became a divided country, even though there
were only the poor and the less poor at the time. Many people
became devoted followers of Marxism overnight.

The labour movement, which had been interrupted through suppres-
sion by the military, quickly picked up with the blessing of the
occupation forces. Official statistics show that labour union
members totalled 381,000 at the end of 1945, which jumped to
4,926,000 at the end of 1946.[1] Labour-management relations during
a decade's time after the war were characterised largely by power-
based confrontations. In fact, the year 1952 witnessed a loss of
15,012,000 man-days due to strike action. This is the largest
figure ever recorded in Japan's labour history that has not been
broken until now. The decade also experienced a number of bitter
conflicts between management and union activists, many of whom were
following the Japan Communist Party line of the time. Incidents
involving violence occurred outside workplaces too, which in many
cases were suspected of being connected with extreme radicalists in
the labour movement.

---

[1] Statistical figures used in this chapter are quoted, unless
otherwise noted, from Japan Productivity Centre, Practical Labour
Statistics, 1981 (in Japanese) (Tokyo, Japan Productivity Centre,
1981), 224 pp.

Let us take just one example, which was not atypical at the
time.   In 1950, Hitachi Ltd. went through a series of bitter conflicts, involving an issue of redundancy and a "red purge".   Many
managers were forced through lengthy hours of open-air "collective
bargaining" sessions surrounded by masses of union activists.
Many "lawful" tactics were devised to press managers for their
compromises.   One tactic made use of sharpened spears made of
bamboo.   They were thrust through the clothes of trapped managers,
very carefully so as not to physically hurt them, and were held by
union negotiators so that these managers could not run away from the
scene.   The spears were shaken occasionally to keep the worn-out
managers awake.   However, most managers stood this and other
ordeals courageously.

While chaos still continued, initiatives began to mount to get
things under control among both managers and selected union leaders.
These managers realised that the co-operation and prosperity of
employees were essential to the survival and growth of their company.
In turn, new union leaders became convinced that their company's
survival and growth were vital to the successful achievement of the
union member's own goals.   This recognition of shared objectives
in a long-term perspective gradually penetrated one enterprise after
another, starting around 1950 and continuing sometimes into the
1960s in the private industry.

Establishment of the Japan Productivity Centre in 1955 symbolised the birth of a new era in labour-management relations.   The
Centre spelled out clearly the need for productivity improvement
with union participation, the need for equitable distribution of
gains from productivity improvement and, most importantly, the need
for a no-layoff policy throughout the entire process.   The
"enterprise-consciousness", or a communal concept of corporation,
which had begun to emerge in the preceding few years, was thus given
a societal sanction and encouragement.   Basically, the concept holds
that an enterprise must function as a basic social unit of wealth-
generation and wealth-distribution and that it is the employees,
from managers to production workers who must first share the fate of
this unit.   This acknowledgement of communality of interests among
longstanding work associates was soon to begin to appeal to a
majority of workers in industry.   With the commitment to a no-layoff
agreement, management was in no position but to encourage this
"enterprise-consciousness".

The growth of this "enterprise-consciousness", however, was
sometimes contested bitterly among union circles.   New union leaders,
who endorsed the "enterprise unionism", always had to fight class-
oriented Marxists, who occupied major leadership roles in the existing unions and believed in the eternal struggle against capitalism.
The new union leaders sometimes organised a "second union" with the
help of those members who had been dissatisfied with the existing
leadership.   This, of course, resulted in open conflict between the
"first" and "second" unions, often creating gaps and cleavages
between union members belonging to opposing organisations.   Even
nowadays, such a "first union" may be found in some companies, much
reduced in size but still keeping its ideological posture.   Laws
do not prohibit multiple unions, and in such cases management must
negotiate with both unions.

It took from 10 to 15 years after the war's end for the features
known as characteristics of Japan's industrial relations system
gradually to become stabilised in private industry.   In a way, what

happened was a re-emergence of the "enterprise-consciousness" after
a wartime and postwar interruption. However, it was not confined
to white-collar workers this time, and in fact all the regular
workers were integrated as a social unit. This is clear even from
the fact that the new "enterprise" union organised all the workers,
with only high-level managers excluded, regardless of types of work
or educational background, into a single organisational unit. The
firm establishment of unions as an actor in industrial relations
ensured a proper functioning of power balance, and was probably the
most important factor contributing to the birth of "career employment".

During the same period, two additional developments occurred,
both having contributed substantially to the improvement of social
and economic status of wage earners and the reduction of income
disparities throughout the nation. One was the inauguration of
the Shunto or "Spring Offensive" bargaining mechanism in 1955 under
the leadership of Sohyo. Shunto has since helped to strengthen the
bargaining position of labour in the national scene by carefully
co-ordinating the activities of major industrial unions and
enterprise-based worker organisations. The other was the tightening
labour market particularly that of new school graduates, which
pushed up the starting wages of young entrants enormously. The
continuous shortage of labour in industrial regions generated an
active geographical mobility and helped to level the wage differentials throughout the country.

In 1960, two significant incidents occurred, both of which in
different ways symbolised the changing spirit of the times. One
was the conclusion of a new security treaty with the United States.
Opponents of the treaty conclusion lost in spite of waves of street
demonstrations which resulted in the death of a student and the
resignation of Prime Minister Kishi's cabinet. The other was the
defeat of the Mitsui Coal Miners' Union in the prolonged Miike strike,
which was staged against the proposed "rationalisation" scheme
including curtailment of employment. The union was the last hope
of those who had worked hard for socialisation of the economy in the
earlier years. The two incidents signified the fact that Japan
made a clear choice to strive for further prosperity in collaboration with the West and within the market mechanism.

By 1960, workers' lives had made some progress but the time was
still the beginning of the "electrification" age. In 1960, among
employee households, 69.8 per cent owned sewing machines, 45.9 per
cent owned cameras, 41.3 per cent owned black-and-white television
sets, 36.9 per cent owned washing machines, and 27.6 per cent owned
electric fans; no statistics were gathered yet on colour television
sets, stereo record players, room coolers and automobiles.[1] It was
the year when colour television programmes started. Sony put on the
market the world's first transistorised radio, and Japan National
Railways reduced passenger classes from three to two to meet the
increasing middle-class aspiration of the Japanese. Of course, the
coming years of economic strides were yet beyond the imagination of
most people, including top leaders in business and political circles.

[1] Japan Institute of Labour, Japan Labour Statistics, 1974
(Tokyo, Japan Institute of Labour, 1974), p. 160.

2. Rapid growth of national economy

Between 1955 and 1979, in less than a quarter century, Japan's gross national product increased 24.59 times in nominal terms and 6.31 times in real terms. The annual growth rate of 8.5 per cent includes the "bad" years after the oil crisis, such as 1974 and 1975, when 0.2 per cent and 3.6 per cent net decreases were recorded respectively.

Particularly, significant strides were made by manufacturing industries, where production increased 11.19 times between 1955 and 1979, expanding faster than the total economy. The Japan Productivity Centre estimates that labour productivity in that industry increased 7.80 times during the period.

As a result, some industries and corporations have surpassed American and European competitors in both capital outlay and performance per employee. For example, let us look at the three industries under study. In the electric machinery industry, the 1977 per employee annual sales figures for Hitachi, GE and Siemens were 19,500,000, 12,250,000 and 9,376,000 yen respectively. In the electric applicance industry, the figures for Matsushita, North American and Thorn EMI were 40,272,000, 15,243,000 and 5,887,000 yen. In the automobile industry, Toyota's per capital annual sales were 51,261,000 yen, and Nissan's 41,993,000 yen. Ford and GM recorded respectively 21,200,000 and 18,517,000 yen, whereas in Europe the figures for Benz and Fiat were 14,092,000 and 8,470,000 yen. Comparable figures were not available for the shipbuilding industry where Japan held a 41.1 per cent share in 1977.

Productivity improvements in Japan have resulted through the complex inter-action of various factors. Among the most important are the timely and continuous application of technological innovations, aggressive capital formation and investment policies, financial systems led by major banking institutions, thoroughgoing marketing research and product development, continuous refinement of production techniques, quality control and resource utilisation, careful cultivation of both domestic and foreign markets, effective and flexible management structure and decision making, and a highly trained, motivated and flexible labour force. To put it simply, Japanese industry has been successful in making good use of natural, technical and human resources within the existing geographical, political, social and economic framework with a minimum of historical and traditional constraints. The widespread recognition of Japan's dependence on international trade, both for food and raw materials supply and for the product market to acquire foreign currency, underlies the citizens' tacit agreement on the need of economic strength for survival and of world peace and co-operation.

As the economy improved, the cleavages in society caused by the destructive war and the succeeding poverty and chaos healed gradually but steadily. Although the notion of "Japan, Incorporated" was exaggerated, governments took an active role in formulating priorities and alternatives in social and economic development at both the national and local levels. Union leaders in the private sector came to accept the importance of corporate growth and profits as a source of immediate prosperity and future security of their union members. Within the framework of career employment, to which both management and unions agreed during the preceding period, the growth of an enterprise simply meant to its members not only better wages and increased future security but also a higher social prestige and more opportunities for promotion and personal advancement. Co-operation in achieving shared objectives, which management helped to foster with the collaboration of respective unions, began to give workers a deep sense of pride, satisfaction and accomplishment as time went by.[1]

3. Changes in socio-economic background

During the quarter-century between 1955 and 1979, the total gainfully-employed labour force increased 1.32 times, whereas the total number of employees multiplied 2.13 times. This more rapid increase of employees in the total labour force means in Japan a faster growth of secondary and tertiary industries vis-à-vis primary industries.

The income of wage and salary earners increased sharply. Compensation per employee rose 15.47 times in nominal terms, or 3.63 times in real terms, while consumer prices multiplied 4.23 times during the period. Another source shows for manufacturing establishments with 30 or more employees that nominal wages increased 13.73 times and real wages 3.32 times.

During most of the period, labour shortages prevailed throughout Japan, helping to induce income compression in several different ways. According to the Labour Force Survey conducted by the Bureau of Statistics, Office of the Prime Minister, the rate of unemployment in 1955 was 2.5 per cent, and dwindled to 1.7 per cent in 1960, reaching the all-time low of 1.1 per cent in 1970. Although the economic slowdown following the oil crisis of 1973 and afterwards again increased unemployment, its rate in 1979 stood at 2 per cent.

Malcom Sawyer reports in his study of income distribution in 12 OECD countries that, between 1962 and 1972, pre-tax income distribution showed a trend towards greater equality in Japan.[2] He also reports, "... three countries (Australia, Japan and Sweden) would seem to record the lowest degree of inequality for a post-tax distribution. At the other end of the scale, France is consistently ranked as the country with the most unequal distribution. The rankings given by pre-tax inequality are not very different. Australia and Japan, in that order, rank the least unequal countries on most measures. And France is joined by the United States at the opposite end of the scale".

Particularly important in the Japanese context was the income levelling that took place between young and older workers between worker groups of varying educational backgrounds. Available data show that the following wage squeezes actually took place between selected years for male production workers (nine years of formal schooling) in manufacturing firms with 1,000 or more employees.

---

[1] Another study by the same author, conducted with A.M. Whitehill, shows that, between 1960 and 1976, production workers' attitudes towards management improved markedly in Japan, whereas they generally declined in the US. See S. Takezawa and A.M. Whitehill, Work Ways: Japan and America (Tokyo, Japan Institute of Labour, 1981). The present chapter overlaps in part with a section in its second chapter.

[2] Malcom Sawyer, "Income Distribution in OECD Countries", OECD Economic Outlook, July 1976 (Paris, OECD, 1976), pp. 3-26.

Assuming the starting wage of a new 17 year old worker to be 100, the wage level of those workers between 50 and 59 years of age with 30 or more years of service was 638 in 1961. The figure declined to 366 in 1970 and further dwindled to 297 in 1979.

Education-wise, one indication of the income levelling, or devaluation of higher education in the labour market, may be obtained by comparing starting wages of junior high school graduates (9 years of schooling), senior high school graduates (12 years), and university graduates (16 years). Ministry of Labour surveys show that in 1955 their ratios were 100:161:261. Comparable figures for 1965 were 100:124:174, and they finally became 100:114:141 in 1980. Since wages increase with age at this career stage regardless of types of jobs, there are practically no compensation differences among age-equals with varying educational backgrounds until workers reach their late twenties, when merit-based differentiation usually starts. In these respects, there is no significant difference between large, medium and small firms.

Improvements took place in working hours too. Monthly scheduled hours in all industries (except services) decreased from 178.3 hours in 1955 to 163.1 hours in 1979. The number of hours actually worked per month also declined from 194.8 hours to 177.4 hours. The number of days worked per month was accordingly reduced from 23.8 to 21.9 days. In 1979, 72.9 per cent of workers were covered by a 5-day work week of one form or another, but those who worked under a complete 5-day plan amounted only to 23.5 per cent of the total.

Average life expectancy at birth in 1955 was 63.60 for males and 67.75 for females. These figures rose to 73.46 years and 78.89 years respectively in 1979. This increased longitivity, plus lower birth rates, have been the major causes for the rapid ageing of the total population and of the labour force. The ageing of the labour force has a particular significance in Japan where seniority, in terms of both length of service and chronological age, is such a vital ingredient deeply imbedded in compensation administration, promotion decisions, retirement allowances and pension programmes.

Another significant change which is demographic and social in nature is the reduction of the size of a family. In 1955, an average household in cities with a 50,000 or more population consisted of 4.71 persons. The figure declined to 3.80 in 1979. When labour unions define a "typical" family for calculating "average" family living costs, a nuclear family is nowadays used with parents and two children. Several factors may account for this proliferation of small families. One is the self-initiated and government-assisted postwar drive for family planning under the prevailing severe economic conditions. Another is the mass-scale geographic mobility of the labour force which was triggered by the concentration and expansion of industrial and business activities in several central zones. Still another is the workers' increased incomes which makes it financially possible for each generation of a family to live in separate locations. Finally, the attachment of the older farm generations to their small "liberated" farms seems to have prevented total family migration to cities, since absentee ownership is prohibited under the postwar land reform law.

Educational backgrounds of the labour force have undergone profound changes as a result of the continuing interest in higher education. Available data show that, in 1956, 42.6 per cent of the new graduates from junior high school directly entered the labour market. The figure decreased sharply and came down to only 3.9 per cent in 1980. As a result, the largest source of new factory workers shifted from junior high school graduates to senior high school graduates with 12 years of education behind them. Even among the high school finishers, those who took up jobs immediately after school dwindled, from the peak of 61.3 per cent in 1960 to 42.9 per cent in 1980. Accordingly, university and junior college graduates, whose share among the new school graduates placed on jobs reached 39 per cent in 1980, have lost much of their former prerogatives in the total labour market.

Public investment in social security also advanced during the period. Major headway was made, for example, when the Welfare Annuity Law, which covers most of the employed workforce in the private sector, was amended in 1973. In the case of a "standard" pensioner family, with a husband who paid premiums for 30 years and a wife with no employment record, their monthly pension was 136,050 yen in 1980. As will be seen in the next chapters, most large firms have government-regulated supplementary annuity funds to provide additional benefits. Some firms also operate voluntary corporate annuity programmes, covering both managers and workers under the same plan. The traditional lump-sum retirement allowance, which is subject to collective bargaining, usually amounts to approximately three years' wages when a production worker retires after 30 years' service.

4. Higher aspirations in life

While workers' economic and material desires were being increasingly met as the total economy continued its expansion, new dimensions of psychological needs and aspirations began to unfold in the workplace and in society as a whole. This means, on the one hand that workers have continued to place a priority on wage increases to meet their expanding desires for new commodities and services. In fact, general "base-ups" and improved material benefits have never lost their importance on the unions' bargaining agenda. But, on the other hand, workers have begun to add new items and dimensions in their demands for improvements. Such improvements may have been simply dismissed as "luxuries" if it had been a decade or two ago.

The first symbolic case was the rise of "my-home-ism" in the early 1960s. At the outset, "my-home-ism" was frowned upon by most management and union leaders as it began to affect younger generations. Concerned managers thought the new trend was a challenge to the all-important, sacred dedication to work. Devoted union leaders suspected that the new fever might erode the basis of union solidarity and militancy. Both positions, however, lost support and the enjoyment of family life has acquired a fair share in the societal value system. A study conducted in 1976 showed that 64 per cent of Japanese workers subscribed to the view that work and personal lives are equally important, whereas only 20 per cent supported that view in the United States.[1]

One key concept, _ikigai_, came to be a focal point in the discussion of newly activated psychological needs, particularly among the youth around the middle of the 1960s. This concept was defined

---

[1] S. Takezawa and A.M. Whitehill, ibid., p. 59.

by Mieko Kamiya as the satisfaction of psychological needs for
existence-fulfilment, change and variety, future anticipation,
human inter-action, freedom, self-actualisation, and meaning and
valuation.[1] In essence, pursuit of a life full of _ikigai_ means
seeking a life worth living; a life that suits the individual
best; a life that is unique to him or her; a life that meets
personal value requirements; a life worthy of committed efforts.
This increased concern with non-material needs was most salient among
young workers at the beginning of the 1970s. Such workers sincerely
sought enriched _ikigai_ in their total lives. As part of this pursuit, they also sought _hatarakigai_ (work-related _ikigai_) in their
working lives and _varigai_ (performance-related _ikigai_) in performing
their tasks.

Another important non-material goal continuously pursued during
the whole postwar period is egalitarianism of a middle-class nature-
Repeatedly, the annual surveys conducted by the Prime Minister's
Office show that more than 90 per cent of the national sample believe
that they belong to the middle class in living standards.[2] The
desire to be equal with others (hitonami-shugi) also found expres-
sion in the demands of labour unions and other social groups for
elimination of previously existing discrimination against certain
groups and individuals. The most successful change seems to have
been the elimination of status differences between blue- and white-
collar workers, which started in the immediate postwar years and
became nearly complete in the 1960s. Nowadays, all the regular
employees in most large companies are monthly salaried, use the
same facilities and are covered by the same benefit plans.

The desire on the part of workers to be equal with others has
also made an impact on promotion and organisational practices. An
accelerated application of meritocracy (noryokushugi), for example,
provided the formerly underprivileged with opportunities for
advancement while depriving the overprivileged of their unjustified
advantages in job promotion and compensation. This management
policy to encourage and reward willing, able, but hitherto less-
privileged individuals (largely due to a lack of proper educational
background) was overwhelmingly welcome by blue-collar workers when
announced and implemented in the early 1960s. In fact, this sort
of social dynamism was often behind the phenomenal growth of enterprises, particularly medium and small ones, throughout the nation
during the period.

Another management response to the rising aspirations as to the
quality of working life has been the introduction of small-group
participatory schemes whereby production workers take a key, con-
structive role in solving production-related problems. Among the
best-known schemes is the QC (Quality Control) Circle movement
which originated in the early 1960s as the formation of voluntary
worker groups to assist engineers in ensuring better quality standards. Nowadays, such problem-solving groups are found through-o
out the manufacturing industry, and also in some of the tertiary
industries. In recent years, this "technique" is accepted as a new
Japanese contribution to the world of management, being "exported"
to other industrial countries as "Q Circles".

---

[1] Mieko Kamiya, On the Subject of Ikigai (in Japanese) (Tokyo,
Misuzu Shobo, 1966), pp. 43-58.

[2] The triannual surveys conducted by the Economic Planning
Agency, which use a slightly different wording for a similar question,
produce somewhat smaller percentages for "middle classes".

In essence, the continuous economic development has entailed changes in the workers' lifestyle, values and aspirations. Workers have become less simplistic, more diversified in life goals, richer in appreciation of individual values, less tolerant of inequality and more demanding in seeking opportunities for self-expression. Many, though not all, of these changes have been incorporated in revised management policies and union-management practices. Certain pressure areas have remained unattended, however, leaving some tensions in society and in the workplace.

5. Disturbances and adjustments

As the growth of economy got on to the track around 1960, the field of industrial relations ceased to be the most troubled major problem area in social relations. In fact, many workers in the large-scale private sector turned increasingly to the right on the political spectrum. Industrial conflicts of the magnitude witnessed during the immediate postwar period were never repeated up until the first oil crisis. Even then, although considerable increases were recorded for man-days lost due to labour disputes in 1974 and 1975, violence was no longer an accompaniment of industrial conflicts. The systematic functioning of actors in industrial relations, such as management and union organisations, governmental institutions and political parties, has apparently produced a self-sufficient, autonomous problem-solving process.

But the single-minded economic expansionism of the 1960s created social problems in several unexpected areas that had not been covered sufficiently by the network of legislation and institutions developed earlier. Sometimes, focus upon an imported problem served as a catalyst, providing an outlet for latent dissatisfactions and frustrations. Sometimes, reaction to such issues travelled quick and far like a contagious disease. The two most important movements with origins outside the country were the anti-Vietnam-war movement and a student movement on university campuses in the latter 1960s. But most other problems had origins in the domestic scene, directly resulting, though to varying degrees, from the rapid economic growth itself.

One problem that has long plagued the wage and salary earners newly migrating into urban industrial areas is the continuous rise in housing costs. As the demand for self-owned houses grew as a result of the rising affluence, the agricultural land reform implemented after the Second World War proved increasingly to be a bottleneck to an accelerated, smooth supply of housing sites. Most farmers around cities preferred not to sell their farms, merely waiting for the land price to rise further. As a result, assistance for home ownership became one of the most serious concerns to management, unions and governments throughout the 1960s and 1970s. Ironically, rising land prices were less of a social problem as a large portion of the total population comes to acquire their own property, however meagre in physical size. Then the owner will, in turn, gain by price hikes. In 1975, a national average of newly acquired housing lots was $225 m^2$ in size, and that of newly built homes was $94 m^2$.

During the rapid growth period, most other social issues did not affect workers' lives directly. Even the rise of consumer prices was swallowed relatively easily, because wages continued to rise even faster. Between 1955 and 1974, prior to the effect of the first oil shock being felt, consumer prices rose 2.90 times,

whereas nominal wages multiplied 8.88 times, allowing real wages
to register a substantial growth of 3.05 times or 6.1 per cent per
annum.   Other outstanding social issues include conflicts between
such parties as pollution victims and polluting companies, National
Railways (Shinkansen) and track-side residents (noise pollution),
nuclear power plants and local citizens, high-rise builders and
neighbourhood residents (sunshine rights), Narita Airport Authority
and nearby farm owners (compulsory purchase of land), and business
firms and consumers (consumerism).   But most workers and unions
in the private sector remained unaffected by such conflicts.

    A major blow hit labour-management relations shortly after the
oil embargo of 1973, when the whole economy had to readjust itself
to the predicted slower pace of growth.   Redundancy became a major
issue in many companies that, with a few exceptions, had until then
continued to enjoy a high-gear growth for nearly two decades.
Although direct layoffs were undertaken by only few companies,
practically all the companies introduced other measures designed to
achieve "employment adjustment".   The most severe one was to
encourage early retirement on a voluntary basis, to which most
unions reluctantly agreed.

    There was even a cry that the Japanese style of management
characterised by career employment came to an end.   This sensation-
al diagnosis proved false in a short time, but manpower reduction,
through one means or another, did take place even in many leading
firms.   One study reports that during the four years between April
1974 and March 1978, 74 per cent of 250 major firms studied experienced a reduction in total employment.[1]   At the end of March 1974,
these 250 companies had 2.32 million employees on their payrolls,
but the figure dropped by 7.5 per cent to 2.14 million after four
years.   The 185 companies registered a net reduction of employment
lost a total of some 211,000 workers.

    Early retirement occurred mostly to older workers.   This was
upsetting to them because many of them believed that they deserved
something better, for they were the ones who had helped most in the
postwar reconstruction of their firms.   Furthermore, as will be
seen in the following chapters, many unions had either begun negotiations or already won concessions on postponement of compulsory
retirement age from management, prior to the oil shock.   It was
believed to be one of the ways to share productivity gains in
society.   The traditional years of age no longer seemed appropriate
as national longevity figures rose, from 50.06 in 1947 to 70.49
in 1972 for males at birth.   This extension of retirement age
picked up its momentum again only towards the late 1970s.

6. Summary

    Over the past three decades, the over-all socio-economic
conditions in Japan have generally taken a course which is favourable
to a continuous improvement of the quality of working life.   When
the transition is viewed in a time perspective, however, it immediately becomes clear that what existed in the late 1940s in the area
of industrial relations was not at all predictive of what was to
follow.   Choices were widely open then, and few people anticipated
correctly what was to come 30 years later.   Indeed, the course
actually taken seems to have been a very narrow path that could have
been missed by anybody at any moment.

---

[1] Sangyo Rodo Chosasho, Changes in Employment in Major Private
Firms Since the Oil Shock (in Japanese) (Tokyo, Sangyo Rodo Chosasho,
1978), 16 pp.

But the fact remains that both labour and management have managed to follow this path to foster a better environment for the quality of working life at every next step.   Both sides have shared the view that a better quality of working life is an asset to both, and a highly competitive economic organisation is the only long-range source of an improved quality of working life.   Particularly, the 1960s and early 1970s were the period when accelerated efforts were made by management and unions jointly to improve the working lives of employees.

The three chapters that follow discuss specific efforts made by unions and management to improve the quality of working life in shipbuilding, electric machinery and automobile industries preceding the decade preceding the time of study.   Here, significant aspects of the quality of working life as seen by workers are first defined by the joint union-management study committee organised for each industry.   Specific cases of improvements are then brought up and discussed that formed the basis of the respective industry report.   Each chapter then ends with a short section on summary and perspectives.

CHAPTER II

THE QUALITY OF WORKING LIFE IN THE
SHIPBUILDING INDUSTRY

This report consists of a number of examples indicative of improvements in the quality of working life brought about by labour and management in the Japanese shipbuilding industry over the last ten years. The research reflects discussions and case studies examined by a committee consisting of both corporate and union representatives. The research took place from December, 1976 to June, 1977.

The initial problem which the study committee tried to solve at its first meeting was that of defining concepts such as "the quality of working life" or "the humanisation of work". It soon became clear that the meaning of these terms as interpreted by certain specialists in English speaking countries was much too limited.

Under normal circumstances any worker knows, more than the professionals in the field, what he desires and expects of his working life. The labour union partially accepts the burden of the worker to fulfil his desires and assists in these efforts. Management also is aware that in order to create a dynamic and productive organisation, it must respect the needs and demands of workers.

The study committee began by attempting to determine what the workers of the Japanese shipbuilding industry have been truly looking for over the last ten years. The workers under consideration were members of the labour unions of the shipbuilding enterprises. This means that all full-time, regular employees are included, with the exception of middle and upper management. White collar, blue collar, professionals and lower ranking supervisors are thus considered workers. Among company and union committee members, it was not long before consensus was reached as to the improvements which workers are truly seeking. We agreed and confirmed that improvements in the quality of working life in the shipbuilding industry have taken place in the following areas:

- traditional working conditions;

- employee benefits and services;

- safety and health;

- work restructuring schemes;

- small-group activities.

During the last decade, along with many other Japnese industries, shipbuilding experienced high growth. This was accompanied by increased employment, with many young workers added to the workforce. There was notable improvement in wages and other working conditions as well as in employee benefits and service programmes. The workforce benefited from widespread progress in basic safety and hygiene conditions, and improvements took place in work organisation. Some of these developments were an outcome of union initiatives; others are products of action taken by management.

The study committee decided that it would be unfair to exclude any one of these topics. Therefore, for each area, the committee reviewed in detail a representative case concerning each topic, and then exchanged information of related cases in other companies. This was finally evaluated from both the labour and management point of view. It was agreed that the research should be undertaken in this way.

In the Japanese shipbuilding industry, especially among the leading enterprises, the technical requirements and working conditions vary only slightly, if at all. There is, moreover, adequate communication between labour and management at various levels within and outside corporate boundaries.

The study committee developed the different themes thoroughly. There was such an abundance of information presented at each meeting, that it was necessary to painstakingly select material for retention. There were virtually no criticisms of efforts made by the enterprises.

The present report can be thought primarily as a description of the actual record attained in terms of improvement in the quality of working life over the past ten years in the shipbuilding industry. It will be left to the reader to make the appraisal; to determine if there are some lessons to be learned, or whether there is room for criticism.

We begin this report by providing a brief introduction to the state of industrial and labour relations as they exist in the Japanese shipbuilding industry.

1. The Japanese shipbuilding
    industry and labour-
    management relations

    (a) The Japanese shipbuilding
         industry

Over the last 20 years the tonnage of Japanese merchant vessels produced has been the greatest in the world. In recent years, approximately 50 per cent of the world's ships have been constructed in Japanese shipbuilding yards.

From the middle of the nineteenth century until 1945, the Japanese shipbuilding industry, rather than a business, was fostered and supported through a sense of mission that this was the only way to protect and maintain the nation. When the four ships of Commodore Perry opened Japanese ports for foreign trade in 1853, there were only wooden vessels in Japan. In order to become a maritime power, the build-up of naval strength was of the most pressing importance. For a nation of scarce resources, there was also the urgent task of putting a merchant marine afloat.

With this type of background, it is easy to understand how national consensus supported the high priority placed on the shipbuilding industry up until the Second World War. The highest quality steels were developed for use in the warships, as were the most sophisticated weapons. In the same fashion, the top engineering students at the colleges chose to make their careers in the shipbuilding industry. The shipbuilding yards were almost completely destroyed during the war, but the technical ingenuity and skills of the engineers survived.

It becomes clear then, that the chief explanation for the spectacular growth of the Japanese shipbuilding industry after the war lay in advanced technical innovations and expertise. Among the technological processes developed or widely applied and improved in Japan were welding and block construction methods, advanced fitting work, precise and exacting production control, computer controls, automated equipment, and economical ship forms (short and stocky type). These processes and methods are now largely employed in other shipyards throughout the world.

Along with superior advancements in technology, there was another major cause of rapid development - a high level of capital investment in plant and equipment. The increase in world oil consumption of course, did much to promote the production of large-scale tankers. Disturbances in the Middle East also tended to lead to a widespread usage of the larger scale tankers. Until the coming of the oil shock, it was Japan that most aggressively pursued high capital investment in production facilities of large-scale vessles. Eight of the ten largest shipyards in the world are located in Japan.

This type of rapid advancement and growth of technological innovation and investment in plant and equipment resulted in strengthening the international competitive position of the Japanese shipbuilding industry. Construction time was shortened, production deadlines were strictly observed and construction costs reduced. Construction capability of large-scale ships in other countries was extremely limited. Under these competitive conditions, the Japanese shipbuilding industry developed steadily right through the oil crisis of the fall of 1973, until the worldwide recession set in.

As the severest recession of the postwar era took hold, however, there came a worldwide, and extremely sharp reduction in orders for new ships. There are prospects that even greater stagnation of long-run demand will prevail. This has been a blow to the Japanese shipbuilding industry, and a whole range of countermeasures, including employment reductions have been underway. There still exists, however, a real edge in international competition in favour of Japan in terms of quality, cost, and payment terms and conditions. The problem of promoting harmonious relations with the other countries having highly advanced shipbuilding industries is an important and growing concern.

(b) Labour relations in the
      shipbuilding industry

Shipbuilding was one of the industries to be highly unionised soon after the war. It took some time, however, before a unified industrial union like that observable today took shape. As in other private industries, the original basic organisational unit of unions in the shipbuilding industry was in the individual enterprise, or production facility. In immediate postwar years, there were two sizable organisations at the nationwide industrial level, each competing with the other. At the time, 75 per cent of total union membership was affiliated with Zenzosen (All Japan Shipbuilding and Machine Workers' Union), while the remainder were a part of Zenkoku Zosen Rodo Kumiai Rengokai (National Federation of Shipbuilding Workers' Unions) under the Sodomei (General Confederation of Labour) umbrella.

Developments in the ensuing period are noted in figure 1.
Put simply, the former main force and movements leaning politically
to the left, which professed socialistic ownership of industry,
became extremely weak.   At the same time the former Sodomei line
industrial centre, has become the overpowering force.   This type
of transition is not at all an exception in Japan's postwar labour
movement.   Similar types of development are observable in many of
the major private industries, including electric appliances, automobile, steel and electric power.

The Zosen Juki Roren (Zenkoku Zosen Jukikai Rodokumiai
Rengokai;   Japan Confederation of Shipbuilding and Engineering
Workers' Unions) of today, has about 230,000 members.   Adherents
of the once influential Zenzosen have decreased to as few as 10,000
members.   Zosen Juki Roren is a leading member of Domei (Zen-Nihon
Rodo Sodomei;   Japanese Confederation of Labour), the major national centre for private industrial unions.   It is also a powerful
force in the IMF-JC (International Metalworkers' Federation -
Japan Council).

Collective bargaining is carried out at the company labour-
management level.   A Shipbuilding Industry Labour-Management
Conference was established in 1969 and convened between the Shipbuilders' Association of Japan, the employers' group, and Zosen
Juki Roren.   Periodic discussions take place there concerning
long-term industrial forecasts and trends.   In making decisions on
working conditions both groups are limited to asserting only indirect influence in terms of providing information, co-ordination
and adjustment, and indirect leadership.   In reality, however,
this upper organisational structure is intended to fulfil a
mediating role.   At the individual firm level labour and management apparently possess only a small area of freedom within which
they are expected to reach consensus.   For example, at the negotiation on working conditions held once each year in the spring and
at the bonus negotiation held in the summer, the eight leading shipbuilding corporations and the labour unions of each company, agree
almost simultaneously to almost the same working conditions.

At many firms, collective bargaining proceeds without work
stoppages.   Furthermore, at all levels, there are opportunities
for various types of negotiations and exchange.   At the company
level, in addition to collective bargaining, several times a year
union-management consultation takes place, in which management and
labour leaders exchange information.   At such times, the company
explains management policies, and labour describes its activities
and plans to the corporation.   There is also union-management consultation at the plant or local branch level as well as collective
bargaining.   Several committee meetings of labour and management
are also held at various levels handling such special topics as
safety and health.

2.   Traditional working conditions

Recently the labour union has shown an interest in the
"Humanisation of Work", as representing an aspect of improving
working conditions.   Consequently, it seems fitting to examine
this in the context of developments in wages, yearly bonuses,
retirement allowance systems, fixed retirement age and working
hours.

(a) Wages and wage systems

The standard wages of shipbuilding industry workers from 1965
to 1976 (not including overtime or work performed on holidays)
appear in table 1.   These are real wages, not nominal, and represent wages after deduction of the consumer price index.   In the
ten year period from 1966 shown on this chart, we see that real
wages increased by 1.7 times.   According to the Monthly Labour
Survey,* the monthly wages of the workers in manufacturing companies
of 500 workers or more increased by 1.8 times in real terms from
1966 to 1975, thus the shipbuilding rate is slightly less than the
average.

Wage increases in the shipbuilding industry, however, can on
the contrary be considered to be fairly high.   The reason is that
throughout this period the average age in the manufacturing industry
generally increased, while in contrast, in the shipbuilding industry
the average age and years of service both decreased.   In the shipbuilding industry in 1966 the average age was 34.9 years while by
1975 it declined to 33.9 years.   Years of service also decreased
slightly from 11.7 years to 11.6.   Reductions in these two figures
in a given industry is an indication that it is a growth industry,
and it also would follow that the industry's average increase
wages would naturally be lower when compared with that of a low-
growth industry.   Therefore, a rise in real wages of 1.7 times can
rather be called a high rate of increase.   Of course those workers
employed throughout this period experienced an increase in age and
seniority.   Therefore, the wage increase during this period of
almost all the workers must have been considerably more than 1.7
times.

The yearly bonus, which is a standard industrial relations
practice in Japan, also increased during the period in the shipbuilding industry.   In 1966 the yearly bonus recieved by labour
union members was 161,466 yen, the equipment of 4.3 months of
standard monthly wages.   In 1975, the sum of 657,119 yen was paid.
This amounted to 4.8 times standard regular wages for the year.

Applying the following formula, Zosen Juki Roren has made an
attempt to calculate the actual hourly pay of a union member including fringe benefits.   The $0.95 of 1966 became $4.43 in 1975.
These figures do not include overtime.

(standard wages + fringe benefits) x 12 + yearly bonus ÷

total yearly working hours

dollar exchange rate = amount paid per hour

1966

$$\frac{(¥37,646 + ¥7,541) \times 12 + ¥161,466}{2,072} \div 360 = \$0.94$$

1975

$$\frac{(¥138,558 + ¥35,704) \times 12 + ¥657,119}{1,968} \div 308 = \$4.53$$

---

* Ministry of Labour.

An even more important improvement was won by the labour unions during the period. This consisted of an improvement in the system of payment and was introduced beginning in 1968 in all the companies. Until that time monthly salaries in the shipbuilding industry were paid to white collar workers, while blue collar workers were paid by the day. The system may be viewed in part as a vestige of the Edo Era in which the Samurai established such a class system. The labour unions demanded an end to it and were successful. The details of the reform measure are as follows:

1. All workers were to be paid by the month with the status distinction eliminated between blue and white collar workers.

2. In distinguishing and classifying workers, the comparative weight of educational background and seniority was to be reduced with a trend toward more emphasis placed on payment by job content and ability.

3. The considerable difference in pay between blue and white collar in favour of the latter group was almost entirely eliminated.

4. Minimum guarantees were built into wages on the basis of age, assuring that for a given age a certain standard of living would always be maintained.

5. A guarantee of yearly promotional raises was established. Before the reform this was only offered to white collar staff.

6. It became possible for workers to pursue more actively their general education and technical training.

(b) Retirement allowance and
     pension

The labour unions also won an increase in the compulsory retirement age. The unions began negotiating for this in 1973, and from 1975 were successful in delaying retirement to 58 years from the previous 55. In Japan there are many workers who feel that they have a duty and right to work until 65 years of age. Consequently, delaying the guarantee of employment in this way is thought to be a measure improving the quality of working life. If an individual does quit his present job, he often finds himself in unaccustomed surroundings, often with inferior working conditions. He may even face the alternative of unemployment. The labour unions had demanded a postponement of retirement until age 60. Although they achieved only a three-year delay, it came before retirement postponements in other industries.

The lump-sum retirement payment, a rather peculiar practice in Japan, also witnessed considerable increases during the period (see table 2). According to one calculation, in 1966 the retired worker with 30 years of service and 55 years of age received a lump-sum payment of 2,456,000 yen. At the exchange rate of the time this came out to US$6,800. By 1975, when one retired under the same conditions he received 7,239,384 yen, equivalent to US$23,500. It is clear that lump-sum retirement payments increased significantly. In 1975, it became possible to work until 58, which resulted in even greater real gains in lump-sum retirement payments.

During this decade, however, the ratio of the retirement
allowance to regular monthly wages decreased.   The ratio has
traditionally indicated the balance of power between labour and
management in the determination of retirement allowances.   In our
previous example, the 1966 retirement allowance, equivalent to 74
months of regular monthly salary, corresponds to only 52 months in
1975, although the actual amount increased to nearly 3 times.
This, however, has a relationship to the decrease in the weight of
the lump-sum retirement payment, the traditional source which
guaranteed the standard of living after retirement.   To put it
more exactly, along with the postponement of retirement age, progress made in the spread of home ownership, and better government
pension systems, have all contributed to reducing the relative
importance of lump-sum retirement payments.

Let us look for example at public welfare pension insurance.
The public pension for workers was established in 1942, but improvements within the system had not always been forthcoming.   It was
not until 1973, the year to "get on with social welfare", that
rapid progress took place.   According to calculations of the
Zosen Juki union, in 1976 when a worker of 35 years of service
retires at age 60, the yearly total pension amount for a married
couple to live on is 2,109,000 yen.   This means that they are
receiving nearly US$600 per month.   At present there are few
retirees receiving this benefit amount, but there can be no doubt
that the improvement in national pension benefits has drastically
reduced the dependence of present day workers on lump-sum retirement payments.

(c) Working hours, days off and holidays

Labour union efforts were also directed toward reducing the
number of working hours.   In 1966 in the shipbuilding industry
there were regularly 69 days off per year and 296 working days.
There was an 8 hour working day with 7 actual working hours, making
for total annual working hours of 2,072.   In 1969, Ishikawajima-
Harima Heavy Industries was the first to employ the 2-day weekend
on alternating weeks, making 94 days off per year.   The other
companies instituted the same pattern of increased holidays one
after another.

The second round began in 1971.   All of the major shipbuilding companies simulataneously adopted a complete two-day weekend
system.   As a result yearly holidays increased to 119 in 1975 and
yearly working days became 246.   National and other holidays are
included, however, within this figure.   From 1966, within a very
few years, these measures designed to increase holidays resulted in
an increase of 50 holidays per year in the shipbuilding industry.
The maximum of paid vacations is 20 days per year.   During this
period the years of seniority qualifying a worker to receive this
maximum were also reduced.   Marriage leave, maternity leave and
absence from work for mourning leave were also increased due to the
demands and efforts of labour unions.

During the decade, however, labour and management co-operated
together so as to avoid any loss in productivity.   For example,
when the two-day weekend was introduced, the labour unions agreed
to increase the actual working hours of each day.   In this manner,
the previous seven actual working hours became eight.   Therefore,

yearly working hours decreased only from 2,072 to 1,968, and no extreme decrease was observable. Moreover, management guranteeed at least the amount of former regular wages. Management strictly promised that a decrease in working hours and days, would not lead to a decrease in income. This commitment was kept.

In addition, labour and management have practiced mutual give and take in a number of areas. For example, the labour unions have co-operated in establishing strict observance of starting and finishing times and in improving workshop attendance. The unions have also agreed to the employment of a new shift system never before tried, with the purpose of making deadlines on repairs and overhauling of rush jobs. On the other hand, management has met labours' demands for a 30 per cent overtime rate, although the labour standards legislation calls for only 25 per cent. More-over, the rates for holiday work and night work were also raised.

An interesting experiment concerning working hours is the flextime system carried out by Sumitomo Shipbuilding and Machinery Co., Ltd. The demand for this was made by the labour union in 1974. It passed through the testing stage in 1975, and is now practised at four research and sales facilities. The major pur-pose is to boost work efficiency, to improve mutual relations in the workplace and to make additional time available for leisure. This is possible by allowing voluntary and self-imposed control in the areas subject to flextime - technology, administration and sales.

The system is presently applied to approximately 1,500 em-ployees and managers out of 13,000 members of Sumitomo Shipbuilding and Machinery Co., Ltd. These workers are free to select and regulate their own hours, with the exclusion of core working hours. Even during the test, over 70 per cent of the workers gave their approval. Today as well, both labour and management feel that flextime is well suited for the daily living of office-type workers in an urban environment. The corporation, however, has no inten-tion of applying and expanding this system further.

In other unions as well, there is a slight interest in adopt-ing flextime. Labour and management, however, are for the most part not in favour. The major reason is that it is felt to be difficult to apply to the blue collar workshop. Flextime defi-nitely has merits for both the individual and the firm, and is possible to apply to people engaged in office administration, research and sales. Since it is necessary first to improve the environmental conditions of blue collar workers, however, there is a strong feeling that the introduction of such a system which bene-fits only white collar workers including managers, would be unfair.

3. Employee benefits and services

The employee benefits and services of the shipbuilding indus-try are an important part of working conditions. The majority of these services are determined and decided in terms of contents and budget appropriations through negotiations between labour and man-agement. These expenditures if converted into a monthly amount correspond to about 20 per cent of fixed monthly pay. Among those outlays, approximately half is legally stipulated and required to be disbursed as welfare service. Formerly, the percentage of welfare costs was lower than the amount required legally. Recently,

however, this trend is beginning to slightly reverse itself.
Between 1966 and 1975, as is made clear in table 3, the employee
benefits and services outlays of the shipbuilding industry have
increased nearly five times nominally.

Due to having absorbed many young workers for manning the new
facilities and shipyards it became necessary to invest large amounts
of capital in new housing, recreation, training and other projects.
This situation was somewhat similar in all the shipbuilding companies. Let us here pursue some of the developments by concentrating primarily on the experience of Mitsui Shipbuilding and Engineering Co., Ltd.

(a) Stability and improvement
     in the standard of living

Mitsui Shipbuilding and Engineering Co., Ltd. spent about 5
billion yen on new capital investment for workers' housing in the
ten-year period from 1965.   This increased bachelor housing from
1,667 to 4,288 units.   Company housing for families increased from
1,545 units to 2,825.   In the latter half of the period, however,
there were some revisions of the system as demands and desires for
private home ownership began to increase.   In the present housing
reserve fund and deposit system, interest is 9 per cent and up to
3 million yen may be saved per worker.   Housing loan financing
differs somewhat with years of service and the region, but the maximum that can be borrowed is 6 million yen at 3.5 per cent interest,
payable within 20 years.   Furthermore, with the guarantee of the
company, it becomes possible to borrow from banks as well.   In this
way, then, a man does not build his home after retirement, as was
previously the case, using the lump-sum retirement payment.   Rather
it has now become the norm to build a home while still employed.

For the purpose of providing assistance in property accumulation, there is the Property Accumulation Savings System.   The savings deposit plan is a special system made possible through legislation introduced by the Ministry of Labour in 1974.   Interest is
exempt from income tax calculation and the plan is employed at
Mitsui Shipbuilding and Engineering Co., Ltd. among others.   The
same corporation in 1968 established a special stock purchase programme whereby employees can buy up to 10,000 yen per month of their
company's stock.   The company matches this with a 5 per cent subsidy as a measure of encouragement.   A similar plan is practiced
at Mitsubishi, Hitachi, and Kawasaki Heavy Industries and at Nippon
Kokan.   Some 15-50 per cent of the employees participate.

As for the traditional area of employee services, there are
company cafeterias and stores.   At all of the shipbuilding companies such activities continue to be practiced.   Their relative
significance, however, seems to be declining.   In Mitsui Shipbuilding and Engineering Co., Ltd., there is a consumers' co-
operative.   The company provided the plot of land.   In the areas
of real estate, insurance, sightseeing and drivers' education, there
are independent affiliated companies which provide the services.
These companies also serve as a second place of work for the
retirees.   In this way then, employee service activities in the
area affecting the workers everyday way of life, have been subject
to a trend departing from the direct control of the company.

We have already commented on the role of the public social security plan in protecting the standard of living of workers after retirement.   At Mitsui Shipbuilding and Engineering Co., Ltd., in addition to this, a private pension fund has been established which is paid by contributing part of the retirement allowance and from deposits made while still working.   This is an optional system. Since it was widely reformed in 1975, subscribing members can receive a monthly payment of 80,000 yen in addition to the national pension.   Payment is made from any time stipulated by the member between the ages of 58-64 until 75 years of age.   In addition, after 75 the company will take on the burden of paying the entire amount of 40,000 yen pension per month until the time of death.

The retired of Mitsui Shipbuilding and Engineering Co., Ltd. have formed a club-type organisation at both the company and union level.   Their major purpose is to cultivate and maintain psychological bonds.   The labour union of the company is also currently planning to set up a project group of "old boys".   If they are successful, they will be in a position to subcontract simple routine work from the company.   This might include such work as the administration of the employee service facilities or the beautification of company grounds surrounding the physical plant.   This would offer an opportunity for the retired personnel to continue working. The same type of experiment is also being carried out in other firms.

(b)   Countermeasure against
        emergency disasters

With the exception of companies located in large cities, the major Japanese companies have displayed a trend towards building up medical facilities.   While this trend continues in the shipbuilding industry as well, rather than concentrating on treating an injury or sickness, these days the emphasis is on promoting everyday measures to ensure health and to early detection of sickness and disease. The firms provide health and diagnostic facilities far exceeding the standards set by the law, and families are enjoying more and more coverage.   The emphasis placed on early discovery and treatment is applied increasingly to diseases common to middle- and old-aged people.

The mutual aid associations began with the assumption that workers should help and support each other in marriage, childbirth, injury and sickness, death, fire disaster, damage from wind, water or other elements, and in time of retirement, to mention a few. Currently, such services exist as a mixture primarily of a variety of corporate, union and independent activities and funds.   There is, however, really little new growth and expansion observable at present.   This is due to the development and improvement in social insurance and in other public and private services.   Discussion here is limited to an introduction of one or two new plans which have been derived from them.

In the shipbuilding industry Surviving Children's Scholarship Annuity is widespread.   This was begun in 1974 at Mitsui Shipbuilding and Engineering Co., Ltd.   In accordance with stipulations of this fund, when a worker dies the spouse receives a pension until the surviving children graduate from college.   The maximum amount of the pension is 15,000 yen per month to the spouse.   For surviving children up to a maximum of 3, each one receives 15,000 yen.

However, when death occurs for some reason not connected with work, the amount and terms of payment are somewhat reduced in accordance with the number of years of service. The payment of course serves to further augment Worker's Accident Compensation Insurance and other compensation.

To provide against emergency disasters the companies encourage subscription to private insurance programmes. This includes all types such as life insurance, cancer insurance, fire insurance, automobile insurance, insurance against injury in traffic accidents and travel insurance as well as others. It is customary for them to have special arrangements with a specific insurance company. Insurance premiums are deducted from salary. The rate of utilisation of these private insurance policies has risen sharply in the last ten years. That is because, unlike social insurance which provides a minimum guarantee, demand has grown for a guarantee that is more substantial and can meet any number of designated and specific insurance needs.

With the movement toward self-contained family units, and because of the consequent difficulty to get necessary help in an emergency when someone becomes ill at home, many companies have a "home helper" system. In Mitsui Shipbuilding and Engineering Co., Ltd., for any situation meeting a certain set of pre-conditions, it becomes possible to request the company to dispatch a home helper who is an employee of the company. For the service there is a nominal charge of 500 yen per day.

(c) Culture, physical education and recreation

Cultural, physical education and recreation activities traditionally had two purposes. First, such activities were meant to provide educational instruction and entertainment for the sake of workers. Second, they were emphasised as a way to cultivate company spirit and feelings of belonging. Over the last ten years, some of these activities may appear from the outside to have been further expanded and because of that a large amount of funds have been invested. Both purposes, however, have experienced setbacks. Outside the company there is no end to the activities available, and because the employees can afford to enjoy these pursuits, it is difficult for the firm to sponsor an activity that is needed by the worker and can be uniquely provided only by the firm.

During the last ten years, particularly at new shipbuilding yards, the increase in the ranks of recruits has brought about an increase and reinforcing of cultural and physical education facilities for club activities and for events involving the workshops in which they participate. Among the events that have become popular are athletic meets, cultural and dormitory festivals, shipbuilding carnivals, camping, various ball games and long distance hiking. A special characteristic of these activities in recent years is that they are more and more run directly by young workers who are making up the great majority of the participants. The company provides the money but it does not become involved in all the preparations and programmes.

Although there is financial assistance, the young people seem to like club activities with completely voluntary and autonomous management. The make-up of these activities are very similar to

the clubs that are popular among university students: namely,
tennis, baseball, soccer, judo, musical bands, chorus and volley-
ball.   Playing fields, tennis courts, gymnasia, and swimming pools
have been built to accommodate these activities.   At Mitsui Shipbuilding and Engineering Co., Ltd., there is also a physical training centre with overnight facilities which can be used by the
workers.

In spite of the great increase in interest in travel, the
number of trips directly organised by the firms are not increasing.
Most trips today are planned by families or by groups of friends.
The utilisation of facilities such as the firm's rest and recupera-
tion centres, and those of health insurance societies, has also
been changing.   The individualisation of interest in travel is
reflected in the short trips taken by the very senior people of long
service (30 years or more) which have traditionally been sponsored
by the company.   At Mitsui Shipbuilding and Engineering Co., Ltd.
the company pays for the tickets, but the senior couples determine
where they wish to go and individually arrange to travel with just
their own members.

(d)   Improvements in the work
      environment

The last ten years has been a period of heightened concern
with the environment and its management.   In earlier years the
shipyard was naturally thought of as a dreadfully hot place to work
under the burning summer skies, and a freezing workshop in winter.
In summer now, workers use heat protection nets, spot air condi-
tioners, ventilation systems, workshop air conditioning (when inside
the ship) and built-in air conditioned clothing.   In the winter
months, the use of inner suits, pocket warmers, and other heating
equipment is becoming widespread.   None of these measures of course
is a complete solution to the problem.

The living conditions of the "houses" used for waiting before
and after work operations, and used for rest during breaks, have
been improved substantially over the last ten years.   Presently
all the houses are air-conditioned, and have large baths and showers.
It has also become common to have a colour television with a place
to have a seat and relax.

Many of the shipbuilding yards are today making agreements
with local self-governing bodies, and are in the process of negotiating on such matters as establishing more green zones for preserving
the environment.   In the last ten years, environment protection has
been one of the most urgent domestic issues.   For this reason the
changes observable in management's attitudes toward adapting to
new environmental demands are great.   Since 1972, the firms have
been particularly active in establishing countermeasure programmes.

If we look only at total amounts spent on new equipment to
improve the administration of the environment at the shipyards by
Mitsui Shipbuilding and Engineering Co., Ltd., we see that in 1972
it was 230 million yen, in 1973, 634 million yen, had gone as high
as 2,301 million yen in 1974 and in 1975, 1,476 million yen.   These
funds were used toward the processing and disposal of smoke exhaust,
water and other industrial wastes, for anti-noise protection
measures and for planting trees, shrubs and grass to improve the
environment.

- 34 -

(e) <u>Increasing ability and personal growth through education and training</u>

In Japan, on-the-job or off-the-job training provided to perfect a worker's skills needed on duty, are not counted as a fringe benefit, and are thought of as one of the routine functions or responsibilities of management. From the moment one is hired, it is thought that it is the company's responsibility to provide as much of the necessary basic and technical knowledge as possible within the limitations of the staff. Retraining to meet changes in job classification and technological innovations could probably be thought of as a fringe benefit if there were a company where none whatsoever had been carried out, and some was then offered. In Japan, however, and in the shipbuilding industry as well, retraining is considered to be such a normal practice that no one thinks twice about it in terms of a step toward the humanisation of work.

Other than ordinary on-the-job and off-the-job training, one of the reported practices at Mitsui related to expanding ability and increasing individual knowledge is the educational scholarship for employees. The domestic exchange student system was begun in 1962 with students sent to universities, graduate schools or junior colleges for one or two years. Furthermore, research studies for one or two years in the laboratories and research institutes in foreign countries also take place. In either case selection is made from among those who would like to go, and every year there are several people selected for each group. The number of people are few, so the effort is to give such a chance to those of ability and desire, all within the framework of lifetime employment. All of their living expenses and travel costs are paid by the company.

One other system at Mitsui is for the benefit of the worker's children in the form of an educational scholarship. In Japan over the last ten years the difference in earnings based on educational level has been receding, but still most workers have a dream of sending their children to college. For those employees who want to send their children to university, a modest amount of money is paid as matriculation and entry funds, and as a monthly scholarship.

4. <u>Safety and health</u>

In recent years substantial technological innovations have accompanied the mass construction of large vessels. Concurrently, there has been rapid progress in improvements in the safety and health aspects of the environment. The most important factor in the background of this development was the rise in the aspiration level of the workers. Workers' expectations of their work environment rose in linkage with their increased standards of living and education. Under the shortage of labour of the high growth economy, and the consequent improvements in work environment elsewhere, it was of course difficult to attract additional manpower, and to hold on to the workers already employed. One of the important background factors, and probably a partial cause, is that the workers underwent a change of consciousness. The labour unions took an active interest in safety and health activities. The case in most of the companies was by and large the same. Concentrating particularly on the Nippon Kokan report, we will now examine some of the changes which took place during this period.

(a) Physical improvement in equipment

First of all there were widerange advances and physical improvements in equipment and machinery. Specifically this can be roughly divided into six major areas.

1. Elimination of heavy manual labour

As transport equipment was strengthened and reinforced, as automatic machinery became widely employed, progress was made in reducing heavy manual labour. Moreoever, with the introduction of advanced fitting work, the necessity for heavy manual labour was further reduced.

2. Making work in high places safe

A most important point was to improve the scaffolding. Each company has its own system. Ishikawajima-Harima Heavy Industries Co., Ltd., for example, developed the work operations platform, and in Mitsui Shipbuilding and Engineering Co., Ltd. there is the rotor system scaffolding. Even in the old shipyards unit scaffolding came to be used. The introduction of the automatic running type lifter has also been helpful. The movement toward utilisation of large scale block construction and increase in the rate of ships fitted out while still at dry dock, have also tended to reduce dangerous work in high places.

3. Making the work environment more pleasant

The problem of noise always associated with shipbuilding yards was almost completely eliminated through technological advances. More specifically, the shaving process by compressed air was altered so as to use gouges powered by gas in electricity. As reported earlier, considerable breakthroughs were also made in countermeasures to summer heat and winter cold.

4. Improvements in operations for greater safety

Maximum implementation was made of safety improvement suggestions submitted by workers in the workshop. This includes, for example, improvement in working tools and equipment, and advancement made in work operations. Developments tended to blend in well with other methods, promoting all-around improved safety.

5. Improvements in construction technology

Efforts have been made to improve design, construction methods and order of assembly with safety in mind. As one example, scaffolding and hand rails, which were once left to the discretion of the local foreman, have now become standardised and a part of the blueprint. Heavy items are calculated at the design or blueprint stage and lifting positions are specified beforehand. Construction procedures are rearranged with safety in mind. Automatic welding machines which can be externally operated have been often utilised.

6. Improvements in safety and protection equipment

Under strong demand from the labour unions, the frequency with which work clothes and safety shoes are exchanged, all free of charge, has been increased. The union has agreed that the use of such safety and protection equipment is obligatory.

(b) The "human system" of
     safety administration

In the shipbuilding industry over the last ten years, the
human system of safety administration has made great strides.   The
major improvements in the system during this period are:

1.   Allowing workers full participation in
     the safety administration organisation

Originally the safety administration organisation was composed
of only managers of the shipyard.   Gradually this came to be up of
rank and file workers as well.   In the case of Nippon Kokan, until
1970, the safety control organisation was composed of only management.   In 1973, supervisors came to be included,   By 1976, a
small group of workers from the construction site was included in
the organisation.

2.   Promotion of safety through the mutual
     co-operation of labour and management

There have been substantial developments made in labour-
management co-operation in the area of safety control.   In 1969,
with the establishment of the Shipbuilding Industry Labour-
Management Conference, including the Special Committee on Safety
and Health, systems of labour-management co-operation have become
possible at every level.   The labour-managemnt based safety petrol
supersedes the level of individual enterprises and each year there
are two inspections of different shipbuilding yards.

3.   Greater participation and training
     in the safety area

This also, as a part of the activities of the small groups
which will be described later, was introduced to encourage the discovery of safety-related problems and workshop activities for solving them.   The standard operating procedures also emphasising
safety, are now drafted by the workers themselves, and are written
up after the whole group has discussed them.   As long as there are
no legal or technical problems, lower management is instructed to
approve these proposals automatically as they are presented.
Suggestions for improving safety are now customarily undertaken by
a group of workers rather than a single individual.

4.   Rehabilitation training

Although not only related to on-the-job accidents, a system of
rehabilitation for the bodily injured or for those who have recovered
from sickness has been established.   One aspect is the continuation
of special periodic check-ups for long-range follow-up.   Another
is the establishment of an affiliated company performing a business
service appropriate for the individual needing rehabilitation.   A
concrete case would be the N.K. Green Service Co., a subsidiary of
Nippon Kokan taking charge of planting grass, shrubs and trees
around the factories.   Employees who are in the rehabilitation
programme make up the workforce of this company.

5.   Promotion of physical fitness

In addition to protection against sickness and injury, there
is a movement toward actively building up physical capacities.   At
Nippon Kokan sports equipment and exercise apparatus were provided.
Seemingly, usage of the equipment has served to reduce the complaints
of backaches.

(c) <u>Safety administration and
    the labour unions</u>

Zosen Juki Roren and the unions affiliated with it, maintain
that "as far as safety is concerned, there is no fence between
labour and management".   Labour and management in the shipbuilding
industry have held a Shipbuilding Industry Labour-Management Conference since 1969, and employment, production and safety have been
handled as important themes of the Conference.   As for the safety
problem, there is a special committee on safety and health which
holds a conference with both labour and management three or four
times a year.

Zosen Juki Roren has within its organisation a safety and
health chapter which is working towards the promotion of safety
control measures.   As a labour federation, it is also involved in
the following activities:

1. Twice a year (summer and winter) it conducts a one month
   safety-health camapign.

2. Holds a safety poster competition.

3. Has safety study courses for union officials at the national
   level.

In the various companies the unions have their own chapters
dealing in safety and health issues.   Moreover, in Nippon Kokan
the labour union officials and representatives participate with
equal rights alongside the management representatives at the regional safety and hygiene committee, a body whose establishment has
been made compulsory by law.

At the Tsurumi branch of Nippon Kokan's Shipbuilding and Heavy
Industries Workers' Union, 16 safety and health committee members
are selected from among 80 representatives.   The individuals so
designated participate in the above-mentioned regional safety and
health committee along with members of the executive council.   They
also conduct the safety patrol at all levels and are members of the
Labour-Management Disaster Countermeasures Conference which is
formed in times of crises.   They also participate in poster contests as judges.   Activities at this level are joined in by the
employees of co-operating companies and the families of workers.

The labour unions are of course well aware that in some respects there is a conflict of interest between labour and management
when it comes to indemnification payments for on-the-job accidents.
Labour has worked hard towards bettering these conditions.   Other
than the compensation paid from the Workmen's Accident Compensation
Insurance, until 1966, there was no system of paying condolence
money, even in the first ranking shipbuilding firms.   In 1967,
Nippon Kokan's union secured a precedent-breaking payment of condolence money in the order of 800,000 yen.   From 1969, the same
system began to spread to the other ranking companies.   Today,
almost all of the firms pay an additional 13 million yen as company
indemnification for death while on duty.

(d) A good record of safety
     administration

     It is readily apparent that safety administration in the ship-
building industry has made substantial progress (see figure 2).
During the last ten-year period both the frequency of accidents
and their intensity have steadily decreased. In the past the
shipbuilding business had one of the worst safety records, and it
became the object of a special Ministry of Labour inspection and
guidance programme. It was clear that when compared to other
industries, shipbuilding could not be proud of its record as there
were a particularly large number of accidents resulting in serious
bodily injury and death. Nowadays, while the severity of accidents
is greater than the average for the manufacturing industry, the
frequency has become less.

     One large problem remaining is the difference in the safety
record between the regular, permanent workers and the employees of
subcontractors. In terms of improvement in this area, it is higher
for the subcontractor workforce. From the perspectives of both
frequency of occurrence and intensity of damage, however, the subcontractors' record is still considerably worse. Looking at 1975
alone, there were 10 deaths among the average number of 154,000
regular workers. Among 55,000 subcontractor workers there were
as many as 21 deaths while on duty.

     With the enactment of the Industrial Safety and Health Law,
it became the responsibility of the parent company to assure that
a plan and programme of safety countermeasures be carried out by
the subcontractors. Concurrently, labour and management of the
shipbuilding industry worked towards safety improvements covering
the supplemental workers of affiliated subsidiaries. The conditions
surrounding these supportive workers, however, including the safety
issue, remain as an important problem in terms of the quality of
working life. There is still much work to be done here by labour
and management in the shipbuilding industry.

5.   Work restructuring schemes

     In the shipbuilding industry, there was a continuous process
of revisions made in job contents and classifications accompanying
innovations in technology from the period of high economic growth.
In other words, the technical changes such as those employed in
large-scale vessels, in block construction and in advanced fitting
work, by expanding the market and increasing sales volume, led to
greater employment of new recruits which in turn lifted the comparative rank and standing of the older workers already in the company.
The regular workers already employed were thereby forced to keep
constantly changing their job categories and skills. In the shipbuilding industry, as in other industries, the widespread practices
of career employment and enterprise unions have played an effective
role when it came to adroitly absorbing and even encouraging and
capitalising on technological change.

     In the last part of the 1960s, however, it became necessary to
make some changes based upon social requirements affecting this
area. The increase in educational and living standards, combined
with a shortage of labour, heightened the expectations held by
young workers towards their jobs and work content. A movement
and demands for "hatarakigai" or "meaning and satisfaction in work

was born.   On the other hand, the insufficient supply of young
workers meant that in terms of personnel composition, the dependency
on middle- and older-aged workers gradually increased.   At this
point it would be instructive to examine a case of job integration
at Hitachi Shipbuilding and Engineering Co., Ltd.   The situation
at Hitachi reflects and arises from these demands for job
satisfaction. [1]

(a) Background surrounding job integration

At Hitachi the initial force motivating a restructuring of job
contents, known by the name of job integration (shokushu-fukugoka),
was the shortage of labour.   In about 1969 the Innoshima factory,
equipped with somewhat obsolete facilities, suffered from an in-
ability to attract a sufficiently large workforce.   Among the new
high school graduates hired, there were many who left the company.
It was here that management began serious consideration of the
possibilities and options available in making the best possible job
use of the middle- and old-aged, and female workers in comparatively
abundant supply.

One of the aims of job integration is to increase the flexibility of a firm's product marketing strategy through a diversification or increase in production versatility combined with increased
adaptability to the working demands of the employees.   With a
decrease in demand for large-scale tankers taking place after the
oil shock, a company seeking to hold a competitive position and
maintain its present workforce, will have to have enough flexibility
to accommodate and allow a sufficient amount of diversification in
product mix.   For that reason it is all the more essential that
the worker possess versatile technical skills and an ability to
quickly adapt to changing job specifications.

Job integration is also meant to meet the need to adapt to the
gradual ageing of workers as more and more young workers become
middle- and old-aged.   Despite a variety of efforts, it is difficult to increase orders for new construction in the shipbuilding
industry.   Obviously, increased hiring should be avoided.   Hitachi
Shipbuilding and Engineering Co., Ltd. had always hired at least
1,000 new high school graduates each year.   In 1976, however, no
new high school graduates were hired.   In addition, since 1974,
the retirement age has increased to 58.   These conditions combined
to increase the necessity to develop new workshops where older
employees can work productively, safely, and handle jobs commensurate
with their declining physical endurance.

One more purpose of job integration is the need to develop a
plan that will give hatarakigai or meaning and job satisfaction to
workers.   At Hitachi Shipbuilding and Engineering Co., Ltd. there
was a high degree of worker expectations as root cause for the
sense of lack of meaning and significance in work and/or dissatisfaction with monotony on the job.   Consequently, it became even more

---

[1] This example of the Innoshima factory of Hitachi Shipbuilding
and Engineering Co., Ltd. was presented at the study committee
meeting by Mr. Toshio Nakayama from the same company.   Because of
Hitachi's distant location, there was, however, no regular committee
member in attendance from that company.

important to reorganise jobs and alter work functions which would lead to increased personal satisfaction.

Figure 3 does not represent the situation at Hitachi Shipbuilding and Engineering Co., Ltd., but does present the degree of feelings of work monotony and job satisfaction for a segment of shipbuilding workers. The survey taken in 1972 at Nippon Kokan's Tsurumi shipbuilding yard, indicates that feelings of monotony are greatest among the general rank and file workers. The data shows, moreover, that it is the younger workers who most suffer from a lack of meaning or satisfaction on the job.

Finally, job integration can be viewed as reformation of the workshop organisation as it adjusts and responds to changes in the social climate of the workplace. With the increase in educational level, a desire to have greater equality in wages and social relationships has intensified in the shipbuilding just as in most Japanese industries. Reduction in job discrimination through job integration and adjustment offers the rationality which compliments and reinforces the growing desire for democratisation of the workplace.

(b) Methods of job integration

Basically the job integration effort at Hitachi Shipbuilding and Engineering Co., Ltd. consisted of two job redesign plans being carried out at the same time. One was a consolidation of job functions with an accompanying decrease in job classifications. If we look at the job of a single individual, his functions and responsibilities were increased. For the individual this means a more versatile and broader job description. The other redesign plan involved partitioning various operations into work units which were suitable for young, middle- and old-aged workers in terms of physical workload and mental and emotional factors and demands. This made it possible to share the workload in a way most beneficial and helpful to the members of the working group.

Let us consider the case of the Innoshima factory where job integration was first developed. The first step was to determine the sphere of job integration. In deciding which jobs would be integrated, emphasis was placed on the relationship between jobs with respect to work processes, operational locations and products to be treated. That is to say, jobs which were closely related in terms of these factors were integrated into large subdivisions.

As the next step job boundaries were removed within each of these larger, expanded job classifications and the job contents were pulled apart and analysed down to the unit of individual work operations. A work operation is the smallest possible independent unit of work consisting of a sequence of specific tasks. The work operation is based upon, and formed after consideration has been made of the type of skill and the type of product with which the operation is concerned.

The next step is to decide the areas of work apportionment based upon age. In doing this, it was necessary first of all to evaluate operations using methods similar to those applied in job evaluation schemes. The amount of physical exertion and fatigue, safety hazards involved in work, the degree of agility, alertness, speed, decision, the precautions and vigilance, degree of emotional stability, co-operativeness and skills required were all assessed

with the use of a point scale.   Some elements evaluated readily
demonstrated that "youth" was required in the given work process.
Others indicated that "maturity" was called for in the operation.
In this way it could be decided what age level was appropriate for
any given work process based upon whether or not the evaluation
suggested a high degree of "youthful element" or "maturity element".

As a result, the following areas of apportionment were established based upon age groups.

	Age	Work apportionment
Young workers	18-24	- Work requiring physical strength and stamina - Elementary work operations
Prime age workers	25-44	- Work requiring physical strength and stamina - Operations requiring skill
Older workers	45-58	- Work not requiring physical strength - Operations demanding skills and experience - Work which can be done by workers of any age

(c)   Developments in job
      integration

Figure 4 is a model demonstrating well the movement towards
job integration, particularly the apportionment of work based on
age differences, as developed at the Innoshima works.   This example
shows the newly integrated job family identified as "upper
structure".   In the past, as listed at the top of the figure, in
the upper structure there were five job classifications: installation, welding, pipe fitting, steel cutting and woodwork.   In the
figure all the operations covered by these five former classifications are listed and have been alloted into work areas apportioned
into three age groups.

For work operations related to the welding process, for
example, we find that the most simple face-down welding tasks are
assigned to young age brackets and older workers.   On the other
hand, the toughest or most physically demanding work, such as face-
up welding, has been allotted only to the younger group.   Critical
welding work of basic structural parts demanding strength and
experience is assigned to older-aged workers.   Workers in their
prime also cover the work allotment areas of older men.   At the
same time, however, they are also in charge of the welding of
pressure resistant and thin materials, both requiring a high level
of skill.   In this way, then, it becomes possible to create a co-
operative allotment of job functions based on age.

At the Innoshima works, there was successful application of job integration based upon a model similar to this. A specific development was that an expert in each of the divisional areas, co-ordinated the workshop activities. Emphasis was on making decisions through considerations and discussions in small work groups. The labour union, moreover, took a completely co-operative stand in this effort in job integration.

In more detail, at the Innoshima plant, 98 skill classifications were reduced and grouped into 35 different integrated jobs. (Originally there were in total 128 job-skill classifications. Among these, 30 functions were excluded from the integration effort.) For the individual worker this meant that new skills had to be mastered. For supervisors, new educational needs arose. How were these changes and shifts in trends brought about?

Figure 5 represents a part of a chart illustrating the "five year after" goals of the job integration programme carried out at the Innoshima plant. Accordingly, the first new job function written is made up of a consolidation of the two old job classifications "marking of shapes" and "gas cutting". Incidentally, workers engaged in the former job function had already been spending about 10 per cent of their total working hours in the "gas cutting" area. On the other hand, those engaged in "gas cutting", had up until now had absolutely no contact with "marking of shapes". After five years, however, the people from both of the old job categories will be working equally in both areas.

In the process of such job integration, skills are acquired almost completely through on-the-job training. Changes in skill levels are rated and reported by the individual himself based upon "skill standards" written up together by the union and management. In this manner, the skill ranking for each individual is decided. This in turn relfects decisions made as to company qualifications and to standards used for treating salary levels, etc. If one were given a totally different work line, and if his skill level consequently decreased, for the first two or three years his former skill level would apply, protecting him against demotion.

Just how much job integration has helped to reduce the physical strain and stress on middle- and old-aged workers and aided in making the best utilisation of their experience, is not as yet clear, as insufficient time has passed since the system was installed. The percentage, however, of workers over 45 is as high as 19.5 per cent in the upper echelon including work suitable for middle- and older-aged workers. In comparison their percentage in electric welding, a job function designed with the young in mind, has decreased to as little as 3.6 per cent. This is evidence that job integration is more than simple job enlargement and that it also is taking root as a useful countermeasure for relief of the middle- and old-age worker problem.

6. Small group activities

Participation in decision making through small groups has made relatively simultaneous progress throughout all sectors of Japanese industry over the last 15 years. Some of this participation has developed as organisational support for statistical quality control (QC circle). Other small group decision making was started with the purpose of bringing about innovations and changes in the leadership style of supervisors. Still other efforts were started with the role of promoting safety in the workplace. Regardless of the original purpose, however, all of these activities of varying labels and names have been integrated through practical application in the various firms.

In the shipbuilding industry there has been the same basic passage of events and small group participative activities have progressed on the shop floor. At the Tsurumi shipyard of Nippon Kokan, for example, the quality control circle was begun in 1963. Promotion of workshop group discussions from the viewpoint of supervisory training was started in 1970. In 1973, workshop conferences for safety administration were established. These activities were drawn together in 1975, and came under the heading of "participation". One can surmise from figure 6 why the safety problem would often be the focal point or starting point of concern for small group participation activities. That is to say, small group participation conferences on safety had the widest appeal for rank and file employees.

Small group activities have two additional aspects worthy of notice. One is their role as an independent and autonomous problem solving forum. In other words there is a tendency that problems are not merely limited to quality and safety but through discussion and debate problems are defined and solved, whether they deal with questions of poor attendance, for example, or allotment of the workload. One other aspect concerns the small workshop groups movement and efforts such as a self-administrative autonomous group or a jishukanri group. Groups in the workplace are gradually beginning to voluntarily assume the function which was traditionally held by the supervisor in the past.

(a) Movement for total participation at Mitsubishi Heavy Industries, Ltd.

The movement for participation in planning by all members at the Nagasaki Shipyard and Engine Works at Mitsubishi Heavy Industries, Ltd. illustrates the tendency towards total engagement of a workforce. At Nagasaki Shipyard and Engine Works, there is a ZD (Zero Defect) group movement rather similar to a quality control (QC) circle. We confine ourselves, however, to an example from the shipbuilding division in the area of behaviour transformation of supervisors and cases of participation in safety administration. This example has been promoted under the leadership of Professor Jyuji Misumi presently of Osaka University.

The plan was begun in 1966, but the goal of the activities has gradually been altered. In the beginning, the effort was to get both the supervisors and employees to become accustomed to talking things out within each work group. In 1970, emphasis was placed on activities stressing greater safety, and progress was made towards solving problems of quality and efficiency. Beginning in 1973, the activities at the newly constructed Koyagi plant facilities of the same shipyard had as their major goal a motto shared by all employees of "Let's make ships". The central theme was to see just how imaginatively a factory could be set up giving job satisfaction and meaning to working life.

During this period from 1970, Professor Misumi introduced the "PM survey". Employees evaluate the administrative and behaviour patterns of the managers and supervisors in each area. All of those

surveyed were assessed by their subordinates in terms of their
leadership behaviour in the two areas of goal achievement (performance) function, and group unity (maintenance) function.   The
results were fed back to the managers and supervisors themselves in
the form of a confidential report.

At the same time, the managers and supervisors set up a special
live-in training programme to heighten their sensibilities and understanding of their own management style.   Through discussion with
other participants in the same circumstances, everyone discovered
points for improvement in his own leadership style, and strove to
set new targets for improvement.   The direct aim of the training
was to have the managers and supervisors create an atmosphere which
would make it possible for rank and file workers to participate
without constraint in the workshop discussions.

Meetings in the workplace were in principle held with the
specific operational group as the unit.   When the operational group
was large, this was divided into smaller groups, with one of the
members chosen as leader.   In the beginning the purpose of the
meetings was to analyse the cause of workshop accidents, and to have
group decisions made in order to avoid them in the future.

Although we do not have the space here to enumerate all the
plans which were conceived and implemented in all the working places,
let it suffice to say that some groups wrote up an operation standards manual adequately reflecting the safety factor.   Other groups
divided up and assigned some sort of administrative and control role
to each employee.   In some areas, the workers themselves inspected
the finished products, applying with pride a sticker bearing the
workshop name.   There were also examples at the factory level where
exhibitions were held demonstrating the improvements made in tools
and facilities throughout the workshops.

Such participative activities leave the labour union with a
favourable impression as the union watches for signs that such
activities are in fact contributing to the purpose of encouraging
a democratisation of the workplace.   The corporations on the other
hand, think of these activities in terms of their intangible benefits such as developing communications, an appetite for work, team
work and creating healthy morale.

(b)   Labour unions and small
group activities

The small group activities carried out at the Nagasaki shipyard of Mitsubishi Heavy Industries, Ltd. are similarly observable
at nearly all the shipbuilding yards.   At Ishikawajima-Harima
Heavy Industries, Co., Ltd. from 1969 on into 1971 "jishukanri" or
the introduction of autonomous management was promoted in all the
factories as one aspect of "the humanisation of work".   The union
at the 1970 convention took up the slogan "Worker comes first is
the foundation to corporate prosperity".   In the 1975 convention
the policy of "We'll give you a yes as long as there's self-
autonomous management where the worker comes first" was adopted.

Based on this policy and in order to check into whether or not
in fact there was "self-autonomous management where the worker
comes first", the labour union formed a project team, and two field
studies were carried out.   One was a combined effort by both labour

and management where the reality of the "humanisation of work" was
to be surveyed as the issue exists in Europe. The labour representatives in particular seem to find a good degree of similarity in
their approach to the doctrines of Sweden, presently in the midst
of developments in this direction. One other is the survey made
of the actual circumstances of self-autonomous management activities
at five plant sites of Ishikawajima-Harima Heavy Industries Co., Ltd.

The union representatives asked to hear the opinions of the
following four groups at each factory: (1) the top management at
each plant, (2) foreman and work group chief, (3) shop steward or
representative and group leader, (4) general rank and file workers.
Along with looking into how the introduction of a self-management
formula has specifically changed matters of workshop organisation,
and operations, this survey also aimed at systematically grasping
the reaction of the various parties involved.

Among the organisational changes observable, was a wide variety
existing in both shipbuilding plants and workplaces. In terms of
important trends, there were the following: (1) A move from group
formation based on job classification to a group composition of
mixing different job classifications. (2) Everyone's contents of
work operations were broadened from those of a single job classification to a mixed or multiple job category. (3) Autonomy within
each work operations group in terms of processes, scheduling and
work distribution was all improved. (4) The former supervisor had
become a sort of technical advisor and more frequently took on a
more staff-like role. (5) There were more spontaneous personnel
movements and support and assistance within and among the various
work groups.

For their own part, the management class of the factories was
naturally very enthusiastic about the promotion of self-management,
and was for the most part satisfied with the results. Moreover,
in terms of the supervisors' organisation as it existed, no one
thought that there should be a change since it was playing an indispensable role in the development of self-autonomous activities.
The supervisor class, along with acknowledging that it no longer
lived in an atmosphere of a workshop expecting directives and orders
from above, found that it had become possible to do more important
work, being freed from routine supervision. It was indicated,
however, that at the assistant foreman level, there was a certain
amount of deterioration in authority patterns.

Among the shop steward group, or frontline representatives of
the labour union, there were many giving very high marks to autonomous management participation. When self-management was first
introduced, however, a number of voices were raised in opposition.
After they were allowed to inject their opinions, and the system
was revised, however, views changed. A typical opinion was that
there is satisfaction in planning your own work operation and putting it into practice. Over-all there was a lighter and healthier
mood; little difficulty was experienced in helping one another
when one's own work was finished and there was little feeling that
diversification of function or versatility of job skills leads to
labour intensification. There were, however, some who complained
of an increased workload.

As for the opinion of the general rank and file, there was
very positive approval. The following are fairly representative
of their opinions. "In doing work on the shop floor, everybody

feels that the administrative style now employed is 'a good way'.
It will completely take root in this shop in the near future.   The
young guys around particularly seem pleased with this way of doing
things."   A high ranking union executive went on to give an example
demonstrating that there was a large change in attitude at the time
of the proposed introduction of new modifications.   He pointed out
that the attitude of "what do I get in return?" was now completely
non-existent.

    The union of Ishikawajima-Harima Heavy Industries Co., Ltd.
gave its whole-hearted support to self-management as a result of
this survey.   It went on to propose that a special committee composed of both labour and management be formed with the purpose of
encouraging its development and the solution to any problems remaining.   One of the labour union's views was to go as far as to set up
as a future goal the concept that the same small ·group could be used
both as a basic unit of work operations and as a block towards union
organising and execution of activities.   They claimed that inasmuch
as the individual is both a unit of the company and the union, it
would be most appropriate that the group be considered in the same
light.   The position and status given to the autonomous group in
the opinion of the labour union is almost completely unprecedented.

7.   Summary and perspective

    The major developments taking place over the last ten years in
the quality of working life of the workers in the Japanese shipbuilding industry have been described in the preceding paragraphs.
Through the overview we become aware of the existence of three special
trends of importance.   These experiences of labour and management
in the Japanese shipbuilding industry, can undoubtedly be of interest
to many people of other countries.

    (a) First of all it should be pointed out that the majority of
the improvements of the last ten years of high economic growth,
occurred in parallel.   This is true in most areas: traditional
working conditions, employee benefits and services, safety and health
and work organisations.   In other words, improvements did not in
any way take place in a vacuum.   They grew out of demands for better
quality in all aspects of working life.

    (b) In the area of established working conditions, there were
not only improvements in terms of quantity during this period, but
attention should also be drawn to the qualitative changes.   These
reflect responses to the workers' social and economic expectations
and demands.   For example, if we look at wages during the period
there certainly were increases in wage levels which catch the eye.
It was also during the same period that a unification of blue and
white collar wage systems, an issue of long standing, was resolved.
Similar changes of importance were the increase in autonomous
decision making on the part of workers in managing benefits and
service programmes, greater union participation in safety administration and a substantial number of other areas worthy of attention.

    (c) At the same time, job integration, small group participative
activities, autonomous management, and other developments in work
organisation definitely represent new progress set against the background of the qualitative changes in the lives of workers during the
past ten years or so.   These were not however born to run in the
face of or to rebel against the past.   Rather they came into being

as the result of efforts of both the enterprise and the union in
pursuit of their respective goals.   While management and the union
were true to their own roles, they both maintained an attitude of
recognising and appreciating the role and efforts of the other.
It should not be forgotten that this was made possible because each
party held a forward looking perspective in coping with and adapting
to the new changes taking place in worker consciousness.

    For much of the period covered by this report, prospects for
ship construction orders were bright.   They were prosperous, even
booming days for the industry.   Today, however, that is not the
case.   Recovery from worldwide recession has been inadequate in
every industrialised nation.   The shipbuilding industry has to
resign itself to continued stagnation.   Both labour and management
of the shipbuilding industry will have to adopt measures for
diversifying operations into alternate types of equipment and products.   Such efforts and shifts in industrial structure and reorganisation are already taking place at an accelerating pace.
What will happen with future labour problems, however?

    In the study group we exchanged opinions on what may be future
transitions and trends in the labour area in the shipbuilding
industry, and, of course, including questions of quality of working
life.   Although no particular effort was made to reach firm agreement on future prospects, the major points which surfaced were as
follows:

    (1)   In the short-run the labour union is most concerned about
employment security.   Although both labour and management desire
to maintain the traditional deep-rooted long-term employment
guarantee, both parties judge that future prospects for this are not
bright.   The shipbuilding industry has grown up with and fostered
certain limited social and geographical areas.   Lay-offs greater
than those already made today threaten to have a large and unfavour-
able influence on the local societies.   Labour and management both
believe that this is true whether or not it is lay-off of the regular workers in a firm (in other words the union members) or whether
it is the employees of co-operating affiliate enterprises.   Management feels that at least it is necessary to maintain an effective
force limited to a smaller key group of workers through employment
adjustment not including lay-off.

    (2)   The labour unions are showing deeper and deeper concern
for problems of older worker groups including a postponement of
retirement and a guaranteed standard of living after retirement.
At the Mitsui Engineering and Shipbuilding Workers' Union, based on
the generally observable trend of a steadily advancing ageing of the
workers, a study is being undertaken of their lives in the year 2010.
Having determined that a good economic foundation after retirement
is already in prospect, a guide book is being prepared to serve as
a reference for workers in the other areas.   Management for its
part, while attempting to reduce to a lean but efficient workforce,
also considers that welfare and safety measure programmes are all
the more important to meet the ageing of the workforce.

    (3)   In the area of job and work organisation, job integration
and self-management developments should become more widespread.
What with the drastic decrease in large-scale vessel construction
which had required a further subdivisioning of labour specialisation,
there has been instead a broadening of technical skills and increasing needs for workers with an ability to plan and inspect their own

work.   Decreases in job mobility between firms will continue to
make it possible to accumulate long-term skills at both the individual
and group level.   With pre-processing equipment (a move towards
numerical control processing) seen to be increasingly introduced by
management, the same would appear to afford a favourable opportunity
to reduce significantly many simple routine tasks.   Trade unions
are also in favour of these developments.

Table 1: Average monthly wages of union members, 1965-76

Year	Yen	Nominal wages Index	Rate of increase	Real wages Index	Rate of increase	Consumer price Index	Rate of increase
1965	33 693	56.9	-	74.2	-	76.7	7.2
1966	37 646	63.6	11.8	79.1	6.6	80.4	4.8
1967	41 431	70.0	10.1	83.6	5.7	83.7	4.1
1968	45 514	76.8	9.7	87.0	4.1	88.3	5.6
1969	51 502	87.0	13.3	93.2	7.1	93.3	5.6
1970	59 233	100.0	14.9	100.0	7.3	100.0	7.2
1971	69 325	117.0	17.0	110.1	10.1	106.3	6.3
1972	79 425	134.1	14.6	120.4	9.4	111.4	4.8
1973	95 231	160.8	19.9	129.1	7.2	124.5	11.8
1974	121 255	204.7	27.3	134.1	3.9	152.7	22.7
1975	138 558	233.9	14.3	136.7	1.9	171.1	12.0
1976	151 289	255.4	9.2	138.7	1.5	184.1	7.6

Source: Zosen Juki Roren.

Wage figures cover regular monthly wages and salaries of the union members of the big eight companies.

Overtime and holiday work premiums and other variable payments are not included.

Table 2: Lump-sum retirement payments (1975)

(Yen)

Union	Length of service (years)					
	15	20	25	30	35	40
Mitsubishi	2 240 000	3 890 000	5 450 000	7 540 000	8 920 000	—
IHI	2 230 000	3 520 000	5 210 000	7 170 000	9 000 000	11 010 000
Kawasaki	1 829 000	3 080 400	4 460 100	6 128 900	6 642 100	6 706 200
Hitachi	1 731 000	2 938 000	4 624 000	6 892 000	7 605 000	6 170 000
Mitsui	1 546 000	—	4 886 498	7 025 885	8 982 371	10 566 069
Sumitomo	1 818 000	3 045 000	5 120 000	7 490 000	8 652 000	—
NKK	—	4 248 600	5 465 500	8 193 000	9 802 400	14 537 500
Sasebo	—	—	5 205 840	7 475 490	—	—
Average	1 899 000	3 453 667	5 052 742	7 239 384	8 514 839	10 397 954

Source: Zosen Juki Roren.

The NKK figures represent payments for lengths of service one year less than those for the other companies.

Table 3:   Monthly costs of fringe benefits per worker

Item	1966		1975	
Legally required benefits and services	4 169 yen	55.3%	17 632 yen	49.4%
Health insurance	2 019	26.8	7 380	20.7
Welfare annuity insurance	1 175	15.6	5 984	16.8
Employment insurance	444	5.9	1 839	5.2
Workmen's accident compensation insurance	496	6.6	2 204	6.2
Seamen's insurance	25	0.3	34	0.1
Children's allowance	-	-	180	0.4
Accident compensation	10	0.1	11	0.0
Voluntary benefits and services	3 372 yen	44.7%	18 072 yen	50.6%
Housing assistance	1 050	13.9	8 227	23.0
Medical services	443	5.9	2 146	6.0
Livelihood services	1 589	21.1	6 027	16.9
Mutual aid services	107	1.4	636	1.8
Property accumulation	-	-	68	0.2
Cultural, athletic and recreational services	146	1.9	789	2.2
Others	37	0.5	179	0.5
Total	7 541	100.0	35 704	100.0

Source: Shipbuilders' Association of Japan.

Note that standard formula for fringe benefits cost calculation currently used in Japan excludes paid vacations, retirement pay-ments, voluntary retirement payments, training time and costs, and regular non-work-related compensation items such as family, trans-portation, housing and meal allowances.

Figure 1: Postwar transition of shipbuilding
          labour unions

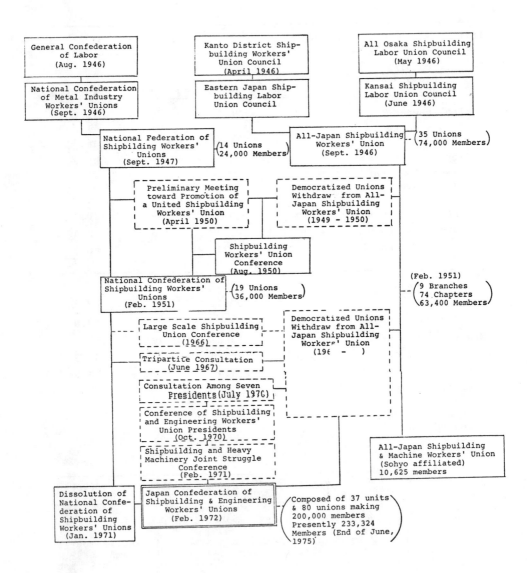

Figure 2:   Accident frequency and severity rates
            in shipbuilding industry, 1965-1975

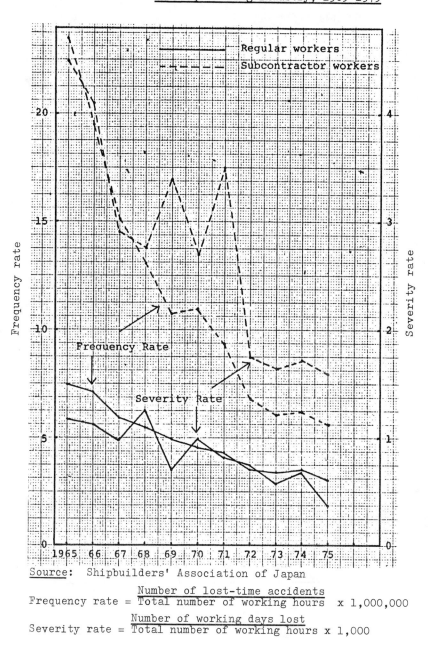

Source: Shipbuilders' Association of Japan

$$\text{Frequency rate} = \frac{\text{Number of lost-time accidents}}{\text{Total number of working hours}} \times 1,000,000$$

$$\text{Severity rate} = \frac{\text{Number of working days lost}}{\text{Total number of working hours}} \times 1,000$$

Figure 3: Job monotony and job satisfaction

I find my job monotonous:

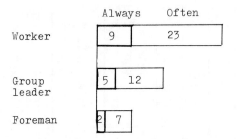

```
              Always    Often
Worker       |   9  |     23      |

Group        | 5  |  12   |
leader
Foreman      |2|  7  |
```

I feel satisfied with my job (I feel the sense of <u>yarigai</u>):

```
Age            Very        Quite
  - 19        |  13  |      32        |

20 - 24       |4|          40            |

25 - 29       |  11  |       48             |

30 - 34       |   19    |        44            |

35 - 39       |     29      |        49             |

40 - 44       |       40        |        43            |

45 - 49       |     35      |      35       |

50 -          |       41        |      41        |
```

<u>Source</u>: Nippon Kokan K.K., Tsurumi Shipyard

- 55 -

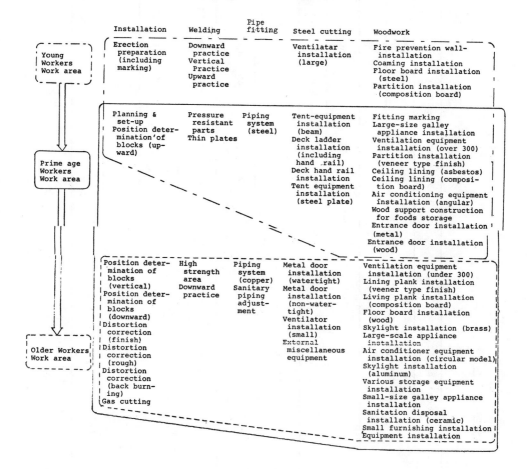

Figure 4: Job integration: task groupings for different age brackets

Source: Hitachi Shipbuilding & Engineering Co., Ltd.

Figure 5: Job integration: five-year goals

Job title after integration	Job title before integration	Feasibility			Rate of integration (%)					
		Sequence	Location	Product	Now			Goal after 5 yrs.		
					A	B	C	A	B	C
Marking	A. Marking	x	x	x	90	10	–	50	50	–
	B. Gas cutting					100	–	50	50	–
Sub assembly	A. Sub assembly fitting	x	x	x	90	10	–	50	50	–
	B. Sub assembly welding				5	95	–	50	50	–
Steel bending	A. Press B				90	10	–	60	20	20
	B. Steel plate bending		x	x	5	90	5	20	60	20
	C. Stiffener, flange, etc. bending				5	5	90	20	20	60

Source: Hitachi Shipbuilding and Engineering Co., Ltd.

Figure 6: Satisfaction with small-group
participation

I draw satsifaction from my participation in:

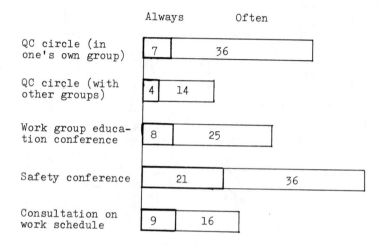

Source: Nippon Kokan K.K., Tsurumi Shipyard

Figure 7: Small-group participation: performance results

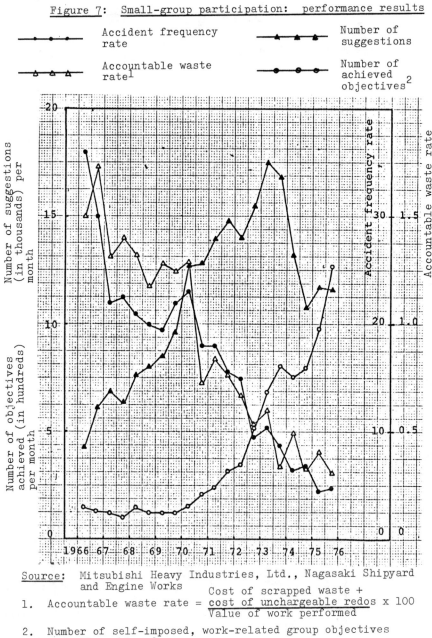

Source: Mitsubishi Heavy Industries, Ltd., Nagasaki Shipyard
and Engine Works

1. Accountable waste rate = $\dfrac{\text{Cost of scrapped waste} + \text{cost of unchargeable redos} \times 100}{\text{Value of work performed}}$

2. Number of self-imposed, work-related group objectives
actually achieved.

CHAPTER III

THE QUALITY OF WORKING LIFE IN THE
ELECTRICAL MACHINERY INDUSTRY

This report covers developments in the area of improvements in
the quality of working life brought about by labour and management
over the last ten years in the Japanese electrical machinery
industry.   The study was undertaken by a committee consisting of
labour and management representatives of two fully integrated manufacturers, two communications equipment manufacturers and one home
appliances enterprise, together with a representative of Denki Roren
(All-Japan Federation of Electric Machine Workers' Union).   Contributions were also provided by three technical experts.   The
committee gathered information on actual cases supplied by related
worker and management representatives.   Discussions were carried
out between June 1977 and January 1978.

Deliberations within the study group began by determining
what was meant by the phrase "quality of working life".   All
committee members were conversant with the industrial relations
practices and working conditions in Europe and North America, and
there was adequate understanding of what quality of working life
meant in those countries.   While it was recognised that the fine
subdivision of labour necessitated by modern production methods
was a problem for some workers, the committee members in general
did not see correction of this labour problem as being of the
highest priority.   The opinion of all members was that the issue
of quality of working life should be treated more broadly and
deeply.

From the beginning the opinion was strongly stressed that
there is a large, even essential difference in what Japanese and
Western workers demand and expect from their working lives.
Within a system of so-called lifetime employment, Japanese workers
are looking for long-term material and psychological feelings of
sufficiency and stability.   This point will be developed in
greater detail throughout the report.   In its review of the
achievements made over the last ten years in improvements in the
quality of working life, the committee decided to consider progress
made in the following areas:

- general improvements in wages and other working conditions;

- improvements in employee benefit and service programmes;

- promotion of employment of the physically handicapped and
  middle- and old-aged workers;

- small group activities;

- work reorganisation schemes;

- worker participation in management.

Although the major electrical machinery and appliance makers
differ in terms of product, location, workforce and other characteristics, there is a surprisingly high degree of homogeneity among

the different companies in terms of working conditions. This is
to a large extent due to the role played by the industrial union,
Denki Roren, in promoting equal and common conditions among individual affiliates.   In addition, over the past half century,
companies have been competing among themselves to improve working
conditions.   While being mindful of the unique features of each
company, the study committee attempted as much as possible to ask
the companies to present case studies which seemed to be representative of trends in the industry as a whole.

Within the study group, there was not always full agreement
between labour and management representatives from the same enterprise.   Nor were there always completely coherent views and consensus among the corporate or union representatives.   This paper
will indicate the major discrepancies as and when they took place.

Let us begin with an introduction to the Japanese electrical
machinery industry and some of its characteristic industrial relations patterns.

1.   The Japanese electrical machinery industry
     and its industrial relations patterns

     (a)   The Japanese electrical machinery and
           appliance industry

Over the last 25 years the electrical machinery industry has
occupied a prominent place among Japanese manufacturing industries
with a continuous record of high productivity.   Directly after
the Second World War, the level of production in the electrical
manufacturing industry was reported to have fallen to about 30 per
cent of its peak output.   By 1955, according to statistics of the
OECD the output of the industry in Japan was only 3 per cent of
that in the United States, 26 per cent of the United Kingdom, and
32 per cent of West Germany.   By 1970, however, Japan had already
out-produced West Germany and the United Kingdom and was up to
40 per cent of the level produced in the United States.

Looking at rates of increase in the production index from 1950
to 1975, the electrical machinery industry has continuously
recorded yearly growth of 20.6 per cent.   This not only far sur-
passes the 12.7 per cent increase of the manufacturing industry as
a whole during that same period, but is a figure higher than the
growth percentages for the other high growth industries - transport
equipment 19 per cent; petroleum and coal products industry 17.5
per cent; and precision machinery 15.5 per cent.   Of course it
was also much higher than other basic heavy industries with steel
at 12.9 per cent and chemicals at 13.1 per cent.   The growth rate
of the electrical machinery industry, presently one of the leading
export industries, stands in sharp contrast to the 8.5 per cent rate
of growth during the same period for the textile industry, the
major exporting industry in Japan before the Second World War.

The growth of the electrical machinery industry after the
War began with the expansion of heavy electrical machinery and
instruments accompanying development of power-generating sources
and other heavy industries.   Later on, there was a remarkable
increase in the use of electric and electronic home appliance
machines and equipment.

---

[1] The description in this section is largely based on:
Planning Department, Policy and Planning Bureau, Denki Roren,
The Second Industrial Policy Measures of Denki Roren (Tokyo:
Denki Roren, 1977), 110 pp.   More recent figures are supplemented
from Census of Manufacturing Firms.

In 1975, production of the electrical machinery industry was valued at 10,800 billion yen (at 300 yen per dollar this is about 36 billion dollars). This corresponds to 8.5 per cent of the total manufactured output for that year, and represents an increase of 145 times over the 1950 figure. In 1950, the electrical machinery industry only comprised 3.1 per cent of total manufacturing industry production. In the following quarter century the number of manufacturing establishments in the electrical machinery industry had increased by 6.3 times while the number of people engaged in the industry rose by 7.3 times. In comparison, the figures for the manufacturing industry as a whole during this same period were limited to a 2.1 times increase in establishments and a 2.7 times growth in workforce.

The application of new technology and well organised and equipped systems of automated mass production were among the major factors underlying the high rate of productivity which brought about the rapid growth of the electrical machinery industry. As domestic market factors, the surges in demand for durable consumer goods and investment in plant and equipment tended to stimulate production. In foreign markets as well, the increase in imports of durable consumer goods by developed industrialised nations, and the expansion of imported equipment and machinery by developing countries also contributed to the rapid growth. Government assistance policies for research and development, export promotion and financing contributed substantially to the growth. Finally, the real key to growth can be said to be the ingenuity and efforts of management and workers which tied all the factors together, making the most of them for maximum productivity.

It is estimated that there are presently about 1,250,000 workers in the electrical machinery industry. According to the Census of Manufacturing Firms of MITI (Ministry of International Trade and Industry), in 1955 there were 230,000 in this industry. By 1970, as many as 1,340,000 were employed. Presently, the workforce has fallen below the peak figure. The percentage of female employees among the total workforce is about 35 per cent for the electrical machinery industry as a whole. It is as high as 60 per cent in electronic parts and acoustical instruments and equipment. In contrast, in heavy electrical machinery and computers, where male employees are predominant, the proportion of females is around 30 per cent.

According to the forecast of the Industrial Structure Council, production growth in the electrical machinery industry until the year 1985 is expected to be maintained at about an 8.5 per cent level. This is about 2.5 percentage points above the macro-economic growth forecast for the economy in general, and is the largest growth expected among all machinery and tool industries. The decline from the high growth era into a period of considerably lower over-all growth seems unavoidable.

In order to cope with changed conditions, the companies of the electrical machinery industry are promoting technology intensification and expansion into international markets. Concomitantly, an even greater strengthening of efforts to reform the financial and manpower structure is also taking place. Probably these efforts to cope with the low growth era will be complicated by movements toward import restrictions and tariff barriers in the markets of industrially advanced nations and by rapidly growing less developed countries who are catching up and moving into

certain consumer product areas. With these prospects in mind,
both labour and management of the electrical machinery industry
face an inevitable restructuring of the industry. New policy
plans and concepts in the area of labour relations are also being
formulated based upon this outlook.

(b) Industrial relations in the electrical
     machinery industry

The Japanese labour union movement in earlier days was
characterised by repeated and explosive strikes in an impoverished
economy and under a radical left wing leadership. From about
1956 things gradually began to come under control, having passed
through a "red purge" (weeding out of extreme communist leaders)
era brought about in a climate of corporate reconditioning, against
a background of national deflation policies, and also through the
instructions and encouragement of the occupation forces. At this
time the electrical machinery industry was on the road to recovery,
being supported by expansion in demand for heavy electrical equipment needed for plant and equipment investments in growing basic
industries. Within a short period of time, the industry would
also profit from the strong home appliance boom. In these
surroundings and forces, Denki Roren (All-Japan Federation of
Electric Machine Workers' Union) was founded in 1953.

Denki Roren is an industrial union affiliated with Churitsu
Roren. Denki Roren is the largest single industrial union in
Churitsu Roren. Its 550,000 members comprise 40 per cent of the
workers in the 1,350,000 affiliated membership of Churitsu Roren.
It should be noted that Churitsu Roren itself has considerable
influence as it is often the deciding power factor among the other
three national centres - Sohyo, Domei, Shinsanbetsu. Since
1959, Churitsu Roren has been a member of the Shunto Joint Struggle
Committee, and to this extent co-operates with Sohyo in pursuing
wage and other demands.

Denki Roren also has an important role due to the high growth
and internationalisation of the electrical machinery industry.
That began when she participated with other major industrial unions
of steel, shipbuilding and automobile in forming the IMF-JC (International Metalworkers Federation - Japan Council) in 1964. Denki
Roren has since been part of the leadership in this movement to
unify the labour front in the metal and machinery workers' unions;
an organisation which has transcended the boundaries of the four
national centres.

The labour movement in the electrical machinery industry is
fundamentally based on the single enterprise unit. This is no
different from the pattern observable in other private industrial
sectors. The workers are organised with the other workers of the
same firm, and most belong to a union operating a union shop type
system. The individual worker is not directly affiliated to
Denki Roren. Rather it is the enterprise union that joins the
industrial union's upper body. Collective bargaining is carried
out at the enterprise level, and labour agreements are negotiated
and signed between labour and management at company level.

The leadership and guidance given by Denki Roren to its
affiliated unions come from two different sources. One is that
in deciding the course of policy actions within the federation,
the 14 major labour unions of the large-scale firms such as Hitachi,
Toshiba, Mitsubishi and Matsushita have an unusually strong
influence.

Another source of leadership derives from the way in which Denki Roren itself operates. Denki Roren has its own independent survey and research capability as well as the ability to formulate effective policies. This in itself wins respect from below and makes leadership initiative possible. Furthermore, Denki Roren's undisputed position in the total labour movement of the nation makes it possible for its influence to penetrate all the way down to the individual union members.

Although collective bargaining in the industry continues to take place at the individual firm level, the unions of the various companies are gradually coming closer together in policy and action. This "strengthening of leadership" initiative by the industrial union occurred in the 1960s. Such a trend on the labour side in turn seems to have led to stronger liaison and contact among employers who already had close connections. This resulted in many similarities in wages and working conditions among makers of approximately the same products and of about the same scale.

(c) The company, the individual,
    the labour union

As mentioned earlier the electrical machinery industry has been through a period of fast growth. Table 1 shows the trends in the productivity indicators of the industry during the period of rapid growth from 1955 up until 1975, in the aftermath of the oil crisis.

According to the table, the total output and the gross value added both increased by about 43 times. The workforce expanded by five times. On the other hand, the number of working hours decreased by 357 per annum. This means that labour productivity per hour rose 9.7 times, and wage earnings per employee increased nine times. We can also see that labour's share of the gross value added climbed by 3.8 percentage points.

From these statistics the following becomes clear. First of all, the jump in labour productivity was shared by workers in the form of higher wages and shorter hours. In other words, the increase in productivity also benefited the workers as well in a very real and concrete way. Secondly, our attention is drawn to the very large increases in the number of workers which took place during the period. Employment practices in the major firms of the electrical machinery industry, as in other Japanese industries, are such that growth of the firm is closely linked with the absorption of younger workers, who in turn push up from below the workers already in the company and thereby provide the latter with promotions in position and status. This is the desirable pattern for the core group of permanent workers, and it is growth that is the key to the process.

This is a classic example of the theory which has everyone sharing bigger pieces of a bigger pie produced by the efforts of both management and labour. Without a doubt, the increase in company profits was large throughout this period. From 1951 to 1974, the ratio of operating profit to gross capital for the electrical machinery industry never fell below the average of the same for industry as a whole. Yet the workers during this period were also able to enjoy a high level of guaranteed employment security, increased wages, improvements in employee benefits and services, and career promotions with accompanying self-fulfilment on the job. Not only the pie increased in size but labour's slice of it also grew considerably.

This is documented in an attitude survey of 3,354 workers undertaken by Denki Roren in 1976. One survey item questioned worker perception of "the union and company relationship". Only 18.5 per cent answered that "the interests and positions of labour and management" are "fundamentally a relationship of antagonism and conflict", a figure close to the 15.3 per cent who answered that the interests between the two "are fundamentally one and the same". The great majority of 58.1 per cent confirmed that they visualised industrial relations as "confrontation and harmony".[1]

In a word, then, the electrical machinery industry has witnessed continuous technological innovation and strong competition in new product development, leading to the achievement of high growth and the realisation of mutual benefit to both the corporation and the individual. The medium which largely brought this about, assuring an equitable distribution of profits, were enterprise unions under the leadership of a strong and influential industry-wide union.

Let us now look at the developments in wages and working conditions in the electrical machinery industry. We can perhaps find in the industry's industrial relations a number of instructive examples of how "co-operation" and "confrontation" were reconciled into mutually acceptable outcomes.

2. Gains made in wages and working conditions

The most important issues needing improvement, and the ones which labour and management in the electrical machinery industry expended the greatest efforts on over the last ten years, concern the working conditions treated in this section and the housing problem described in the following section.

(a) Wages and bonuses

The changes in average cash wages (excluding variable payments such as holiday and overtime premiums, but including allowances for dependants) over the last ten years for workers in the electrical machinery industry are seen in table 2. Between 1968 and 1977, average cash wages increased by 3.9 times nominally and 1.7 times in real terms. This figure is comparable to the monthly wage payments for the manufacturing industry as a whole (companies with over 30 people) as compiled in the Government's Monthly Labour Survey. According to this, between 1968 and 1976 there was a real wage increase of 1.65 times. The rate of wage increase of workers in the electrical machinery industry, therefore, was slightly above the average for the total manufacturing industry.

Union demands and settlement regarding the annual bonus in the period from 1968 to 1977 appear in table 3. As is observable, the bonus of each year was consistently in the neighbourhood of five to six months of average monthly wages. (In the electrical machinery industry bonus payments have been demanded and negotiated on an annual basis since 1967.) This means that yearly cash income combining wages and bonuses has been between 17 or 18 times monthly salaries. If compared with the figures for all manufacturing industries, this record also would probably be somewhat higher than the over-all average.

---

[1] Denki Roren: Values and Perceptions of the Union Among Electric Machinery Workers, Research Report 131 (Tokyo, Denki Roren, 1977), p. 91.

The amounts of the wages and bonuses as revealed in tables 2 and 3 may not appear to be inordinately high. This is because in the electrical machinery industry there is a large percentage of young female workers who are paid low wages. Among male workers there is a comparatively small proportion of highly paid middle-aged and older workers. In Japan of course large numbers of young graduates from schools are recruited at the lower, entry wage levels.

Changes in the wage structure and payment schemes will be touched upon next. Until now the wage system has been undergoing continuous changes reflecting and reacting to the high growth era when huge numbers of young male workers joined the companies at about the same time. The current situation is one in which those large numbers of employees are growing older in an economy which is growing slower. This creates new challenges and causes new problems.

The wage system of Japan's major corporations, dating from the first half of the 1950s, is a seniority based scheme in which all workers were allotted fixed incremental increases. In the latter half of the 1950s and even later there were massive hirings of young school graduates which tended to boost starting salaries. Technological innovation, moreover, was already modifying the old job patterns and skill systems. All this tended to increase pressures for change of seniority wages. This led to management efforts in the areas of job pay and payment by ability. The moves originally came from the management's side, and in the beginning almost all of the labour unions displayed attitudes of opposition.

In the electrical machinery industry the bulk of the predominantly semi- or even non-skilled workforce consisted of very young workers and workers hired mid-career from other industries. As to the method of wage increases, the preference of both groups was the "base up", or across-the-board increases with little regard to length of service or job or skill differences. From 1959 through 1964 wage increases were centred around the base up. Meanwhile, the workforce matured enough in both age and skill composition to question this method of wage increases. From about 1965, a wage structure based upon job classification, with a minimum wage guarantee linked to the age factor, was proposed under the leadership of Denki Roren. By 1970, all of the major firms had adopted a wage system based on job classification.

Although there are differences among companies of the electrical machinery industry in terms of specific aspects of job classification wages, the basic concept involved is the same. It was decided at the 1968 Denki Roren convention to establish a minimum wage throughout the industry with a 25-year old worker as the standard. All workers over 25 years would be paid more than that figure. In addition job functions were analysed and evaluated in order to establish wage differentials and different payment rates depending on the occupational or job classification, and this was added to the minimum 25-year old wage figure. In 1970 that type of minimum wage floor was established at another age point of 40 years so as to guarantee higher standards for middle-aged workers.

In these ways, the wage systems in the electrical machinery industry changed, adapting and responding to the demands of management, changes in the labour market and changing needs among the

workers.   Such efforts and policies reflecting the needs of the
workers preceded similar developments in other industries.   This
is clear when we consider that the wage systems of the electrical
machinery industry served as important models for wage systems in
other industries.

(b)   Reduction in working hours

The electrical machinery industry, with its large numbers of
young workers began efforts to reduce working hours, particularly
in terms of the realisation of a five-day work week, sooner than
such efforts were taken in other industries.   One labour leader
reports that during the last ten years or so, pressures for a
reduction in working hours were as important as wage demands.   In
the 1963 Shunto, Denki Roren adopted a policy of for the time being
getting Saturdays off every other week.   By 1970 all the major
companies had adopted a complete five-day work week with Saturday
off every week.

The 1960 announcement by Matsushita Electric Industrial Co.,
Ltd., that it would adopt a five-day work week no later than 1965
stirred interest throughout Japan to the issue of shortening the
working hours.   In 1965, Matsushita actually entered into a
complete five-day work week.   The other major firms, however,
moved into an alternative Saturdays off scheme between 1963 and
1965.   After experimenting for half a year with a complete five-
day work week between 1966 and 1968, they moved fully into the
system between 1967 and 1970.   Since then every year demands for
reduction in hours continue and the drive for gaining more holidays
progresses.

Working hours per year are 2,032 for communication equipment
makers, 2,010 in the large-scale home appliance area, and 2,000
hours for the heavy electrical equipment area.   As a result of
progress made here pressure from the workers for shorter hours
seemed at one point to have largely subsided.   Movements towards
reduced working hours in other less advanced industries have since,
however, been taking place under the guidance of the Ministry of
Labour, and substantial progress has been made in the 1970s.
This has led to the achievement of even shorter working hours in
some industries which surpass the earlier record of the electrical
machinery industry.   In reacting to these developments, some
workers in the electrical machinery industry are once again
interested in a still further reduction of hours.

(c)   Retirement system and lump-sum
retirement allowances

In most of the companies the retirement age had been fixed
for male workers at 55 years and for female workers at 50 years.
From 1962 it began to be extended concurrently with the revision
of the labour agreement for the whole electrical machinery industry.
In the major enterprises by 1972, a 60-year retirement age for
male employees and 55-60 for female workers was realised.   Conditions concerning the extension of the compulsory retirement age
(1970-76) in unions affiliated with Denki Roren are found in
table 4.   The changes occurring during 1962-72 among the companies
participating in this study group are presented in table 5.

The demand of Japanese workers to extend the retirement age from the traditional 55 years comes from factors such as the lengthening of life expectancies in the 1960s and the trend towards a nuclearisation of the family unit (fewer older people were in the position of being able to dwell together with their children's families and thus lacked financial support from the family in old age). In addition, public welfare pension payments usually started at age 60 for males (55 for females). Substantial improvements took place after 1973 in the public welfare pension scheme. It had been most inadequate until then. This was still another reason why workers pressured for an extension of the retirement age. Among Japanese workers there is a developing trend demanding the right to work until age 65. This means that yet another extension of the retirement age may be in the offing.

The first extension of the compulsory retirement age occurred in 1962, when Matsushita Electric Industrial Co., Ltd., increased it to a uniform 57 years regardless of sex. Among the leading corporations of the industry, there has since been steady progress made in experimental systems of finding work for retirees through part-time hiring or special assignment for one or two years. In 1968 most of the top companies followed a pattern of retirement between 56 and 58 with 2-3 years of re-employment. With the revised labour agreement of 1972, a compulsory retirement age of 60 years became the widespread rule. The fourth section will touch upon the establishment of separate subsidiary companies to absorb some of the excess middle- and old-aged workers.

In extending retirement ages in this way, there has not been the accompaniment of automatic incremental seniority wage increases. Wage increases have often either stopped at the previous retirement age level, have decreased in amount or at times the rate of increase in salary has fallen off. The reason is that in the process of the negotiations between labour and management, there is a trade-off between employment and wages. The wage developments can also be said to be in line with demands for something closer to payment by job content, as appeared in the demands for more wage equality expressed by the younger workers. It can also be looked upon as appropriate and fair from the perspective of wages paid to meet actual needs and expenses encountered in running households and supporting family dependants. Such obligations are generally not so great for the workers in retirement status as they would be for some younger employees.

Table 6 describes the typical conditions of the lump-sum retirement allowance practices as they exist in the leading firms. In an electrical machinery industry having a very high percentage of young workers employed, there had not been much interest in lump-sum retirement bonuses. Among the middle- and older-aged workers, however, dissatisfactions are currently on the upswing. The reason is that the linking formula between the amount of wage increase and the lump-sum retirement bonus is divergent, varying widely by company. Because of this the difference in lump-sum retirement allowances among companies has become greater since 1969. As revision of the lump-sum retirement bonus is only possible once every two years, this makes solution of the problem even more difficult for the union.

From the foregoing view of recent trends and changes in working conditions it should be clear that in terms of wages, biannual bonus payments, working hours and retirement systems, labour and

management of the electrical machinery industry have been among
the pioneers of reform and progress in Japan.   By developing new
concepts and redefining priorities, the industry has stayed ahead
of the times, and has met and solved basic problems with considerable imagination and foresight.

3.   Employee benefits and services

Activities in the employee benefits and services area of the
electrical machinery industry were originally initiated by management.   They were developed as necessary policies and facilities
to attract and retain workers.   Today, however, both management
and labour have a common interest in these matters which have
become gradually integrated into the industrial relations systems.
Many employee benefits and services are considered important
supplements to working conditions.

This section will begin with an examination of the efforts
made by both labour and management in this area by first looking at
a case study at Hitachi, Ltd.   This is a typical example of a
corporation having factories located outside major cities, with a
primarily male workforce.   Next we shall look at the "Green
Communication Movement" as it is practised at Nippon Electric Co.,
Ltd.   The increase in the variety of workers' demands in a new
climate of high economic growth is likely to create new expectations
for the improvement of the employees' working lives within the firm.
These may not always fit into the framework of traditional industrial
and labour relations practices.   The "Green Communication Movement"
is a good example of a policy of adaptation or countermeasure taken
by a corporate community in an urban environment which helped to
meet these needs and changing expectations.

(a)   Actions taken in the employee
       benefits and service area

Employee benefits and services at Hitachi, Ltd., are varied
and numerous as can be seen from figure 1.   Among those listed,
compulsory programmes or legally required benefits are not included.
Programmes for which there is controlling legislation, but in which
participation is voluntary are included however.   This would
include, for example, National Health Insurance, the Property
Formation Savings System and the Welfare Annuity Fund.

Figure 2 represents the progress which has been made in recent
years in employee services at Hitachi, Ltd.   From 1970 to 1976
employee service expenditures increased from 13.8 billion yen to
31.3 billion yen, an increase of 2.3 times.   During the same
period, total payroll or personnel expenses increased by 2.2 times,
so the rate of growth in employee benefits kept closely in line
with personnel costs.

Also during this period, all the firms placed strong emphasis
on providing housing.   Major causes of the housing shortage were
destruction from the war and unprecedented mobility of the population between different areas of the nation caused by rapid industrialisation.   As land prices in Japan are among the highest in the
world, it is not at all easy for an unassisted individual to
acquire a plot for building his own house.   Expanding demand
tended to boost land prices.   Behind the increase in demand for

housing were the rising income levels enjoyed by workers.   For
the worker, ownership of his own house had become possible and it
had become a realistic goal he was determined to attain.

At Hitachi, Ltd., a housing problem subcommittee was set up
within the Central Employee Benefits and Services Committee with
representatives from both labour and management.   In 1964 a comprehensive housing policy was formalised with a major policy change
from emphasis on company housing to the promotion of a system to
assist workers to acquire their own homes.   With this in mind, the
programme made provision for setting up a savings and loan association, and procuring housing lots and ready-built houses for sale
to employees.   In 1968 a housing loan system, fully financed by
the company, was set up and the following year a system of home
owner insurance was established.   By 1977 a Property Formation
Savings System was introduced.   At present, if one takes advantage
of these facilities, up to 15 million yen can be borrowed.   With
this type of financing the union maintains that it is not impossible
to buy and have a house even in the Tokyo or Yokohama area of high
real estate prices.

Two results are observable.   One is that there has been
remarkable improvement in the housing environment of the working man.
After the Second World War, there had been legal restrictions on the
size of homes because of an insufficient supply of building
materials. ✿ Moreover, adequate national housing policies were not
forthcoming, and even as late as 1963, 60-70 per cent of the
workers' dwellings were 35 sq. m or less.   At present this figure
has risen to approximately 80 sq. m.

Another change is the decrease of worker dependency on company
supplied housing.   We note in figure 3 that at Hitachi, Ltd., in
1967, 38 per cent of the male worker householders were living in
company-provided housing.   By 1976 this had decreased to 27 per
cent.   Moreover, among male householders, the rate of private
ownership in the worker's name increased from 44 per cent in 1965
to 62 per cent in 1976.   The comprehensive housing programme sets
as its goal, home ownership by the age of 35 with the repayment
of the housing loan to take place by the compulsory retirement age.

As for the future system of employee benefits and services
there are basically two outlooks, both of which are equally likely.
One forecast would be that the relative weight of the traditional
system which tended to assist and directly support the worker's
livelihood (e.g., food, shelter and transport) will decrease.
The other is that the percentage of benefits required by law will
increase, while the proportion of optional or voluntary private
services will in turn decrease.   Probably the only exception to
that will be in the housing area.   As these trends become reality,
the relationship between the individual and the corporation which
had always had the worker dependent on the firm will likely change
so that there will be a more equal interdependence.

Finally, some reference will be made to activities and developments in the safety and health area at Hitachi, Ltd.   The safety
and health programme again has developed in conformity to policies
set out by labour and management in a special committee on
safety and health.   One of the characteristics of the movement
in recent years is that authority and decision-making influence
have been granted to those operational officials responsible for
safety and health, and this starts from the level of machine and

equipment selection. Another outstanding trend is that the
present-day safety and health activities tend to involve all the
personnel including those at the top echelons, line management,
supervisory and worker levels. Still another recent feature is
that there is a greater awareness of the importance of continuous
health maintenance, and regular check-ups. Over the past ten years
the safety and health administration record at Hitachi has constantly improved as is shown in figure 4.

(b) Toward more pleasant surroundings

     The "GC (Green Communication) Movement" as developed and
carried out at all of the Tamagawa establishments of the Nippon
Electric Co., Ltd. (total number of employees involved - 9,000)
is a diverse corporate programme that defies easy labelling. It
consists of employment benefit and service activities, policies to
cope with and improve local community relations and schemes of
communications and participation in management. There are also
activities to beautify the natural environment.

     According to the company's explanation, the GC Movement
represents one aspect undertaken in Tamagawa of what is really a
larger company-wide "Q strategy". This "Q strategy" stands for
a company-wide movement of increasing "Q (Quality)" in management,
product and service, the working environment, the surrounding
society, human behaviour and action at all levels and in all
situations, and the corporate image in the eyes of the public.
The GC Movement was started in 1973 in Tamagawa for promoting the
over-all "Q strategy" programme under the workers' motto "Let's
get together, participate, work toward making everything beautiful".

     In the background of these developments there were several
factors probably responsible for getting the movement under way.
There had been a deterioration of mutual support and ties with the
local community as was evidenced by a declining public corporate
image and an increase in the voices of protest of residents against
local industry. A decrease in "community consciousness" or in
worker morale and corporate identity among employees was also
apparent from low interest and attendance in company-sponsored
cultural, social and recreational activities. Despite this,
however, it was the company's impression that the workers had
potentially strong inclinations to discuss and participate in the
solving of problems encountered both on the job and in the
surrounding community.

     The movement evolved as displayed in table 7. Each of the
activities listed there has its own entity and label. To introduce
some of them, "GC Hour" is a 30-minute discussion session held in
the workshop once a month. "Green Club" and "Pub Ingle" are the
names of bars for alcoholic beverages which are located within the
company. "Green Home" is a lodge with cafeteria and overnight
facilities which all members of the company can use for meetings
and social gatherings. "Management by Ideas" and "GC Suggestion
Box" are schemes for eliciting new ideas and novel proposals.
Collection of "Bell Mark" Stamps is a drive to gather trade stamps,
the proceeds of which are to be used as a donation to local
elementary schools.

As can be seen from these activities, the movement not only tends to deepen contact and friendship between the workers of the company, but by participating in such socially significant actions, the individual enhances his own feelings of pride and dignity while making a valuable contribution to the community.   The union is looking upon these developments somewhat favourably and is taking a wait and see attitude watching the moves and overtures the company makes towards employees.   Depending on the issue, the company will at times consult with the union, and in some instances action has only been taken after the company has been given the nod from the union side.

The GC movement of the Tamagawa facilities of Nippon Electric Co., Ltd., is the product of a critical study and amalgamation of employee services and education-training programmes which had existed at least in part before, in the light of new social needs, requirements, and changing expectations and wants on the part of the employees.   Most of the firms in the electrical machinery industry are carrying out similar "make our workshop brighter and better" type campaigns.   Also the GC concept of participation and contribution of good works to the local community has become widespread.   Labour and management often undertake jointly a variety of cultural and club-type activities for the employees' benefit. There are also cases in which the union on its own has built recreational facilities and established sport programmes.   The diversification of the employee-community activities is not limited to the experience in the electrical machinery industry.   They can very well be considered characteristic of a trend observable in industry throughout Japan.

4.   Employment of handicapped, disabled
     and older workers

Policies to assist handicapped and disabled workers are among the most important measures that must be included in any meaningful treatment of improvements in the quality of working life.   During the period under consideration the national Government had been promoting measures to increase the employment of the handicapped and of middle- and old-aged workers.

In this section a few examples shall be presented as they occurred in the electrical machinery industry.   The examples are not necessarily similar in nature nor were they motivated by the same reasons.   There are also differences in the institutions sponsoring the policy measures.   The first case is one of an employment promotion plan for the handicapped;   the next is the establishment of special corporations for middle- and old-aged workers.   Finally, a union arranged counterplan to assist those with incurable diseases, those requiring prolonged medical treatment and the handicapped is described.   This section is an attempt, then, to take a look at several progressive moves made towards creating employee services to help workers in such special circumstances.

(a)   Employment of the handicapped

(1)   At the Hachioji branch factory of
      Oki Electric Industry Co., Ltd.

The first programme was started in the outskirts of Tokyo at
the Hachioji facility of Oki Electric.   The branch factory is under
Oki's direct jurisdiction, and was opened in 1973 by a desire
expressed by the local community.   The motivation for constructing
the mini-facility was that it would make a significant and useful
contribution to the social welfare of the local community.   The
factory building is small in scale, an area of only some 130 sq. m.

At present the workshop is staffed by nine male workers and
five female workers, excluding the general supervisor.   All the
workers are mid-way career entrants (not hired directly from school
graduation) and all are in some way handicapped.   They all commute
from in and around Hachioji, and their attendance records are
excellent.   In addition, four workers have resigned either due to
moving out of the area or because their disability has considerably
worsened.   None has quit or left for other reasons.   Working
conditions are the same as for any temporary employees.   Working
hours have been shortened for each day at the request of employees.
Instead, the workers take off only one day a week.

Work operations in which they are engaged have been selected
based on three conditions: (1) operations involving only one
individual (not team work);   (2) work not involving the use of
dangerous materials and chemicals;   and (3) operations which can
be executed by the power of and the manipulation of the hand.   The
main work in which they are engaged now is the visual inspection of
printed circuits.   At times the workers perform drafting operations
and additional inspection jobs such as continuity tests.   Although
it takes a little longer than usual to become accustomed to the
work, once they have the experience the workers have achieved high
levels of performance with 10 per cent more efficiency per hour
than standard workers.

(2)   Employment promotion of the handicapped
      at Matsushita Electric Industrial Co., Ltd.

This example concerns a social welfare workshop for the
handicapped which is attached to the Kotonoura Rehabilitation
Centre, a public welfare corporation in the city of Wakayama.
The factory was completed in 1973 with the co-operation of the
welfare corporation, the national and prefectural governments and
Matsushita Electric Industrial Co., Ltd.   The purpose and induce-
ment to establish such a factory came from the determination to
provide work to those handicapped who had the ability to work yet
faced obstacles and difficulties in obtaining employment.   It was
hoped that by opening such a factory these people could lead
normal, healthy and happy lives.   The factory has a floor space
of 1,177 sq. m with an adjacent dormitory facility of 1,230 sq. m.

There are 12 staff employees in the workshop, one of whom is
on loan from Matsushita.   Additionally there are some 40 workers
coming primarily from the seriously handicapped.   Among the
workers, 30 must use wheel chairs.   All of them live in the
dormitory nearby.   Working periods are 7.5 actual working hours
per day with a 5.5 day work week.

Matsushita Electric has been co-operating by being in charge and responsible for three aspects of the programme - construction of an efficient and functional factory, the development of sound and profitable management practices, and manpower development through appropriate training and guidance. The work involved the assembly of dry cell parts, and from 1977 production of pocket warmer parts was included. In terms of business performance, the operation has been consistently profitable. The two transferees from Matsushita have now been reduced to one, due to the training and development of leaders within the handicapped workforce. Every autumn the handicapped workers are invited by the union members to a "cultural festival" (a kind of fair with food, games, singing, etc.) sponsored jointly by management and labour of the battery and dry cell division of Matsushita, the organisation directly backing up, advising, and assisting the workshop for the handicapped.

Recent legislation stipulates that 1.5 per cent of the work-force should be from the ranks of the handicapped. Matsushita is making an early achievement of this one of its top policies. More specifically the company is striving to find jobs within present operations which could be handled by the disabled, and is also in the process of redesigning certain jobs to suit the specific needs of the handicapped. Special consideration is also being given to their personnel and human relations needs as well as to safety features necessary for the handicapped. Before employing individuals from a school for the deaf and dumb, for example, much time was spent in preparation with the people at the local Public Employment Security Office (unemployment office), the school, parents and the individual to be hired. In prepara- tion for the entrance of the deaf-mutes, other employees in the workshop learned the hand signals necessary for communication. Such active and positive implementation of programmes are being promoted throughout the company.

(b) Policies of employment of middle-
     and old-aged workers

In 1970 the composition of the labour force in Japan was such that among males from 15 to 64 years of age, the percentage of those 45 to 64 was 26.8 per cent. By 1975 that had increased to 30.1 per cent. It is projected that that proportion will further increase to 33.9 per cent in 1980, and 37.0 per cent in 1985. Reflecting the past period of rapid growth, the electrical machinery industry is still an industry made up of a particularly young work-force. In spite of that the rise in the number of older workers and the provision of jobs and positions for them are becoming a major concern of both labour and management. One answer to this problem has been rapid and widespread extension of the retirement age to 60. (Refer to tables 4 and 5.)

The growth in the percentage of middle- and old-aged workers has really put management and labour, traditionally accustomed to employing a majority of younger workers, at a loss. What is to be done with seniority wages, promotions and raises? Many questions are left unanswered. There also is a limit to the number of older workers who can be transferred and absorbed into affiliated or subsidiary corporations as was effectively practised on a modest scale in the past.

The establishment of such subsidiaries originally took place
out of economic considerations rather than for the humanitarian
purpose of setting up workshops to accommodate older workers.
With the emergence of an excess supply of elderly workers, it is
probable that creation of the subsidiary companies has been strongly
motivated by the economic factors involved. Even if such subsidiaries are founded to assist the aging worker groups, it is
essential that the new company functions and survives on its own
as an independent corporation. Actually, it is only through such
a display of independent strength and vitality that the livelihood
and income of the company's workforce is stabilised and guaranteed.
On the other hand, in preparation for future consolidations there
is a lot of pressure on the subsidiary to operate profitably.
There is no doubt that an effective utilisation of middle- and old-
aged manpower resources is becoming critically important in both
the parent company and its subsidiaries.

The need for establishing healthy subsidiaries is becoming
widely recognised, and while effectively utilising surplus elderly
talent there, the same will also have to take place in a systematic
way in the parent corporation. For this purpose, essential tasks
include a reassessment and updating and strengthening of the older
workers' skills and production capabilities, along with perhaps a
second look at reorganisation of work processes. Some companies
already provide work space and a production set-up within the
larger factory purely for the use of the middle- and old-aged
workers. Following are descriptions of the establishment of
subsidiaries, the assignment of a workshop exclusively for senior
workers and a re-employment or job placement consultation service
as they are actually carried out at Nippon Electric Co., Ltd.

(1) Nippon Electric Welfare and
     Service Co., Ltd.

This company was founded in 1970 for the purpose of taking
charge of the mailing service, custodial service, and aspects of
the employee benefits and services programme. Among the 867
employees, 516 (60 per cent) are over 45 years of age. The
breakdown of employment by job function is mail sorting and delivery
(52 per cent), food preparation in the dining hall (19 per cent),
custodial and maintenance (8 per cent), boiler room attendants
(6 per cent), and sales personnel in company stores (6 per cent).
The remaining 9 per cent are in management and supervisory positions
throughout the company. On paper the company is composed of
temporary transferees from the parent company. If an employee of
the parent over 56 years of age so desires, however, he may
officially switch his affiliation over to the subsidiary. Should
one join the subsidiary in this way, he is guaranteed a job until
age 62. Workers at Nippon Electric Welfare and Service Co., Ltd.,
are not members of the labour union, but working conditions are
determined after consultation is held with Nippon Electric Workers'
Union.

(2) Nippon Electric Warehouse and
     Distribution Co., Ltd.

Established in 1972, it takes custody of the products and
materials used at Nippon Electric. It is also in charge of
packaging, cargo handling and delivery. Of the 1,088 workers
employed, 51 per cent are over 50 years old. These workers,
however, are allowed to handle only light-weight products and
materials.

(3) Nippon Electric Machinery Tool Co., Ltd.

Of its 224 employees, 105 are over 45. Work consists of
the custody, maintenance and lending of machinery tools.

(4) Nippon Electric Komu (Plant
Maintenance and Construction
Service) Centre Co., Ltd.

Among 80 personnel, 45 are over 45. Operations here include
maintenance of factories, offices and buildings, construction of
and changes in floor plans and layout, and care of the gardens
and grounds.

(5) Allocation of a specific workshop or
job solely to older workers

These senior workers are in charge of only the midnight shift
(10 p.m. to 6.30 a.m.) of the operation and inspection of the
furnace equipment used in making transistors. Actual working time
for some 64 employees, however, is only 7.5 hours.

(6) Placement service for senior workers

This is a service to re-employ usefully workers who reached
the age of 56, and would like to work at a new or different job
until the compulsory retirement age of 60. Information on job
offers and possibilities (from both within and outside Nippon
Electric) is centrally maintained by the personnel department where
efforts are made to place the job candidates.

At Nippon Electric a survey of worker morale and satisfaction
was undertaken among the middle- and old-aged workers in the above
companies (1) to (3) and in workshop (5). Seventy to 73 per cent
answered that they had a "sense of worth doing (yarigai)" their
present job. When asked if they were satisfied working at the
present company, positive replies ranged from 59-70 per cent.

(c) Voluntary activities of the labour union

As a result of the rise in workers' expectations, there is no
longer tolerance of what used to be a reconciliation to the
unhappiness and hardship resulting from accidents, fire, natural
calamities, etc. In such instances if the individual involved
does not have sufficient resources to get by on his own, relief
must be provided, whether it comes from a public source, the
corporation or the union. The Matsushita Volunteers' Club is an
example of a union programme.

The club is an organisation directly run by the Matsushita
Electric Industrial Workers' Union and is independently financed.
It was founded in the autumn of 1977. After making a comprehensive
survey of 60,000 union members over a one-year period it was found
that as many as 1,500 members (2.5 per cent) had someone in their
immediate families suffering from a chronic illness or a handicap.
In view of this it was decided to begin a programme of services,
including voluntary activities on the part of union members, through
an organisation as presented in figure 5.

Celebrating its thirtieth anniversary, the Matsushita Electric Industrial Workers' Union is now planning for the opening of a kidney dialysis centre. It has always been difficult for the employees working in places other than the head office and factories around the Osaka area to make business trips to Osaka because kidney dialysis is not readily available for them. Moreover, because it is not very convenient for workers living in Osaka to have treatment in the evening, there have been many instances of time off from work to receive the treatment during the daytime. The programme of the dialysis centre is being designed to meet these needs.

5. Small group activities

In the 1960s small group participation and autonomous activities sprang up in the atmosphere of Japanese industrial relations, rapidly taking root in corporations throughout the nation. These activities are now observable in some areas of Korean and Taiwanese industry. Small group activities are often found under such names as QC (quality control) Circles and ZD (zero defects) Movement. There are also many examples in which individual firms have created their own unique, organisational names. Although there are small differences in function and substance, basically the units have been set up on the initiative of the corporation, and are participative activities usually aimed at some improvement in the workshop and operational methods with optional participation of employees and some degree of self-management.

In the electrical machinery industry, these small group activities had an early start. Our focus will be primarily on developments that took place at Hitachi. As far back as 1930 a scheme of official commendation for employee suggestions was started. In 1937 a number of cross-departmental volunteer study groups were organised made up of the company's technical staff and engineers. This well demonstrates that Hitachi has been strong on worker initiated, autonomous management tradition since well before the war. After the Second World War there was a revitalisation of training for managers and supervisors. Subsequently, senior management began actively to promote productivity improvement campaigns, with line managers and supervisors being held responsible for the results. Such campaigns obviously promoted and strengthened the self-initiating capabilities of production departments and sections.

In the mid-1960s QC and ZD activities were introduced at Hitachi, Ltd. QC first appeared at the Kameido factory (presently at Narashino) and ZD at the Tochigi manufacturing plant. The adoption of small group activities throughout the company was promoted by the company-wide MI (Management Improvement) campaign begun in 1968. In order to make the MI campaign more effective, all the upper managers at the plant locations strove to develop small group activities at the workshop level. The greatest spur to widespread use of these groups came between 1971 and 1972.

By 1976 small group activities were being carried out at all of Hitachi's 27 factories. There are presently as many as 6,182 circles and groups, with about 10 members in each one. At each factory a small group activity office with a full-time or part-time staff has been set up. Currently there are 85 such staff offices. Activities are organised by the factory centred around this office.

Participants in the groups are recruited through the managers and
supervisors.   Participation is voluntary and the activities
themselves are generally carried out through self-rule and consensus
of the group.

It is hoped that the campaign will be given further stimulus
by the holding of periodic meetings at the factory which are used
as opportunities to present and obtain recognition for any progress
made by the groups in the management improvement area.   Among the
factories there are exchange meetings of MI results, with five
factories having taken part in 1973.   In 1977 the number of
exchanges among factories was increased with 17 plants participating.
There are plans for a company-wide exchange convention in the
future.   One of the results of the small group activities is that
the number of improvement suggestions per employee has been on the
increase, as recorded in recent years.   (The number of suggestions
per employee of the entire company for the half year's measured
period.)

1973	1.5
1974	1.8
1975	2.3
1976	4.7

Small group activities were originally launched by management
with the purpose of improving management.   Widespread adoption of
the groups grew rapidly because the autonomous activities in the
small groups helped give the workers "yarigai", a sense of worth
in doing, and "ikigai" or a sense of fulfilment in living.   Workshop organisations in Japan have always had a tendency to develop
strong characteristics of feelings of community, solidarity and
team play.   If one adds autonomous, self-rule through democratic
dialogue as promoted in postwar education, plus the working man's
expectations brought about by rapid economic growth, it can be
understood why there has been so much action in this area.

In 1974 when the All-Japan Federation of Electric Machine
Workers' Union conducted an opinion poll, there was some diversion
of views among union members concerning small group activities (see
table 8).   One-third of those surveyed worked in shops where such
activities were not practised.   Of those exposed to the groups,
some two-thirds felt some dissatisfaction.   Is it likely that the
spread of the movement since the survey has reduced further the
negative reactions or "dissatisfaction among the majority"?   Or,
has the cause of the discontent been remedied?   Thirty per cent
of those familiar with the scheme were very much in favour of it.
Does this suggest that there were big possibilities for the
practice?   Any attempt to answer these questions would merely end
in speculation.   In reality, since 1974, there has been an even
more impressive diffusion of these small groups at all the companies.

The self-autonomous groups, however, are presently facing an
important transition period.   The largest problem they are
encountering is the gradual diminution of the utility of these
schemes from both the corporation's and the individual's viewpoint.
That means that the edge of excitement becomes dull and this could
lead to loss of enthusiasm for the campaign in general.   What this
probably tells us, however, is that within limited areas the
practice of making decisions through small groups in the workshop
has firmly taken root.   If there are further developments in this
direction these will probably take the form of a greater degree of
voluntary self-management, that is to say, more autonomy in the
small groups, as will be described later on.

In the beginning the attitude of the unions towards small
group activities was one of considerable criticism.   The unions
felt that such activities would tend to divert some of the energy
which they thought should instead be spent on the union's programme.
When it became clear, however, that there was no such danger in
reality, the widespread position became one of neither hostility
nor enthusiastic support.   Today there is no opposition providing
the group sessions do not lead to an increase in the workload or
overtime work without pay.   The union is, however, reluctant to
grant that small group activities organised with management
initiative and leadership are in themselves an example of an
improvement in the quality of working life.

On the contrary, the unions are seriously examining how to
cope systematically with the dramatic change in worker consciousness
which must underlie such a rapid diffusion of management inspired
activities and the widespread worker participation they enjoy.
Shifts in worker consciousness of themselves probably have a
relationship as well, and lead to worker demands for the democratisation of labour union activities.   A successful and satisfying
experience with one's role in small group activities in the workshop as an employee of the company also leads to a heightening
of eagerness to participate in the decision-making process as a
union member.   In this way the union, sensing the pressure from
within, has had to carefully size up and begin to face the issue
of participation in management as shall be related in section 7.

6.   Reorganisation of work

In this section we consider improvement in the quality of
working life in the electrical machinery industry as it relates to
work restructuring schemes.   The period discussed is one in which
there was rapid progress made in shifting to production of larger
scale with the accompanying technological innovations often leading
to monotony or intensification of work functions.   Attention will
be turned to questions such as what was the level of job satisfaction
among workers during this period, what measures did the company
employ to adapt to such changes in job structure and organisation,
what degree of emphasis did labour and management place on attaining
job satisfaction and what are their plans for assuring it in the
future.

(a)   Job satisfaction

In the electrical machinery industry, as shown in table 9,
there was already a move to large-scale production.   The survey was
performed in 1969 by Denki Roren and it covers the affiliated unions.
Among 66 unions surveyed, 54 reported that within the past year
there was a significant expansion of the production process.   In
57 unions there were reports of new types of product models, and at
56 unions there was an intensification of labour (more work per
hour).   Twenty unions reported that the conveyor belt speed was
accelerated.   This was probably only symptomatic of what would
follow because the real rationalisation (application of new labour
saving technology) at the mass production sites and highly automated
electrical machinery factories took place after the oil crisis.

The issue of a "life and job worth living" became the focus
of great concern in the mid-1960s as a result of the heightening
and diversification of values and expectations on the part of
workers living in a rapid economic growth period. The small
group activities at the initiative and leadership of the corporation were welcomed as a way to inject meaning and purpose into
the workshop, even if at the same time their original aim was to
improve work methods and labour efficiency.

Denki Roren surveyed the attitudes of her members six times
between 1969 and 1977. The following is a look at the worker
perceptions of job satisfaction as revealed in a survey collected
in August 1974. Table 10 shows how the workers reacted to a
question on "yarigai" or "sense of worth doing" their present job.
According to the table, 65 per cent responded that they feel
"yarigai" either very much or quite a lot. The fact, surprisingly,
was that there were a large number of workers who were satisfied
with their work. In particular the satisfaction ratio for males
was as high as 70 per cent. Among female workers many of whom are
engaged in conveyor assembly work, however, this ratio was less
than 50 per cent.

The same survey asks workers about complaints and discontent
they sense in their workshop social and human relations context,
as well as other aspects of their working lives. As is observable
from table 11, again there were many girls (41 per cent) indicating
that there is "monotonous and boring work". Among those working
at the conveyor belt, this dissatisfaction runs as high as 46 per
cent. A different question illustrates that there are many workers
on the assembly line who experience the following feelings. (This
represents the combined responses of "always feel that way" and
"sometimes do".)

Bored and fed up	81.5%
Feel powerless and like a cog in a machine	77.8%
Working just because I have to in order to live	73.7%
Feel like the machine is operating me instead of my running it	64.3%
Feel lonely, isolated and helpless	43.8%

With the exception of the last choice "Feel lonely, isolated and
helpless", those working on the assembly lines complained of a
sense of alienation more than workers in other production jobs.

As was also clearly confirmed by the Denki Roren survey, the
female workers in the production facilities where the mechanisation
and division of labour are very minute with each job limited to a
narrow and specific function, there is the greatest lack of job
satisfaction. The decision, however, of how to evaluate the
problem and of how promptly to remedy the situation, varied greatly
between labour and management of the different companies. Even
within the same company there were differences depending on the
area of work in question.

Among the companies participating in the research, Mitsubishi
Electric Corporation, Hitachi Ltd., and Oki Electric Industry Co.,
Ltd. carried out experiments in which jobs and the organisation of
work were directly revised in areas subsequent to the setting up
of small group activities. Some of the highlights of this process
as unfolded at Mitsubishi Electric will now be reviewed.

(b) JEL assembly method and autonomous
     management

In 1964 the Mitsubishi Electric Workers' Union demanded that
the wages paid for simple, monotonous job functions be reassessed.
This was the first time that the problem of monotonous work was
articulated as such from the union side.   In response, some minor
revisions of the wage system were made, but the re-evaluation of
the routine and monotonous work was not as yet settled.   The
demand of the union was to have a greater weight placed on the
characteristically inherent psychological burden which goes along
with such dull assembly line jobs.   The movement towards
eliminating monotonous work itself through the application of
remedial production technology was initiated by management and was
an approach different from the union one of merely winning higher
compensatory wages.

The reorganisation of work and job restructuring through
careful application of production technology to this end began at
Mitsubishi Electric in 1968 at the mass production factories under
the lable of the JEL (job enlargement) method.   Later on such job
restructuring was carried out at a number of factories, but here
we look only at the JEL method as practised at the Fukuyama plant,
as well as the autonomous management programme of the Nakatsugawa
factory and the Iida manufacturing facility.

(1) JEL (assembly) method at Fukuyama

Basically the JEL method is an attempt at expanding job
functions and eliminating monotony by adding steps or operations
to the work cycle.   It was first introduced and tested at the
Fukuyama plant and applied to the assembly of fuseless breakers
and watt hour metres.[1]   As can be seen in table 12, application
criteria for the JEL method were established at Mitsubishi Electric.
The idea was to see that all of the job redesign efforts satisfactorily meet these standards.   A look at the standards will
reveal that JEL assembly methods offer possibilities for job
enrichment, small group autonomous management and job rotation.

At the Fukuyama works the success of the JEL method is well
illustrated by the 10 per cent average rise in productivity and
the 50 per cent reduction in factory defects.   There were also
signs of growth in the workers' sense of responsibility, and an
increase in workers' morale.   The number of suggestions for
improvement of the workshop and work process also increased.   As
for demerits of the JEL method, one was that excessive competition
was bred between the top workers.   Another was that workers of
less capacity preferred not to be made part of the new programme
but to continue doing their old jobs of a shorter cycle (fewer
manipulations or steps) at the pace determined by management
standards.   It was also admitted that the favourable effect of
the JEL method was only temporary, soon giving way to renewed
monotony.

(2) Autonomous management at
     Nakatsugawa factory

In 1971 in the assembly of gas clean heaters, a new product
susceptible to a high defect rate, there was a switch over from
continuous line method to small autonomous group management.

------

[1] This is briefly covered by Shin-ichi Takezawa: "The Quality
of Working Life: Trends in Japan", in Labor and Society, Vol. 1,
No. 1, Jan. 1976, pp. 29-48.

(See figure 6.)   For that purpose the gas heater was redesigned
so that it could be divided into several independent "modular"
parts, and the subassembly of each module was left to an autonomous
management group.   Each group was made responsible for carrying
out the complete work process design ("plan") and inspection ("see")
as well as execution ("do").   In other words, responsibility for
quality, regulation of work speed and the working methods were all
broadly entrusted to the discretion of the independent, autonomous
work group.

In making this transition to autonomous management, however,
meticulous and thorough preparation was required.   One step was
to arrange for the systematic distribution of authority and
responsibility among those parties directly involved, such as
line departments, auxiliary services, management staff and subcontractors.   A second was the need to establish an intensive
industrial engineering training programme known as the IE school
for supervisors.   Thirdly, preparations were made to make staff
technological assistance readily available without delay whenever
it was called for by line management.   Finally, a new skill testing
programme was installed for production workers.   Certain key
operations were designated as such so that only those workers who
qualified themselves in the specific skill areas could engage in
these tasks within each autonomous group.   Those who were directly
involved in the programme emphasise that the autonomous management
system became workable only after such preparations were made.

When the organisation of the group had taken place, a leader
was selected and training continued within the group.   Quality
standards were formulated and tools were fixed and serviced.   As
the last step, there were meetings with superiors and concrete
targets were set in terms of production volume, rates of productivity, percentage of product defects, reduction of costs and losses,
and safety.   This brought the groups directly into the actual
production phase.   As one result achieved in the production area,
the assembly time was reduced by nearly 70 per cent, and it is
reported that factory defects were cut down by almost 90 per cent.
Moreover, in addition to co-operative and friendly relations among
the workers, job improvement suggestions exceeded the target by
40 per cent.

(3)   Autonomous management at Iida factory

The Iida shop is a branch factory of the Nakatsugawa plant.
It is a new manufacturing installation specialising in the mass
production of ventilation fans.   One of the unique features of
this factory is its extreme degree of automation with widespread
use of labour-saving devices.   The amount of capital investment
per worker in such plant and equipment is 2.7 times that of the
previous ventilation fan producing facility.   Material labour
productivity is also reputed to be high - 2.8 times.   The break-
even point is at only 50 per cent of operational capacity, making
it indeed a high performance production facility manned by only
156 personnel.

Another unique characteristic is that from the beginning the
factory was designed with "the humanisation of work" in mind,
that is to say, with an aim towards making job enlargement,
autonomous worker management and job rotation standard features.
The conveyer belt assembly system has been abolished with the

small group autonomous management of three to four employees taking
its place.   Each member is in charge of the full assembly process,
which used to consist of 25 different functions on the assembly
conveyor used in the past.   Each group fixes its own production
targets daily.

The operational efficiency of this method is 25 per cent higher
than the previous conveyor assembly.   The percentage of defects
has decreased to 0.2 per cent or one-tenth of what it had been
before.   Only one person has resigned from the factory in the
three years since it has been in operation and the reason was to
obtain a higher education.   Furthermore, there is no sales clerk
in the factory store and the workers completely serve themselves,
pay on the honour system, and run the store through the same
autonomous management method.

Several examples have been examined of work reorganisation and
restructuring at Mitsubishi Electric.   The management presents the
following points as problems which are encountered in these changes
and developments:

(1)   Some workers are left behind.   There are some who do not look
       favourably on the new methods due either to limitations of
       ability or due to personality characteristics.   In some cases
       all three - JEL assembly methods, autonomous management, and
       the conveyor system - have had to be made available, giving
       workers an option to choose.   None the less, what can or
       should be done with those who are left behind?

(2)   No matter what system or method is employed, there will
       eventually be the problem of diminished enthusiasm.   What can
       be done about it?

(3)   Is it in fact true that lightening the feeling of monotony,
       or making a given job more complicated or enlarging it leads
       to significant improvement in the quality of working life?

(4)   What is the best way to treat monotonous work in terms of
       wage administration?

The Mitsubishi labour union, since 1966, has been studying
these matters through a committee dealing with work alienation.
The union maintains that the practical and efficient utilisation
of workshop meetings for such discussions should be encouraged.
The precedents set at Nakatsugawa and Iida are very special cases
much in the forefront.   Management involved is to be commended
for its revolutionary innovation and courage to try the untried.
Success was reached, however, because of long and conscientious
preparation including the founding of the industrial engineering
training programme.   The union does not feel, however, that this
kind of autonomous management should or can be immediately introduced
at other manufacturing facilities.   Rather it would be necessary
first to prepare carefully the development conditions that would
permit establishment of these activities in other factories as well.

(c)   The future of job satisfaction

The hypothesis that positive intrinsic job factors and
negative job factors are among the most important determinants of
job satisfaction seems also to hold true for Japanese workers as

supported by a study in which the workers from Oki Electric
Industry Co., Ltd. participated.[1] According to the study, the
intrinsic QWL (quality of working life) factors denote the difficulty of work as a difficulty which breeds challenge and interest,
task variety and change, degree of autonomy, sphere of influence,
opportunity to create, chance to enhance ability, enjoyment, and
finally, sense of accomplishment. For negative QWL factors there
are physical and mental exhaustion, monotony, loneliness, boredom
and weariness. The results of this research have been summarised
as in figure 7. Intrinsic QWL factors show the strongest positive
relationship to job satisfaction. The strongest negative relationship is demonstrated by the negative QWL factors. In this
diagram it can also be seen that organisational climate factors,
leadership factors and working conditions as extrinsic QWL factors
have an important relationship with job satisfaction.

Within the study group it was agreed that job satisfaction is
certainly one factor affecting the quality of over-all working life,
but there were strong views expressed that its importance should
not be over-valued or over-emphasised. Such doubts concerning the
importance of job satisfaction do not at all negate or undermine
the efforts and success at Mitsubishi Electric looked at earlier.
This can be said because if such management efforts result in cost-
saving production while also contributing to improvement in job
satisfaction, and aid in improving the quality of working life in
other key aspects, then such experiments should be rewarded with
the praise of both labour and management. If moves towards work
reorganisation and autonomous management do not succeed in meeting
these conditions, they will probably not be welcomed and approved
by management and labour.

It is a fact, none the less, that there is strong discontent
over the monotony of work, although admittedly mostly among the
female workers. According to the "Work groups and worker attitudes and consciousness" research of Denki Roren, the conveyor belt
speed is not unilaterally controlled or accelerated by management
and there is also a positive assertion in this report that the
functional autonomy of workshop groups is also quite well retained
and preserved.[2] Job satisfaction, in spite of that, is certainly
not very high. Denki Roren's attitude on the situation appears
in the 1976 report of the Industry Countermeasures Committee
entitled, "Research Report on the Humanisation of Work".

The report can be summarised in a few words. First of all,
the union by no means disavows or opposes technical solution
policies such as job enlargement, job enrichment, job rotation,
technical training, and small autonomous groups. Secondly, the

---

[1] Systems Analysis Office, Policy and Planning Division,
Labour Minister's Secretariat: A Study of the Amelioration of the
Human Work Environment (unpublished, 1977), p. 25. The research
was undertaken by Shoichi Kajiwara of the Ministry of Labour, and
Takao Kondo of the Occupational Research Institute (with Rikkyo
University at that time) as principal investigators. Both of
them served as observers on the present study committee.

[2] Denki Roren: Research Report 116 (Tokyo: Denki Roren,
1975), pp. 61 and 99.

union maintains that human relations problems in the workshop should be solved through participation in leisure time or community social activities. As a third point, the position is taken that improvements in working conditions and the working environment should be brought about by the routine activities of the union. Finally, however, the point is emphasised that the solution to job alienation only becomes possible by the participation and efforts of the majority of the workers. This brings into question the problem of worker participation both at the management and at the workshop levels.

7. Worker participation in management

The question of worker participation has received much attention in Japan. In particular the problem of worker participation gathers interest as an important key to assist and ensure that stable progress is made in improving the quality of working life. Among the different political parties, and between management and labour there are large discrepancies and for the time being there is almost no prospect for the establishment of legislative provisions for worker participation as have occurred in Western Europe.

The workers of the electrical machinery industry have been among the most aggressive, clearly expressing demands on the matter of participation. In this section we shall first of all examine the way Denki Roren is dealing with the issue of participation in decision making. Next a case study will be made of Matsushita Electric as an example of the most serious and thoroughgoing joint effort by labour and management towards worker participation in the electrical machinery industry.

(a) Denki Roren and management participation

Denki Roren is currently placing substantial emphasis on the issue of participation. The industry-wide union is of the opinion that participation is the key to the improvement of the workers' life in society in general, and that participation is also pivotal to the achievement of a humanisation of working life. Denki Roren maintains that at the four levels of national and local government bodies, industrial policy, corporate decision making and workshop level, the workers should directly participate in a mechanism allowing them to express their desires and make decisions in order to bring about changes in political and economic policy, the democratisation of industry and management, a fair distribution of wealth, and the humanisation of work. Within the larger perspective we shall focus on Denki Roren's attitude towards participation at the corporate and workshop levels.

Presently worker participation in management at the corporate level consists of collective bargaining and labour-management consultation systems. Among those two there are no plans to revise or change the way collective bargaining operates. It is thought, however, that there is a need to reinforce the system of joint consultation between the two parties. With that in mind, labour's attitude is that the areas subject to joint action and consideration should be expanded, and rather than merely reporting or perfunctorily discussing issues, the status of joint consultation should be elevated so that actual decisions are made in real

and important areas.   In particular, Denki Roren's policy is one
of having thorough and decisive consultation placing emphasis on
such matters as the establishment of new subsidiaries, partially
contracting out existing operations, mergers and acquisitions, plant
construction abroad, integration and consolidation of factory and
production facilities as well as decisions regarding plant production cut-backs and factory close-downs, and finally all plans
involving personnel actions.

The union places the highest priority on workshop participation,
and feels that it should be started immediately in order to achieve
the humanisation of work and democratisation of the company and
workshop.   This is based upon labour admitting after careful self-
reflection that although there are specific needs for participation
at these levels, the labour unions have not as yet been successful
or made the effort necessary to make the most of the existing
potential.   As for methods to realise this kind of participation,
the union sees establishing and strengthening labour-management
consultation councils, at both the plant and the workshop levels,
at labour's initiative.

(b)   Matsushita Electric Industrial Workers' Union and management participation

At Matsushita Electric over the years industrial relations have
taken shape around a system of labour-management consultation.
After the oil crisis, however, many union members saw limitations
in what could be accomplished through this system.   That was
because the labour-management consultation system tended to discuss
matters only in terms of implementation after the decision had
already been made by management.   It became clear that it would be
difficult for the labour union to influence adequately and exercise
power under these conditions.   The flaw in the system was not very
apparent during the era of high economic growth, but it became most
clear as the post oil crisis recession settled in.

At this point the union painfully realised that what was needed
was a consultation forum in which discussion could take place with
management at the step before actual decisions were firmly reached.
The hope was to be able to inject, and to have management take into
consideration, the intent and views of the workers as union members
represented by the union.   To this end the system sought by the
union was called the Management Participation System, and its
realisation was presented as a demand to the company.   This demand
was submitted to management in July 1976 as a clause to be entered
into a revised collective agreement.   The main points demanded
were:

(1)   Several representatives of the labour union should be given
      the right by the company to be present and express their views
      at the highest management policy decision-making meetings at
      the head office, factory and other levels.

(2)   Management should agree to add the following items for con-
      sideration and discussion in the labour-management consultation
      system: rationalisation schemes to increase efficiency and
      productivity, the expansion, revitalisation, construction and
      improvements of plant and equipment, the establishment and
      close-down of affiliated companies and subsidiaries, domestic

and international investment and market entry decisions, decisions on corporate organisational structure and management hierarchy, and matters related to the hiring of temporary workers.

(3) The company will make contractual commitment in the labour agreement to provide for workshop labour-management councils; this will be in line with the union's effort to strengthen its checking function on management decisions.

In summary the demand for management participation comes down to: (1) a strengthening of the union's influence and role in receiving information, and in expressing its position; (2) reinforcing labour's effectiveness and influence in concrete decision making by adding teeth to the labour management council, and finally (3) building real substantial workshop participation through including it in formal contractual agreements.

Reacting to these demands, the company would not give approval to revising the labour agreement along the lines requested. Finally, developments were confined to the following written confirmation of agreement between labour and management:

(1) A Management Participation Study Committee be founded for one year with five representatives each from labour and the management sides.

(2) Informal discussion meetings take place between the company president and the three top union officers.

(3) Informal management discussion meetings be held at the factory and head office general manager level between these top company managers and the corresponding union executives at that level.

(4) Efforts will be made to further substantiate and strengthen existing labour-management consultation councils.

As can be seen from the above, management participation at Matsushita Electric is only gradually taking form against the background of long, consistent, and generally good industrial relations. There were no overly dramatic elements of change observable here in arriving at the present stage of worker participation. Rather one might expect that the actual and substantive progress is for the future. In the near term there are the strongest possibilities for the actualisation of a contractualised workshop labour-management conference. Already at Matsushita Electric since around 1970 there has been de facto development of workshop labour-management conferences in a number of plants. In the forthcoming contract clause, it is likely that both labour and management will agree that such a body should be separate from the collective bargaining function. Probably the main objects of the consideration in the workshop labour-management conference will be such items as safety and health, workshop environment, and holiday and vacation arrangements. If this new conference concept is contractualised, the agreement of both management and labour will be necessary in order to make decisions in these areas.

Participation in top management decisions will probably remain difficult for the union to realise, at least in the form which the union is demanding. If, however, unions are merely looking for an

increase in influence in the decision-making process, and a forum
to air union views and needs with management, there are possibilities for the realisation of this. Moreover, the fact of the
matter is that the labour union is not after participation of a
co-determination order. Here again the probability is higher
that there will develop a de facto substantive advancement made in
the use of existing channels fit to the local reality and needs,
rather than the invention of drastic formal schemes.

In the foregoing paragraphs an analysis was made of the
initiatives and developments of labour and management at Denki
Roren and Matsushita Electric in the area of management participation. These developments represent only a very small dot on the
international scene, so small that it would not even be visible had
the above efforts not been taken to carefully trace its path of
progress. There is a possibility, however, that these unprecedented
changes will serve as leading indicators of what is to follow in
Japan at the industry and corporate level. In particular the
workshop labour-management conference, which seems to have the most
immediate chance of being realised, is considered to be of potentially great value in achieving a useful and needed balance in the
workshop role of the worker as both an employee and a member of the
labour union.

8.   Conclusion and a look at the future

In the "Work groups and worker attitudes and consciousness"
research conducted by Denki Roren it is held that worker consciousness is not primarily determined and formed directly by feelings
of alienation coming from the present conditions of the production
and work process, but rather by the personal attributes and
characteristics of the workers (age, education, sex, etc.), their
"life stage" (whether married, with family, etc.) and work factors
(the social structure and organisation of work and the production
process, the form of industrial relations and personnel management
and its philosophy). At the same time the union research also
maintains that worker consciousness is strongly affected by the
attitudinal values which the worker holds in regard to his future
in terms of work, position and status.[1] Certainly for the worker,
"the quality of working life" can only be judged and understood by
his putting into proper perspective and evaluating for himself his
experience and relationship to all of the above factors over the
long passage of time going back from the past and on into the
future. Looked at from this perspective, what changes in the
environment surrounding the "quality of working life" actually did
occur over the last ten years?

The outstanding growth and prosperity in the last quarter
century of the Japanese electrical machinery industry is by far
the number one factor in having a decisive influence on improvements in the quality of working life in the industry. High
economic growth was not only the source of improvements in the
various working conditions but it also brought about a guarantee
of employment security, opportunity for promotion, shifting of
personnel to challenging new work and new facilities, and an
opportunity to develop ability and skills. High growth also gave
the workers of the industry satisfying prospects for the future.

[1] Denki Roren: Research Report 116, op. cit., p. 101.

This needs emphasising as a fundamentally important fact. Even
if there were some minor complaints concerning their working lives,
such as discontent with monotonous work, that was not something
that posed a critical threat to the workers' basic life goals.

In these circumstances, efforts made at improving the quality
of working life initiated by labour and management on an individual
enterprise basis over the last ten years have touched all aspects
of working life. The increases in wages, bonuses, and other cash
earnings during the period of high growth were of direct interest
and concern to most workers. Consequently, this was an important
issue between labour and management just as it was in the other
industries; during the period cash wages of the electrical
machinery industry increased as much or more than the cash wages
in other industries. It must be said, however, that the single
most significant improvement in the quality of working life of the
electrical machinery industry would rather be the very early realisation of "non-wage level" aspects, those qualitative and quantitative
improvements in response to changes and new horizons in worker
consciousness and attitudes. Put differently, "the quality of
working life" in the electrical machinery industry is the basic
characteristic of its leadership and initiative - inherent in both
management and labour - to be way out in front in time and to bring
about an improvement a step ahead and before all others.

In terms of wages, quality change was apparent in the
restructuring of the wage system. As for other working conditions
and employee benefits and services, outstanding quality improvements
are mainly concentrated around reduced working hours, the system
for the promotion of home ownership, and an extension of the
compulsory retirement age. All of these concrete improvements in
specific conditions become after all only natural, in that after
they were achieved the patterns they set were soon followed in
other industries. If we look at any given point in time we are
impressed with the achievements of the workers in the electrical
machinery industry which "were to be seen nowhere else, were the
very newest, finest, and most advanced". It was the economic power
of the industry and the foresight of labour and management that
made possible the breakthroughs in the quality of working life
responding to the changing needs of workers. Thus, the workers in
the electrical machinery industry not only have been able to enjoy
a higher level of working life at any given point, but in the long
run have benefited from the improvements accumulated from year to
year.

Quality improvements in working life are also visible as the
result of individual efforts on the part of companies and labour
unions. Innovations from the corporate side were obviously
targeted at increasing management effectiveness and productive
efficiency. In order to attain this, it must be possible to meet
the changing demands made by both the society and the workers.
As for imaginative improvements coming from the corporate side,
we can mention the establishment of a better workshop atmosphere,
small group activities, JEL assembly methods, autonomous management,
and factories exclusively for old- and middle-aged workers and the
handicapped. Moreover, the voluntary activities of the labour
unions also fall within this category. If these activities in
themselves did not have the tendency to enhance the quality of
working life then certainly it would have been difficult for the
activities to have taken root in the industry.

There will probably never again be an age that can boast of the continuous reform and revolutionary developments experienced up until now. The reason is that an age of low economic growth will tend of necessity to place limits on the economic power of the electrical machinery industry. In such circumstances, improvements in the quality of working life will have to be thought of in even broader terms. For example, a very basic problem such as the stability of employment may emerge also in the electrical machinery industry in certain types of product and model production areas. Furthermore, issues such as those evolving around Shunto, bonuses, and lump-sum retirement allowances, will probably become points of more fervent dispute between labour and management than they were in the easy days of growth and prosperity. In the midst of an increasingly austere economic environment, it is very likely that the rationalisation schemes to improve efficiency, with their inclination towards labour saving and intensification, will become the focus of even sharper attention and perhaps growing opposition from labour. In these ways, the issues of "quality of working life" may for one thing conceivably broaden their boundaries to include more basic labour problems as the economy at large slowly settles into an era of modest growth.

On the other hand, slow but steady quality improvements in working life which were made necessary by the rise of worker expectations and consciousness, will probably not weaken in their importance in the future. Japan is now at a stage when the workers are more interested in the quality than the quantity of food served in the company dining hall. In the workplace there probably will be worker complaints and suggestions brought to the attention of management and the union reflecting their views and consciousness on working hours, the staffing of work, days off, holidays, unpleasant jobs, monotonous tasks and any number of other matters of concern to them. The increase in the ranks of the middle- and old-aged will naturally give rise to the challenge of finding and designing jobs for them. The recognition of the importance of the quality of working life problem of better providing for and accommodating the needs of those requiring prolonged medical treatment, the handicapped, and the chronically ill or incurable, will also probably increase. Changes in worker consciousness are behind the raising and forwarding of all these challenging and troubling considerations, and those changes are irreversible.

As an influential factor determining future change - particularly the long-term ups and downs of corporate prosperity and the more familiar changes directly affecting the worker and his working life - in the electrical machinery industry, the importance of management participation, more than anything else, comes to mind. Even if the realisation of labour union participation in management at the corporate policy level is still very remote, union participation at the factory and workshop level is already well within target range. Participation at this level has already been systematised and can be seen in progress at many of the companies. If participation mechanisms at these levels developed into a forum of not mere co-operation, but also an institution where conflicting interests are adjusted and resolved, the long-range influence of the development on working life would indeed be great, and would in all likelihood reach out and affect other industries as well.

Table 1: Productivity indicators of the electrical machinery industry
1955 and 1975

	Unit	1955	1975	1975/1955
Total output	¥1 000 000	249 506	10 821 261	43.46
Gross value added	¥1 000 000	110 605	4 779 996	43.05
Total employment		229 344	1 214 082	5.29
(Female employees)		63 346	445 186	7.03
Working hours	hrs. per yr.	2 312	1 955	-357 hrs.
Shipment per employee	Yen	1 087 912	8 913 122	8.19
Gross value added per employee	Yen	482 266	3 937 128	8.16
Labour productivity	Yen	470	4 559	9.70
Wage earnings per employee	Yen	188 046	1 684 011	8.96
Labour's share of gross value added	%	39.0	42.8	

Notes: 1. 1955 figures based on establishments with 4 or more
employees; 1975 figures cover all establishments.
2. Total output, gross value added and employment figures
cited from Census of Manufacturing Firms.
3. Working hours cited from Monthly Labour Survey.

4. Labour productivity = $\dfrac{\text{Total output}}{\text{Total employment x working hours}}$.

5. Labour's share of gross value added computed with the
formula provided in Census of Manufacturing Firms.

Sources: Ministry of International Trade and Industry, Census of
Manufacturing Firms.
Ministry of Labour, Monthly Labour Survey.

Table 2: Average cash wages in the electrical machinery industry
         1968-1977

Year	Nominal wages (yen)	Index	Rate of change over previous year (%)	Real wage index	Rate of change over previous year (%)	Con- sumer price index	Rate of change over previous year (%)
1968	32 112	100.0	–	100.0	–	100.0	–
69	38 188	118.9	18.9	113.0	13.0	105.2	5.2
70	45 209	140.8	18.4	124.3	10.0	113.3	7.7
71	52 883	164.7	17.0	137.3	10.5	120.0	5.9
72	62 163	193.6	17.5	154.1	12.2	125.6	4.7
73	74 548	232.1	19.9	165.3	7.3	140.4	11.8
74	98 353	306.3	31.9	175.5	6.2	174.5	24.3
75	109 973	342.5	11.8	175.5	△0.0	195.2	11.9
76	118 562	369.2	7.8	173.0	△1.4	213.4	9.3
77	124 388	387.4	4.9	167.2	△3.4	231.7	8.6

Note: Average cash wages exclude variable payments such as
      holiday and overtime premiums, but include allowances for
      dependants.

Source: Denki Roren Wage Survey.

Table 3: Annual bonus negotiation, union demands and settlements

Year	Union demand standard	Average demand in multiple of monthly wages	Settlement		Over previous year		
			Multiple	Amount	Change in multiple	Amount increase	Percentage increase
1969	Minimum of 5-month average with 4-month guaranteed as individual minimum	6.14	5.66	¥231 336	+0.16	¥+ 35 604	18.2
1970	Minimum of 6-month average with 4.8-month guaranteed as individual minimum	6.32	5.49	263 335	-0.17	+ 31 999	13.8
1971	Goal set at 6 months, minimum of 5.5-month average with 4.4-month guaranteed as individual minimum	6.07	4.92+α (5.01)	272 270+α	-0.57	+ 8 935	3.4
1972	Minimum of 5.5-month average with 4.4-month guaranteed as individual minimum	6.03	5.24	337 370	+0.23	+ 65 100	23.9

1973	Minimum of 6-month average with 4.8-month guaranteed as individual minimum	6.37	5.98+α	472 863+α	+0.74	+136 302+α	40.5+α
1974	Minimum of 6.3-month average with 5.04-month guaranteed as individual minimum	6.33	5.33+α (5.42)	554 454+α	-0.56	+ 93 885+α	20.4
1975	Minimum of 5.5-month average, previous year's settlement set as minimum at more prosperous companies	5.57	4.98+α	575 835+α	-0.44	+ 21 186+α	3.8+α
1976	Minimum of 5-month average, previous year's settlement set as minimum at more prosperous companies	5.44+α	5.17+α	659 272+α	+0.19	+ 83 437+α	15.5+α
1977	Minimum of 5-month average	5.42+0.06	5.07+α	710 326	-0.1	+ 51 096	7.76

Note: The symbol "+α" means that the preceding figure is the minimum amount or multiple of demand or settlement observed among the unions concerned. The figure that follows in some cases in parentheses is the actual average computed after settlement.

Source: Denki Roren.

Table 4: Extension of compulsory retirement age - No. of unions

	1970		1972		1976	
	Male	Female	Male	Female	Male	Female
No age limit	1	1	1	1	1	1
60	22	8	61	22	82	39
59	-	-	-	-	3	1
58	34	17	15	13	11	7
57	8	7	6	5	7	14
56	16	19	8	16	3	26
55	42	36	34	44	22	32
54-50	-	25	-	16	-	15
49 or less	-	10	-	8	-	4
Unidentified	1	1	-	-	-	-
Total	124	124	125	125	139	139

Source: Denki Roren.

Table 5: Negotiation on extension of compulsory retirement age

Name of union	Retirement age in 1962	1964	1966	1968	1970	1972
Hitachi	55	One-year employment extension with base wage remaining at 55 level for willing worker with sufficient health for his work assignment	Re-employment in special worker category or referral to affiliated company from 56 until 60	Compulsory retirement extended to 56, re-employment in special worker category until 60	Compulsory retirement extended to 60 (male) and 56 (female), effective September 1973, in newly established extended worker category	Improvements made in conditions of work for extended workers
Mitsubishi	Male 56 Female 55	Wages to be improved for workers on yearly contract after compulsory retirement	Union demands to be reflected on yearly contract system, ad hoc union management committee to be set up if necessary	Employment for 2 years in special worker category after compulsory retirement	Compulsory retirement extended to 58 (male) and 55 (female), re-employment in special worker category for 2 years thereafter	Compulsory retirement extended to 60 (male) and 56 (female)
Matsushita	57	Re-employment up to 58 on yearly contract basis	Ad hoc union management committee appointed, compulsory retirement to be extended to 58 in 1967 with additional 2-year re-employment	None	None	Compulsory retirement extended to 60
Nippon Electric	Male 55 Female 50	Re-employment of willing and healthy workers for 2 years	Compulsory retirement extended to 56 (male) and 51 (female) with additional 1-year re-employment	Re-employment made to 2 years	Compulsory retirement extended to 58 (male) and 53 (female) with additional 2-year re-employment	Compulsory retirement to be extended to 60 (male) and 55 (female), effective October 1973
Oki Electric	Male 55 Female 50	Re-employment on yearly contract basis until 58 of healthy workers deemed appropriate by management	None	Compulsory retirement extended to 56 (male) and 51 (female)	Compulsory retirement extended to 58 (male) and 53 (female) with re-employment until 60	Compulsory retirement to be extended to 60 (male) and 55 (female), effective October 1974

Source: Denki Roren.

Table 6:   Lump-sum retirement payments (1976)

Union	Length of service (years) (yen)		
	30	25	20
Hitachi	8 311 800	5 940 800	4 257 700
Toshiba	8 310 000	5 735 000	4 135 000
Mitsubishi	8 310 000	6 390 000	4 560 000
Matsushita	10 790 000	8 570 000	6 490 000
Sanyo	11 191 600	8 612 100	6 217 200
Fujitsu	8 593 100	6 334 800	4 360 200
Nippon Electric	8 542 300	6 576 700	4 250 700
Oki Electric	8 501 056	5 807 325	3 862 734

Note: Senior primary school graduate (8 years of formal
         education), male, factory worker, compulsory retirement
         at age 55.

Source: Denki Roren.

Table 7: "Q Strategy" and "Green Communication" Movement at NEC

"Q Strategy"	"Green Communication"		
	Dialogue	Participation	Beautification
"Quality" Management	Top management speeches Management News Green Club	Management by Ideas	
"Quality" Products and Services		Management by Ideas	
"Quality" Environment	"G.C. Hour" Good conduct awards	Management by Ideas "G.C." Suggestion Box Morning Music Request	Flower bed building Tree planting by company division Housekeeping days Dining-hall beautification Coffee snack bars
"Quality" Community	Community Association Plant tours by children	Bazaars Collection of "Bell Mark" stamps	Beautifying Mukogawara Station
"Quality" Behaviour	Top management speeches "Pub Ingle" Beer parties "Green Home" "G.C. Hour" Good conduct awards "Green Concerts" Birthday parties for newcomers Plant tours by mothers and children	Management by Ideas "G.C." Suggestion Box "Green Voice" Hobby Corners Lady's Culture Sessions Sports festival for newcomers	Trash Clean-up Campaign
"Quality" Corporate Image	"Green Concerts"	Management by Ideas	

Source: Nippon Electric Co., Tamagawa Works.

Table 8: Attitudes towards small group activities

Do you participate in voluntary small group activities designed for work and methods improvement such as ZD Movement and QC Circles?	Denki Roren - total membership (percentage)		
	Male	Female	Total
I actively participate and I am satisfied	19.3	12.9	18.1
I participate but I am not satisfied	45.2	34.0	43.0
I do not participate because I'm opposed	2.8	3.5	2.9
There are no such activities	28.7	39.1	30.8
No answer	3.9	10.4	5.2

Source: Denki Roren, Research Report 114 (Tokyo: Denki Roren, 1974), p. 117.

Table 9:   Union views on production scale expansion (1969)

		Number of answering unions
Was the production scale expanded during the past year?	Expanded No change	54 12
Were new product models introduced during the past year?	Yes No	57 9
Did the new product models cause changes in the production system?	Yes No	46 18
Were belt conveyors sped up during the past year?	Yes No	20 34
Do you have continuous, simple and repetitive operations?	Yes No	53 13
Are individual workloads on the increase?	Yes No	56 8
Are production time standards in use?	Yes No	49 17

Source: Denki Roren, Research Report 76 (Tokyo: Denki Roren, 1969), pp. 135-136.

216236

Table 10: Job satisfaction (1974)

Do you feel the "sense of worth doing (yarigai)" in your present job?	Very much	Quite a lot	Not much	Not at all	No answer
Total	14.3	51.0	29.5	4.2	1.0
Male	16.5	52.7	26.5	3.5	0.8
Female	5.3	43.9	41.7	7.0	2.1
Job category					
1. Production	12.7	45.9	34.8	5.6	1.1
(a) Conveyor assembly	8.7	38.8	43.0	7.8	1.7
(b) Machining	10.7	47.5	35.3	5.3	1.3
(c) Panel control	16.8	44.6	30.7	7.9	-
(d) Maintenance	13.6	55.6	28.4	1.2	1.2
(e) Supervisory	23.3	52.6	21.1	2.4	0.5
(f) Auxiliary service	13.0	47.8	39.1	-	-
(g) Others	9.4	44.1	38.5	6.9	1.1
2. Technical (production)	13.0	56.3	26.8	3.1	0.7
3. Technical (R & D)	20.9	63.2	14.4	1.4	-
4. Office (EDP)	17.1	59.5	20.7	2.7	-
5. Office (clerical)	13.3	48.6	33.1	3.2	1.8
6. Sales and service	19.5	60.0	16.8	2.2	1.6
Not available	10.5	49.1	26.3	12.3	1.8

Source: Denki Roren, Research Report 114, op. cit., pp. 134-135.

Table 11: Dissatisfactions with working life (1974)

Name three dissatisfactions or concerns which seem important to you in your working life

	1. Incongenial atmosphere	2. Monotonous and boring work	3. Nobody to truly depend on in workplace	4. Work is too difficult	5. Early morning, night work, overtime	6. Bad working environment	7. Poor supervisory practices	8. Insufficient holidays and vacations	9. Occupational safety and health hazards	10. Unfair and unequal wage payment	11. Little responsibility and authority	12. Dead-end job anxiety	13. Inadequate employee benefits and services	No answer	Sub-total
Total	24.7	23.0	23.2	3.4	7.4	25.0	27.9	14.0	7.0	22.8	19.3	22.4	21.7	7.4	249.2
Male	22.1	18.7	21.7	3.6	8.7	25.7	29.9	14.4	6.8	24.7	20.9	21.9	22.6	7.3	248.9
Female	35.3	40.5	29.1	2.6	2.4	22.1	19.7	12.4	7.7	15.5	12.6	24.5	18.1	7.9	250.5
Job category															
1.Production	24.2	28.2	22.1	2.3	5.9	31.4	27.6	11.1	9.5	25.6	17.5	26.3	17.9	6.3	255.7
(a) Conveyor assembly	27.0	45.6	22.7	1.2	5.0	29.3	24.8	13.0	5.7	22.7	15.6	32.4	16.3	5.4	266.7
(b) Machining	24.6	25.4	19.5	2.3	7.8	37.0	28.2	9.9	11.6	29.3	16.0	21.4	16.6	5.5	255.0
(c) Panel control	21.8	27.7	20.8	5.0	10.9	40.6	23.8	13.9	16.8	19.8	22.8	19.8	18.8	6.9	269.3
(d) Maintenance	28.4	16.0	25.9	3.7	11.1	25.9	35.8	17.3	6.2	25.9	19.8	18.5	18.5	3.7	256.8
(e) Supervisory	19.2	17.3	23.3	2.4	4.3	22.8	29.0	11.1	7.0	25.2	22.0	23.3	20.3	11.4	238.8
(f) Auxiliary service	13.0	17.4	21.7	4.3	-	21.7	34.8	-	17.4	30.4	8.7	21.7	39.1	13.0	243.5
(g) Others	25.4	27.0	22.7	2.1	4.1	33.5	27.7	9.8	11.0	25.5	16.3	30.1	17.4	4.4	256.9
2.Technical (production)	23.7	12.9	23.2	5.1	7.8	26.8	33.5	14.9	7.2	22.8	19.6	9.7	25.0	5.8	248.0
3.Technical (R & D)	21.8	8.3	26.7	4.9	13.4	19.1	30.1	22.0	2.7	24.0	24.9	17.3	29.8	8.1	253.2
4.Office (EDP)	33.3	23.4	25.2	4.5	18.0	22.5	29.7	15.3	10.8	13.5	19.8	8.1	18.9	5.4	248.6
5.Office (clerical)	28.3	30.5	21.8	3.3	5.7	14.2	22.5	14.9	2.1	17.0	19.7	20.5	22.3	10.9	233.6
6.Sales and service	17.8	10.3	28.6	5.9	8.6	14.1	31.4	15.7	2.7	20.5	22.2	20.0	31.4	7.6	236.8
Not available	35.1	15.8	24.6	1.8	5.3	24.6	17.5	14.0	28.1	19.3	8.8	21.1	17.5	10.5	243.9

Source: Denki Roren, ibid., pp. 166-167.

Table 12: Criteria for JEL assembly method application

1. Parts

   (a) Output   Minimum of several hundred products per month

   (b) Size of parts   Easy to handle with one hand while sitting; final product weight less than 10 kg

   (c) Number of parts   20 to 30

   (d) Cycle time   10 minutes in total

   (e) Number of tools   7 to 8

2. Operation

   (a) Difficulty   All electrical and mechanical adjustment operations and operations prone to defects should be included

   (b) Potential loss   All waste possibilities, balancing losses, handling losses and set-up losses should be included for possible future improvement

3. Quality

   (a) Test   All test and inspection should preferably be included

   (b) Fluctuation   Individual skill differences should be within a reasonable rage. Operational steps and key points should be clearly expressed

4. Information

   (a) Feedback   Line management should feed back output data, work errors and their causes to individual workers as quickly as possible

   (b) Group   ZD, QC and other small group activities should also be employed

   (c) Cost   Cost information should be provided for voluntary cost reduction efforts

   (d) Communication   Each group should be able to communicate with other groups

5. Human factors

   (a) Work pace   Workers should have experience with standard pace

   (b) Training   Work should have a training function

   (c) Rotation   Job rotation should be made possible

   (d) Responsibility and authority   Each group should have responsibility and authority

   (e) Planning   There should be room for creative work

   (f) Knowledge   There should be opportunity to gain specialised knowledge

   (g) Self-management   Self-management by objectives should be made possible

Source: Hiroshi Hayase, Self-Management at Mitsubishi Electric Nakatsugawa Works (unpublished article, 1977).

Figure 1: Employee services for Hitachi Workers

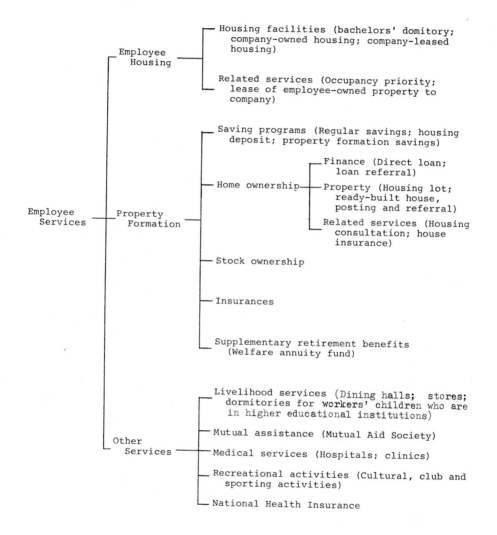

Figure 2:   Direct labor cost and cost of
            employee services

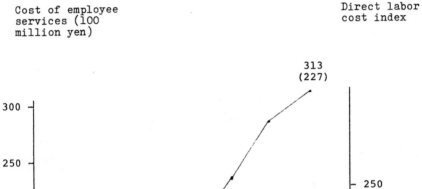

Cost of employee
services (100
million yen)

Direct labor
cost index

Source : Labor Union of Hitachi Workers

Figure 3: Home ownership and company housing
at Hitachi, Ltd.

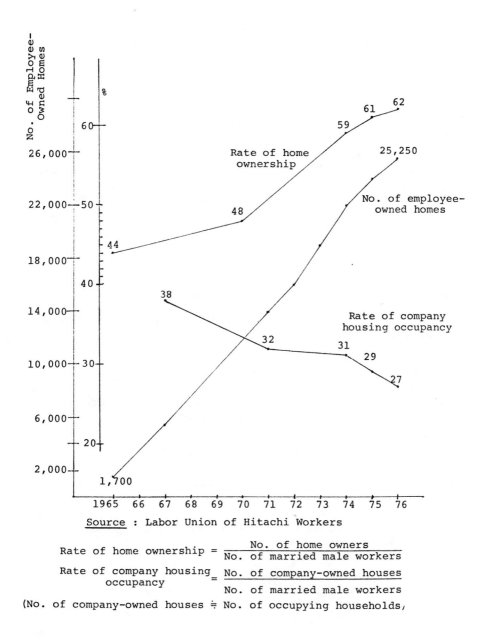

Source : Labor Union of Hitachi Workers

Rate of home ownership = $\dfrac{\text{No. of home owners}}{\text{No. of married male workers}}$

Rate of company housing occupancy = $\dfrac{\text{No. of company-owned houses}}{\text{No. of married male workers}}$

(No. of company-owned houses ≒ No. of occupying households,

Figure 4: Safety and health records of Hitachi workers

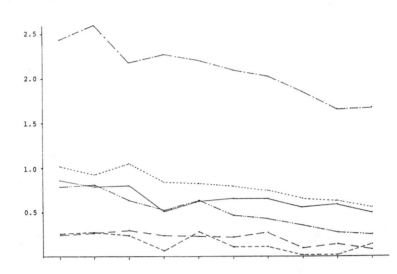

Sickness and Injuries-Non-Occupational Cause										
Rate of comtraction (%)	1.02	0.93	1.05	0.84	0.82	0.79	0.74	0.65	0.62	0.55
Rate of absence (%)	0.86	0.79	0.80	0.51	0.62	0.65	0.65	0.55	0.58	0.49
Industrial Accidents										
Hitachi										
Frequency rate	0.79	0.81	0.63	0.52	0.63	0.46	0.42	0.35	0.27	0.25
Severity rate	0.26	0.28	0.24	0.07	0.28	0.11	0.11	0.02	0.02	0.14
Entire electric machinery industry										
Frequency rate	2.44	2.60	2.18	2.27	2.20	2.09	2.02	1.85	1.65	1.67
Severity rate	0.25	0.27	0.30	0.24	0.23	0.22	0.27	0.10	0.14	0.08
Year	1967	68	69	70	71	72	73	74	75	76

—·—·—·— Accident frequency (for entire electric machinery industry)

················ Rate of contraction (%), sickness and injuries, non-occupational cause

———————— Rate of absence (%), sickness and injuries, non-occupational cause

—·—··—··· Accident frequency (Hitachi)

— — — — — — Accident severity (Hitachi)

— — — — Accident severity (for entire electric machinery industry)

Source : Labor Union of Hitachi Workers

Figure 5: Volunteer activities of Matsushita Electrical Industrial Workers' Union

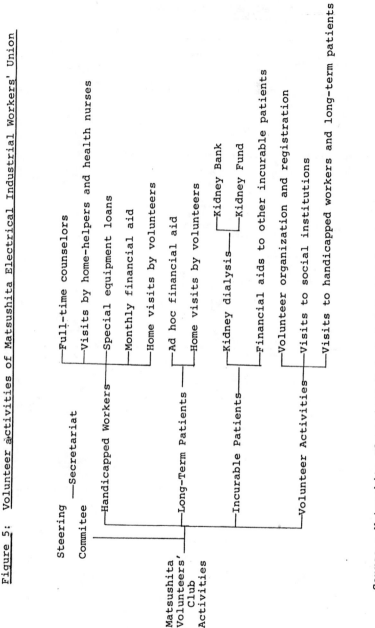

Source : Matsushita Electrical Industrial Workers' Union

Figure 6: Shift of gas clean heater assembly
to self-management

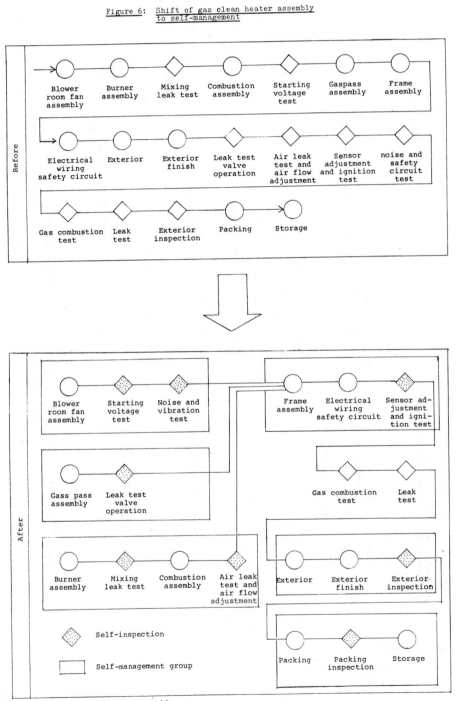

Source : Hiroshi Hayase, Ibid.

Figure 7: Intercorrelations among quality of working life factors

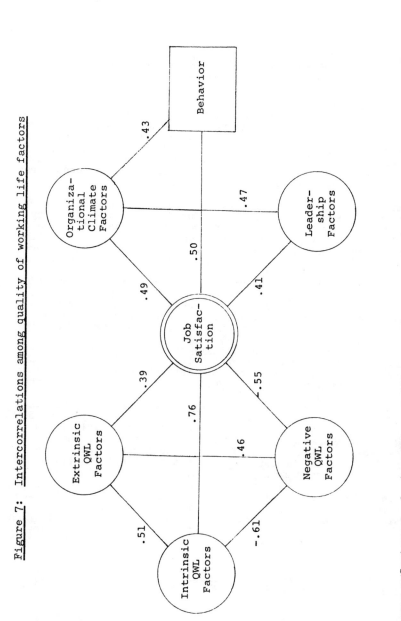

Source : Systems Analysis Office, Policy and Planning Division, Labor Minister's Secretariat, A Study of the Amelioration of the Human Work Environment (Unpublished, 1977), p.25.

Note : Intercorrelations are expressed in canonical correlation coefficients.

CHAPTER IV

THE QUALITY OF WORKING LIFE IN
THE AUTOMOBILE INDUSTRY

This report presents the trends in improvements in the quality
of working life in the Japanese automobile industry over the last
ten years.   Labour and management representatives from five companies, all having passenger car assembly divisions, participated in
the deliberations which were conducted from January to May 1978.
Japan's two largest automobile manufacturers were included among the
companies.   There were as well two participants from Jidosha Soren,
the Confederation of Japan Automobile Workers' Unions.

Substantial efforts are made every year to improve working
conditions and the work environment.   The first problem faced by
the study committee was thus one of narrowing down and selecting
what should be treated under the theme "improvements in the quality
of working life".   After discussion, as in the case of the other
two industries studied, shipbuilding and electric machinery, it was
decided to consider first the trends in working conditions during
the decade.   The committee members later presented and discussed
other areas which have important relationships with working life,
centring chiefly on actual cases at the companies with which the
study committee members are affiliated.   This report is thus a
summary of the trends and case studies presented and examined.

Concerning questions of the quality of working life, it is the
automobile industry which has attracted the most notable attention
throughout the world in recent years.   Automobile assembly work was
one of the focal points of research done on work alienation in the
early 1960s.[1]   The strike in 1972 at the Lordstown, Ohio, factory
of General Motors became a world-wide symbol of worker alienation.[2]
Although the scale of operations was modest, the assembly work of
the Volvo Kalmar plant in Sweden received widespread publicity as a
technological breakthrough in automobile manufacturing methods.[3]
In Japan as well, in the period of labour shortages prior to the oil
crisis of 1973, the automobile industry had great difficulty in
attracting an adequately large workforce.

For these reasons the study committee paid very close attention
to improvements in the quality of working life as related to the
organisation of work and job content.   As a common understanding on
the part of both labour and management, however, it became clear

---

[1] Robert Blauner: Alienation and freedom: the factory worker
and his industry (Chicago, The University of Chicago Press, 1964).

[2] Bennett Kreman: "Search for a better way of work: Lordstown, Ohio", in Roy P. Fairfield (ed.): Humanising the workplace
(Buffalo, NY, Prometheus Books, 1974), pp. 141-150.

[3] Stefan Agurén, Reine Hansson and K.G. Karlsson: The Volvo
Kalmar Plant: the impact of new design on work organisation
(Stockholm, The Rationalisation Council SAF-LO, 1976), 40 pp.

that during the period in question, from the workers' point of view, there were other areas more important than the problem of monotony in work. In order to assess properly the improvements made in the quality of working life during the ten-year period which reflected as well the changes in worker consciousness, it was considered necessary to cover all of the following areas:

- automobile industry and union-management relations;

- general trends in working conditions;

- employee benefits and services;

- employee education and training;

- relationship between men and jobs;

- small group activities and self-management.

Competition among companies is extremely sharp in the automobile industry since they all operate at much the same level of technology. As a result, it is relatively a homogeneous industry in terms of working conditions and work environment. Especially in the area of working conditions, a high degree of standardisation has been brought about at the industry-wide level through the influence and efforts of Jidosha Soren, the Confederation of Japan Automobile Workers' Unions. Throughout this report most of the data or case studies will generally apply to the industry as a whole. Cases unique to a particular union or company will be identified as such.

An introduction to the Japanese automobile industry and the patterns and trends observable in industrial relations follows.

1. Automobile industry and
   union-management relations

   (a) The Japanese automobile
        industry

The first four-wheeled vehicle powered by a gasoline engine was produced in Japan in 1907. During the next 25 years and as late as 1932, however, the number of automobiles manufactured annually in Japan never exceeded much more than 2,000. Some two-thirds of these machines were three-wheeled vehicles. The increasing military production during the Second World War reached its peak in 1941 when there were over 50,000 three- and four-wheeled vehicles (98 per cent were trucks) manufactured primarily for military use. By the end of the war in 1945, however, production had fallen to 7,500 vehicles.[1]

Growth in the industry after the War was spectacular. In just six years the 1945 production level increased ten times. Nine years later, in 1960, that figure had again multiplied tenfold. In 1976, 16 years later, production had once more increased ten times. This means that in 30 years production increased 1,000 times. The Japanese automobile industry in 1977 produced 8.8 million vehicles,

---

[1] Association of Japanese Automobile Manufacturers and Nikkan Jidosha Shimbunsha, eds.: Automobile Almanac (in Japanese) (Tokyo, Nikkan Jidosha Shimbunsha, 1978), pp. 72-73.

production figures exceeded only by the United States.   Japan
produces more than West Germany and France combined, and about four
times as many vehicles as either England or Italy.

Table 1 presents the productivity indicators of the Japanese
automobile industry over the last ten years.   They show the trends
in the number of cars produced and exported, total production, total
employment in the automobile manufacturing industry, per capita
physical and value productivity and the labour-equipment ratio.   It
can be seen from the table that, although there were almost no
changes in total employment, there were large increases in the
number of cars produced per worker, in total production and in the
labour-equipment ratio.

Table 2 indicates clearly the progress made in labour productivity in the automobile manufacturing industry.   During the
period 1962-73 the number of man-hours needed to produce one compact
four-wheeled vehicle decreased from 82 to 28 hours.   The reduction
in man-hours required was largest in the machining production process
which experienced the greatest advances in automation.   The smallest
man-hour savings took place in foundry, forging and press operation
processes.

The automobile industry has become the largest industry in the
domestic economy.   In the area of export, it has also come to be
one of the strongest industries in the face of international
competition.   According to the 1977 Economic White Paper, for
example, the optimum production capacity of an automobile factory,
estimated at 20,000 units in two shifts per month, was already
reached on an average in 1970 (figure 1).   Incidentally, the Volvo's
Kalmar plant was constructed in 1974 with a forecast of annual one
shift production of 30,000 units (monthly production of 2,500
vehicles).[1]   This rapid growth of the industry has, of course,
created a number of new problems both within the country and abroad.

Rapid growth in the automobile industry brought about the
problems typically represented by gasoline exhaust pollution and
traffic congestion.   On the international scene, the trade imbalances
due to the increase of exports to advanced industrial nations has
become a problem of the most serious dimension.   On all of these
issues, legal and technological countermeasures are being promoted.
Both labour and management of the automobile industry are seriously
working toward solving the problems from their respective viewpoints.

(b)   Industrial relations in
       the automobile industry

Within six months after the Second World War, when the labour
unions were allowed to reorganise, all of the major companies of the
automobile industry were unionised.   In 1948 such enterprise-based
unions formed a nation-wide organisation, Zenjidosharoso (All Japan
Automobile Industry Workers' Union).   In 1952, however, radical
disputes broke out under the Union's leadership and in 1954
Zenjidosharoso was dissolved as a result of the efforts for
democratisation made by the individual affiliated unions.   Along
with the growth in the automobile industry came a more pronounced
trend toward reorganising, at the industrial level, the workers of

---

[1] Stefan Agurén, et al., op. cit., p. 7.

the automobile industry.   Jidosha Rokyo (Automobile Workers' Union
Council) was established in 1965 as a council of the unions of
automobile makers, parts manufacturers and sales companies.   The
present Jidosha Soren (Confederation of Japan Automobile Workers'
Unions - JAW) was formed in 1972 as successor to Jidosha Rokyo.

Jidosha Soren is an industrial union made up of 550,000 workers
engaged in automobile production, parts manufacture, sales and
product transport.   The members, which directly comprise the
industrial-wide body, are 11 different federations of labour unions
and a federation of labour unions of parts manufacturers.   Each
federation is in turn made up of individual enterprise unions and
their regional organisations.   Each labour union member is directly
affiliated to the labour union at the enterprise level.

Jidosha Soren's aim, as a labour union in a free economy, is to
bring about a democratic society with high social welfare standards.
In order to achieve this, the social role of the labour union must
expand.   As a union, it must fulfil its social responsibilities and,
through its surveillance, ensure that the company lives up to its
social responsibilities.   Jidosha Soren's position is also to
promote the democratic participation of the workers at the national
industrial, corporate and local community levels.   As for its
relationship with other domestic unions, Jidosha Soren is one of the
cornerstones in the solidarity of the labour movement in the private
sector, and is a key body in the IMF-JC (International Metalworkers'
Federation-Japan Council).   The international character of the
automobile industry also makes it possible for Jidosha Soren to seek
co-operation with free labour movements in both advanced industrial
nations and developing countries.

Collective bargaining on working conditions is carried out at
the individual enterprise level.   Also in each of the companies,
in addition to collective bargaining, management and the labour
union executives maintain consultation schemes whereby they discuss
current problems and issues of importance face to face several times
a year.   At the plant and workshop levels, moreover, there are
consultation forums for labour and management to discuss issues
related to the workshop environment, production planning and safety.

Since the days of Jidosha Soren's predecessor, Jidosha Rokyo
(Automobile Workers' Union Council), an industry labour-management
conference has been held regularly between labour and the Japan
Automobile Manufacturers Association.   The first time the two
bodies convened was in 1968 when they discussed problems at the
industrial policy level, such as capital liberalisation, parts
production and marketing.   More than 11 labour-management conferences were held since Jidosha Soren was formed in 1972.   The matters
covered on the agenda included such items as trends in the automobile industry, countermeasures to reduce the amount of harmful
gas emissions, automobile taxation, employment security, trade and
the establishment of international fair labour standards, multi-
national corporations, wages, vacation and holidays, and extension
of the retirement age.   Jidosha Soren also holds similar conferences
with the three other management associations in the automobile
industry.

Labour disputes in the automobile industry have become extremely
infrequent.   Industrial relations with an emphasis on talking things
over through collective bargaining and labour-management consultation
is becoming the general rule.   This can be seen in the following

example. Around 1972, when Jidosha Soren was formed, about half of
the unions of the manufacturers would conduct a strike vote and give
the executive committee the authority to call a strike even before
wage negotiations were begun. Currently, however, this type of
before-the-fact strike vote and the adoption of an antagonistic
posture before entering negotiations occurs only rarely. Indeed
in 1977 and 1978 there was no major union which went on strike for
wage or bonus increases.

(c) Union-management consultation

The automobile industry has one of the most highly developed
systems of union-management consultation. In particular, the
system between the Nissan union and the Nissan Motor Co., Ltd., will
be examined for an understanding of the general conditions and
developments taking place in recent years. The high degree of co-
operation observable is particularly significant when we note that
the Nissan union was formed in 1953 in the aftermath of the
"100-day strike".

The Nissan union and Nissan Motor Company carry on union-
management consultation through several layers of consultative
activities. According to a Nissan union statement, there are three
purposes to the system of union-management consultation. First of
all, there is the common goal of increasing the amount of funds
available for distribution to the workers. Secondly, there is the
democratisation of the industry and the company by making management
reflect and be responsive to the workers' opinions and needs.
Thirdly, there are the efforts aimed at assuring that the industry
and the enterprise live up to their social responsibilities. At
Nissan, a clear line of distinction is drawn between the systems of
union-management consultation and that of collective bargaining.
During consultation, for example, wage and working condition issues
are not on the agenda.

At Nissan, as can be seen from table 3, union-management
consultative activities are carried out at all levels. At the
company-wide level there is the Central Union-Management Consultation
Council. There are also branch meetings and specialised committees
handling consultation in specialised areas. At the plant and workplace levels there are various meetings held either periodically or
in answer to a specific need when it arises. At the industry level
the union-management consultation system at Nissan becomes a forum
for talking things over between labour and management of the entire
Nissan group including the sales and parts subsidiaries. It also
spills over into consultation at the entire automobile industry
level.

The following four points are representative of the major trends
of recent years occurring in Nissan's union-management consultations.

(1) At the central level talks have not been mere formalities.
They have rather been penetrating exchanges between a small
number of individuals.

(2) The importance of consultation at the industry level has
increased more than in earlier years.

(3) Activities at the community level, such as the signing of agreements to cut down on pollution, have been growing in importance.

(4) Conferences and informal sessions between union and management are rapidly gaining ground at the workplace.

These basic trends can also be observed at other unions.

2. General trends in
    working conditions

Personnel staffing in the automobile industry is now primarily made up of male, full-time, regular employees who have graduated from high school.   In recent years, among the new recruits of the major manufacturers, college graduates represent a little less than 10 per cent, senior high school graduates about 70 per cent, and some 20 per cent of the new hires have been junior high school graduates scheduled to receive apprenticeship training.   In 1960 approximately one-fourth to one-third of the total workforce were temporary employees.   None remain, however.   Other than a small percentage of the workforce who are seasonal workers, all in the automobile manufacturing industry are at present regular, full-time employees.

In this section we propose to examine trends in the working conditions of the automobile industry over the last ten years. Let us start by tracing the path of changes in wages, bonuses, working hours, holidays and vacations, the retirement system and lump-sum retirement payments.

(a) Wages and the wage system

The average standard monthly wages (not including premiums and other variable payments for shift work, overtime and holiday work) of workers in the automobile industry from 1967 to 1977 can be seen in table 4.   As this chart reveals, monthly wages have increased by four times from 36,433 yen to 146,820 yen.   Particularly toward the end of the decade the increase in consumer prices was extremely rapid.   If we take this into account and deflate for a calculation of real wage increase, one sees that they rose by 1.63 times.   This yields a yearly average of 5 per cent net increase for the entire period.

As for summer and year-end bonus, in 1967 the yearly total was 188,500 yen (5.18 times monthly wages).   By 1977 yearly bonuses had risen to 791,800 yen or the equivalent of 5.4 months of basic wages. A calculation of total annual wages based upon 12 months of basic wages and yearly bonus payments gives an increase from 1967 to 1977 of 625,700 yen to 2,553,600 yen.   An approximate calculation of the US dollar equivalents at the prevailing dollar-yen exchange rate of respective years reveals annual wages of $1,740 in 1967 and $10,640 in 1977 or a nominal increase of 6.11 times.

In terms of the dollar equivalent of wages per hour, as the following calculation reveals, an increase of 6.35 times or $0.84 to $5.33 took place.   As these figures do not include premiums for overtime, holiday or shift work, real wage income would actually be more.   (In the common case of the worker who has been assigned to

shift work, even without including overtime and holiday pay premiums,
monthly cash wages will often be some 20 per cent more than the basic
monthly wage.   Keep in mind that there are also employee fringe
benefits coming to an additional 40 per cent or so of basic monthly
wages.)

1967:

$$\frac{¥36,433 \text{ (monthly wages) x 12 (months)} + ¥188,500 \text{ (annual bonus)}}{2,078 \text{ (scheduled hours/year)}}$$

$\div$ ¥360 (exchange rate) = $0.84/hour

1977:

$$\frac{¥146,820 \text{ (monthly wages) x 12 (months)} + ¥791,800 \text{ (annual bonus)}}{1,996 \text{ (scheduled hours/year)}}$$

$\div$ ¥240 (exchange rate) = $5.33/hour

The corresponding 1978 figure would be $6.72 at an exchange
rate of $1 = ¥205.

During the period there are two conspicuous trends in all of
the companies in the area of the wage package and compensation
system.   First, the weight of age, years of service and education
level achieved in school decreased in importance as determinants of
individual wages.   At the same time, there was a growing trend to
have wages more closely reflect differences in job contents and
skill levels.   The tendency to move in the direction of job pay and
payment by ability actually began about 1955.   It was not until the
late 1960s, however, that there was a real acceleration of change in
this direction.   The change was made possible due to the shortage
of young recruits with an accompanying rise in starting wages.   To
this was coupled the technological innovations which undermined the
assumption that seniority naturally leads to an accumulation of
useful skills which should be rewarded.   In recent years, however,
there is a reverse trend, one toward seriously reflecting on the
wisdom of further de-emphasis of seniority pay and years of service.

The second observable trend is the move toward trying to secure
a greater degree of stability in wage income.   Originally in the
automobile industry, while the relative importance of incentive
wages was not very great, many companies employed a system of
incentive bonuses to workplace groups or larger organisational units,
though not to the individual worker.   A reduction or end to this
practice was sought by the unions shortly after 1945.   Since 1965
the move toward reducing or eliminating the incentive component has
been intensified.   Also when it comes to bonuses, a new yearly
bonus formula has been adopted which prevents large or season-to-
season variations in the amount paid by making use of the multiple
of basic monthly wages.   Such developments have contributed to
stability in the standard of living of union members.

It may be informative to look at an example of how individual
wages are determined at Toyota Auto Body Co., Ltd.   The major
components of monthly wages are personal wages (increasing in an
S-shaped curve as age advances), job wages (determined by job
evaluation), and ability pay (reflecting differences based upon an

evaluation of the skill level and ability with which the worker executes his duties). These three wage components have a ratio of 4:5:1 in determining the wage. (At present there is a proposal from the labour union that some of the emphasis on job wages be reduced with the weight shifting over to ability pay and that ability pay be more closely related to years of experience. These concepts are to some extent being adopted by the company into the wage system.)

Among the three wage components, the determination of job wages is made by a Workplace Labour and Management Job Classification Committee established at each workplace. This is an unusual practice. In most cases the union merely preserves its right to enter grievance proceedings, and does not participate in decision making on individual wages. In Toyota Auto Body Co., Ltd., however, as can be seen from figure 2, classifications are determined by the managers, supervisors, union members and members of the Workplace Job Classification Committee who are elected by union members. Of course, it is possible for union members to appeal any dissatisfactions which they have.

The union and management of Toyota Auto Body developed their present system between 1966 and 1970. In addition, both sides have conducted separate surveys on worker attitudes almost every year. The surveys have, in turn, been used as references in revising and improving the wage system, all in all giving the company a unique history of serious and progressive industrial relations. The reforms in the wage systems during the period in the automobile industry also have common aspects observable in all the companies. Wages, for example, have the same three basic components throughout the industry. Household costs and actual expenses incurred are considered (mainly as reflections of age assuming its relationship to family responsibilities) as substantial items for consideration. Along with this, the other two elements of job contents and ability and skill on the job are individual wage determinants common to all manufacturers. And the relative weight of all three elements still continues to change as it reacts to new pressures and needs.

(b) Shortening working hours

At the beginning of the period there were already some initiatives toward shortening working hours coming from both union and management quarters. Until 1971, however, not much progress was made. From 1967 to 1971, annual holidays increased only from 72 to 74 days and working hours showed a very modest decrease from 2,078 to 2,064 hours. The reduction of working hours and increase in holidays picked up momentum only after 1972.

Taking the lead from Jidosha Soren policy makers, the unions conscientiously addressed themselves to shortening working hours and implementing the five-day work-week. Efforts resulted in an alternating system of Saturdays off every second week at most companies by 1972, and just one year later the five-day work-week every week was introduced. At present the great majority of the corporations in the automobile industry, including parts manufacturers, have instituted the five-day work-week. This has meant that the number of holidays in the industry have increased by 43.5 days to 115.5 days in the ten-year period since 1967. During the period there was an increase in working hours per day resulting in a decrease of only 82 working hours per year from 2,078 to 1,996 hours. The reduction in working hours was accomplished without a decrease in wage income to the workers.

(c) The retirement system and
     lump-sum retirement
     payments

During the survey period the fixed retirement ages at most of
the companies in the automobile industry were extended from 55 to
60 through union and management negotiation.   Briefly, ten years
ago at most of the companies, labour agreements fixed the retirement
age at 55.   Workers reaching 55 would retire from the company.   If
they had the desire and ability to work, it was common practice for
them to seek a second career.

In leading companies such as those of the automobile industry
workers enjoyed high wages and superior working conditions on
reaching retirement age.   Obviously, it was very difficult to obtain
equally lucrative re-employment at a standard to which one had become
accustomed.   The percentage of middle- and old-aged workers was
comparatively small, however, and in good times when subsidiary
companies were expanding and growing, the industry as a whole had a
high capacity for absorbing such employment, so this did not present
an insurmountable problem to those jobseekers.   Extension of the
retirement age was initiated by labour unions as an employment
security issue.

The unions of the automobile industry addressed themselves to
extending the fixed retirement age first in 1965, making it the
first industry to do so.   Efforts were rewarded with a two-year
extension of employment at most of the unions by 1967.   In 1970
unions succeeded in establishing a system of re-employment to age 60.
By 1973 this was taken one step further and retirement was extended
to 60, securing regular and full employment until age 60 when one
becomes eligible for the national pension or social security benefits.
Table 5 presents the model lump-sum retirement payments of affiliates
of Jidosha Soren.   It shows the payments made to union members of
various years of service.

3. Employee benefits
    and services

Throughout the period under study, each labour union worked
largely from its own intrinsic needs and position toward improving
and building better employment benefits and services within its own
company while maintaining close ties with other unions in the same
industry.   Let us first assess the trends observable in employee
benefits and services for the entire automobile industry, and then
look at the areas emphasised and changes in the substance of employee
benefits and services at Toyota Motor Co., Ltd.

(a) Growth in benefit
     and service costs

Trends for corporate expenditures on employee benefits and
services in the automobile industry appear on table 6, as compiled
in a Nikkeiren (Japan Federation of Employers' Associations) survey.
Costs approximated for employee benefits and services are about
13-14 per cent of monthly personnel costs per individual, and this
has not changed significantly over the last ten years.   Over the
last ten years the rate of increase in labour costs has been 4.08
times while increases in employee service costs have risen at almost
the corresponding rate of 3.92 times.   As can be seen on the

two lines at the bottom of table 6, however, in the preceding period
(1957-66) the rate of increase in employee service expenditure (2.98)
was much higher than the rate of increase in per capita monthly cash
wages (1.54). From 1967 to 1976, the larger proportion of expenditure went to cash wages rather than to employee benefits and services.

Moreover, throughout this decade the increase in legally required
costs was larger than that in voluntary benefits and services, unlike
that in the previous ten years. In other words, within total
increases in employee benefit costs, between 1955 and 1966, the share
of voluntary benefits and services was greater. In the last ten
years, however, the share of legally required benefits and services
has become larger. This was due to increasing costs imposed on
corporations in the area of legally required services and funds
available had to be re-apportioned to cover this. Although disburse-
ments for voluntary benefits and service costs increased, that
percentage of increase ended up being less than the increase for
legally required benefits and services.

As much as 75 per cent of the cost of voluntary employee
benefits and services is accounted for by housing assistance and
subsistence services. Among the programmes of the latter,
especially large items of expenditure are company subsidised dining
facilities and the transportation allowance which covers the costs
encountered in commuting to work every day. These items are
gradually approaching the regular working conditions which are
decided by negotiation between union and management. Looking at
developments in recent years, it can be said that investment in
housing has begun to fall off. In contrast, the proportion of
expenses allotted for cultural, athletic and recreational services
has been increasing rapidly although the actual amount is not large.

The above trend is also found at Toyota Motor Co., Ltd. At
this company employee service outlays are 35,500 yen per month per
employee. This is a nominal increase of 3.8 times compared with
the figure of ten years ago. During the same period the legally
required portion of these benefits increased by 19,400 yen or almost
4.7 times. Voluntary benefits and services grew by 3.1 times or
by 16,100 yen. Among the voluntary benefits and services, 90 per
cent were distributed among housing (33 per cent), commutation
(31 per cent), company subsidised meals (15 per cent), and 12 per cent
on cultural, athletic and recreational services.

(b) Changes in employee
     service policies

A look at employee service policies at Toyota Motor Co., Ltd.
reveals that in recent years emphasis has been placed on attaining
different but related social goals. First of all, there has been a
goal of meeting the needs of employees to establish a base of
economic security early in their working lives. This would include
the institutionalisation of systems to promote home ownership and of
providing health services for the entire family. The second thrust
of employee service policies has been toward measures that will be
beneficial in terms of both the physical comforts of life and an
anxiety-free psychological balance. Concrete programmes designed
to this end would include cultural, sports, recreational, company
dining and resort activities and facilities. The third concept on
which such services are oriented would be the aim of shielding workers
from insecurity and fear of such things as old age, sickness and death.

Efforts in this area would include various insurance policies and systems of assistance for surviving children and scholarship funds.

The employee benefits policies at Toyota Motors can be thought of as having changed in answer to the following types of shifting needs of workers which were a product of general economic growth and the concomitant rise in the standard of living.

(1) The need has surfaced for the types of goods and services which before were either low in priority or simply given up.

(2) New needs have arisen for higher quality benefits or services which are not satisfiable by the existing programme or policy.

(3) Workers' desires and demands have diversified and rather than being satisfied with standardised and uniform programmes, workers have come to seek benefits more in line with their specific needs and tastes.

Let us review from among Toyota's programmes and policies a few concrete examples of new systems of revised and improved benefits which have been instituted in response to the changing needs and aspirations of workers in recent years.

(1) Bachelor quarters were converted to individual private rooms where multiple occupancy had been the rule before. Although there had previously been central heating, summer air-conditioning was also introduced into the housing areas.

(2) Reacting to changing needs and desires for home ownership rather than living in company housing, housing instalment saving and housing loan systems along with Housing Friends Society and referral services were established. In addition, a subsidiary company, Toyota Housing Corporation, was set up to promote home ownership.

(3) Commuters switched over to the use of private automobiles instead of public transportation. The former assistance given in the form of company subsidised commutation passes took a new form of gasoline subsidy for nearly the entire amount required for such communication. Other assistance to auto commuters includes car purchase referral services, direct purchase loans, trade-in referrals and used car concession stores.

(4) Company subsidised food and dining plans shifted to quality rather than quantity which had been the overriding concern in less affluent days. Menus were diversified with selection becoming possible for company lunch services and for dormitory cafeterias. Facilities for providing hot meals were also installed.

(5) Cultural, sports and recreational activities and facilities were improved and enlarged. A sports centre (300,000 m^2), Toyota clubhouse (consisting of a club for employees, library and restaurant), and welfare centres and grounds at each factory were constructed and equipped.

(6) In terms of the way in which cultural, sports and recreational activities and events were conducted, in addition to the company-wide or factory-wide events carried from the past, the smaller operational basis also gave workers an opportunity to work things out independently on a small group workplace basis.

(7) Happy Life Insurance was instituted covering a complete range
of needs including life insurance, long-term leave of absence,
accident and injury, and insurance against sequelae or diseased
conditions which are an outgrowth of previous diseases or
injuries.

(c) The role of employee
benefit and service
programmes

One important development occurring with respect to employee
benefits and services was the emergence of an integrated framework
through which employee services were to be reappraised from the
viewpoint of workers' needs.   There are three possible ways to meet
the workers' needs, namely, through greater consumption of their
own income, through provision of benefits by the corporation and
labour union, or by way of national or regional government instituted
programmes.   The burden of both expense and initiative is largely
determined through the natural course of history.   The system of
apportionment in terms of effort and responsibility, however, must
have a logical consistency at any given time.   Moreover, as far as
the worker is concerned, it must enable him to realise some balance
between his independence and mutual dependence needs.

In a continuously changing society the life cycle of each worker
further adds to the diversity of workers' needs.   The normal cycle
will start at the time an individual first begins his working life
as a bachelor.   Then he will marry and raise a family, educate the
children and finally return to the life of a couple living together.
The aspirations and needs of people change in reaction to the various
steps their lives take.   In a nation such as Japan, where severe
social change has been experienced based upon a rapid period of
industrialisation, differences in consciousness based upon age
inevitably create social conflicts in the form of generation gaps.
From this kind of perspective, the trend to think of labour-related
issues as a function of the life cycle is gaining ground in recent
years in Japan.

Figure 3 presents the main points of "A guide to worker benefits
and services" as compiled by the labour union of Toyota Motor Co., Ltd.
The horizontal line at the top of this figure displays steps of the
workers' life cycle.   On the left side, the benefit and service needs
of the workers are classified according to aspects of daily living.
On the right side of the figure are the various programmes or services
provided by the national and local governments which are available
to the workers of Toyota Motor Co., Ltd.   In the centre of the
figure are portrayed the outlines of the various plans and programmes
which have been instituted by the corporation and the union.   Those
offered by the union are indicated in capital letters.

The Toyota Motor Workers' Union conceived of a life cycle
perspective before designing this guide.   Based upon the perspective
the various programmes within and outside the company and union are
rearranged and evaluated.   Facilitating union members' understanding,
acceptance and utilisation of the programmes is one of the aims of
this guide of life cycle and welfare services at Toyota.   Another
purpose for devising such a chart is to use it to help identify what
might be missing, making it possible for the union then to begin
discussions to help clearly determine what are important themes on
which the union should act.   Efforts would have to be extended toward

determining the concrete programmes and also selecting the best
group or organisation to take responsibility and carry out the programmes.

4.   Employee education and training

     The members of the study group showed the most interest in
employee education and training.   The automobile industry is one
with an unusually high degree of involvement internationally in terms
of product and technology.   The contents of work are unique for
their high degree of mechanisation and division of labour.   In
Japan, however, the great majority of workers in the industry are
male and possess the "special quality of Japaneseness" which is
especially true of male workers in large enterprises.   In other
words, such workers expect long-term employment and growth and
progress in the course of their careers.   They are well-educated
with over 12 years of schooling and are all quite homogeneous coming
from much the same cultural and exactly the same ethnic background.
In the field of education and training there is thus a direct
confrontation of the contradictory forces of "universalism" and
"particularism".

     To sum up the discussions to follow, it can be said that in the
education and training field all kinds of efforts are being made to
achieve a satisfactory long-range integration between the needs of
workers and corporate requirements.   Workers planning to work at the
company for a long time have a desire to attain a high level of growth
and personal development both in terms of technological skill and
position in relation to those younger workers who join the company
later.   In answer to this desire, the company assists by providing
opportunities for continuing education and further growth of skill
capacity.   Promoting workers based on their ability tends to lift
employee morale and results in strengthening the organisation.
This interest which is common to both workers and management
flourishes in the automobile industry as manifested in its thoroughgoing programmes for employee education and training.

     (a)   Basic concepts behind
           employee education
           and training

     Employee education and training are among the most emphasised
aspects of the field referred to as "organisational behaviour" in
Europe and America.   A consensus was reached by the study committee
that employee education and training have very important contributions to make to improvement in the quality of working life.   This
realisation was not only made by the committee members coming from
the corporate side.   As long as there was no problem presented in
the area of working conditions the union committee representatives
actively supported corporate efforts in the education and training
areas.   That is to say, fundamentally, union and management do not
see education and training as areas of conflict.

     With reports on education and training coming from all the
companies, and with differences in history and development at each
company, there are special features and characteristics peculiar to
each company both in terms of basic policies and concrete plans and
programmes.   In this subsection, we will see case examples at
Isuzu Motors, Ltd., Toyota Motor Co., Ltd., Honda Motor Co., Ltd.,

and Nissan Motor Co., Ltd.   Before we move on to this, however, let
us briefly summarise the characteristic concepts common to the
education and training plans and programmes of all five companies
including Toyota Auto Body Co., Ltd.

(1)   Education and training are absolutely indispensable to the
      organisation.   The concept is not that the organisation
      creates the need for education and training but rather it is
      continuous education and training that will build up and expand
      the organisation.

(2)   Education and training must be provided to all the employees,
      giving an opportunity for growth and progress throughout one's
      lifetime.   It is believed that this should apply to all people
      engaged in office, technical and production work.

(3)   Education and training are fundamentally seen as responsibilities
      of line management and supervisors.   Managers and supervisors
      should be appraised by their superiors concerning the effective-
      ness of their efforts as educators and trainers of their subor-
      dinates.   There is a strong conviction that this is an
      important mainline function, not something that can be done
      haphazardly.

(4)   Education and training are intrinsically activities in which
      the individual voluntarily takes his own initiative.   All
      agreed that education and training activities are based on the
      assumption that there is a strong desire for self-development
      and improvement on the part of each employee.

(5)   All corporate education and training plans and programmes taking
      place outside the workplace are thought of as promoting and
      supplementing on-the-job training and self-improvement.

(6)   The accumulation of ability and skill has a real and practical
      value to both the company and the individual which far exceeds
      the direct demands imposed by the task at hand.

(7)   Through education and training the individual also gains a
      feeling of accomplishment since he realises that he is learning
      and growing as a result of the training.

   Although the following presentation of actual implementation of
these concepts will differ somewhat with the company, let us now
look at developments at Isuzu Motors, Ltd., Toyota Motor Co., Ltd.,
Honda Motor Co., Ltd. and Nissan Motor Co., Ltd.

   (b)   Employee training at
         Isuzu Motors, Ltd.

   Isuzu Motors, Ltd. specialises in trucks but also manufactures
passenger cars.   General Motors of the United States has acquired
approximately one-third of the stock ownership.   Although GM offers
some assistance in various aspects of management, employee training
plans are almost entirely left up to Isuzu.   With this said, let us
move on to an overview of the training system and philosophy behind
employee development at Isuzu Motors, Ltd.

   The education and training programme at Isuzu has five goals:

(1) The formation and maintenance of a corporate organisation of
     flexible structure that ensures responsive adaptation to changes
     in the outside environment. In order to cope with the changes
     it is necessary to prepare a large number of personnel trained
     to react quickly and effectively.

(2) The building of higher levels of professional knowledge in the
     ranks of individual employees will not only equip the enterprise
     for changes in the environment but will also prepare the workers
     for technological innovations. It will give each employee the
     feeling that he is growing as an individual and make it possible
     to obtain satisfaction on the job.

(3) By concentrating on development of production people who are
     technically competent and sound in judgement, it is hoped that
     the over-all skill level of company personnel will increase.

(4) Fully drawing out the workers' potential skills and satisfying
     their desire for improvement within the present organisation
     will give them immediate feelings of "hatarakigai" or sense of
     meaning in work and "ikigai" or sense of worth in living.

(5) Education and training not only involve the relationship
     between the individual and his work. A goal is also to
     develop an organisational climate in which expansion of the
     individual's faculties will positively tie into and improve
     the relationship between individuals and between individuals
     and the group.

     In order to achieve these goals, employee education and training
programmes are classified according to three major job content
families: administrative, technical and production. For each
classification, from the newly hired recruits to the managers, there
is a systematic education and training plan designed to promote
continuing education. Figure 4 presents the training and education
system for administrative and technical employees, while figure 5
shows the programme used for production employees. In actual
practice the training system for both groupings is unified and
centralised under the same authority. That is to say that the
supervisor appearing in the figure for production employees can be
promoted to the department manager class as is on the other figure.

     The system of employee education and training at Isuzu Motors
has taken shape over a long period of time. Among the various
programmes, those which have been established only recently or those
which have increased in influence would be organisational development,
the development of international businessmen (through, for example,
assignment to General Motors Institute) and "family" training. By
"family" training, we mean here voluntary meetings held at the workplace as the organisational unit. Here problems are presented (and
solutions evaluated) on topics which the participants determine on
their own - anything from productivity, human relations or quality
control and improvement. The members next set about considering
how to solve the matter.

     (c) Continuing education
          at Toyota Motor

     The main role of Toyota Motor's education and training programme
is based on the following assumptions and objectives:

(1) Motivation for self-development and personal improvement is
absolutely indispensable on the part of each employee as a pre-
requisite for effective personnel development policies.

(2) It is necessary that human and organisational systems and line
management function so as to promote the personal development
of all employees.

(3) And finally, staff education and training activities exist as
supplementary programmes which assist with aspects of the two
preceding conditions.

The system of education and training based upon the above
conceptual framework is outlined as in figure 6. Unique features
are as follows:

(1) The system covers both production employees and administrative
and technical employees on up to managers. The over-all plan
has long-term career development in mind.

(2) Of course, the programme is designed to meet directly present
work requirements but it is also intended to go beyond this,
and to contribute to the growth of the individual.

(3) The programme adapts to the different needs of the corporation
and the individual by offering both compulsory and elective courses.

Let us now look at a few of the special features at Toyota Motor
concerning its personnel and organisational systems as well as line
management which support the formal system of education and training.

At Toyota Motor, "formal education" (planned and systematic
off-the-job education and training) and various human relations
activities have been implemented as training programmes occurring
outside of the workplace. In the area of human relations there are
activities of various groups within the company, the "Personal Touch"
movement, the movement to improve the company dormitories, and the
Toyota Club. In order for education and training to be as effective
as possible and to take firm root it is essential to have mutual
trust. Human relations activities not only serve the policy function
of promoting mutual trust but also serve to educate employees
(figure 7). As these activities are conducted with the employees'
voluntary planning and participation, they are also useful in developing personal initiative and self-management in the human relations,
organisational behaviour and leadership areas.

From a staffing and placement perspective one of the factors
promoting education and training for all individuals is the consideration which must be given to developing and assigning the right man
with the required skills for a particular job. There is a system of
job assignment which takes into account both the aptitude and performance test results of the individual as well as his desires.
Job rotation is also encouraged and it is possible for the skills
of one job family to be fully learned within a period of about ten
years. A second important point is to have a system of promotion
that is well-matched with aptitude and ability. There are no
limitations on the promotion of production workers. In the last
five years, for example, there were 37 promotions to section manager
from those ranks.

Finally, the role of managers and supervisors in training and development should be noted. The growth and training of subordinates is an important duty of all managers and supervisors, and they are rated on this score in their performance appraisals. The work assignment can be made by superiors regardless of the job classification of the employee. There is an emphasis on eliciting suggestions and proposals in the workshop. In line with this every effort is made to encourage workers to express their opinions and to promote mutual understanding through means of individual meetings with superiors and informal group inter-actions. Moreover, each manager keeps a training and development chart and every year individual discussions are held with subordinates as to their career plans, desires and the best way to use effectively the ability and skills of each worker.

(d) Training and development at Honda Motor Co., Ltd.

Among the companies participating in this study, Honda Motor Co., Ltd. was the most recently established. As a result the employees including top and middle managers are comparatively young, and in both a good and perhaps not so good sense this means that the company has not inherited long-standing traditions. Free, then, from rigid precedents, Honda has been successful in establishing its own distinct approach to training and development. Honda has a practical, realistic and innovative approach to the development of individual talent. Of course, the emphasis on training and development at Honda is also characteristic of automobile manufacturers. The view is jointly held by all the firms that training is an activity primarily to be carried out by the individual and is the responsibility of each employee. Corporate responsibility lies in providing fully the appropriate opportunities for the workers to cultivate and make use of their abilities.

Upon the completion of the training period to which all new company entrants are subject, all of the new recruits are assigned a number by superiors which identifies their level of job skill. This number is called the "on-the-job training (OJT) step". All new recruits qualify for step 1. From that point on based upon an OJT programme, consisting of about 300 different job category models, the line supervisor provides not only guidance but he also evaluates the progress and skill acquisition and growth of each individual. The OJT steps range from a rank of 1 to a rank of 6. The OJT programme clearly identifies the job skill requirements at each level for each different job classification. An OJT programme text has also been written for each classification. This text was produced by the specialists of each "trade group" within the company.

According to Honda Motor Co., Ltd. training and development follows a five-step cycle. It is a constant and gradual process leading up to and culminating in a higher rank.

(1) Identifying the ability and aptitude of each individual worker.

(2) Establishment or revision of training policies and plans for the individual.

(3) Job rotation for optimal development and utilisation of his ability and aptitude.

(4) Evaluation of ability and job performance with feedback
     provided to the individual.

(5) Individual finally attempts to qualify for a higher company-
     wide designated rank.

     Among these steps, 1-4 are carried out by the superiors. The
result of the evaluation in the fourth step will be connected with
wages, bonuses and rank promotions. Authorisation of the qualifica-
tion in 5 is a system applying after the trainee has achieved a
certain level of the OJT step. The individual of his own volition
will apply for testing to a higher qualifying level or rank title.

     Differing from the OJT step, the "rank title" is a company-wide
title which more formally indicates the skill or ability level. On-
the-job training is available to all employees, blue-collar and
white-collar workers. (At Honda no distinction is made between
blue- and white-collar.) At most other firms, the rank title would
be a system which applies only to a specialist staff or to those
managerial groups at least above the supervisor level. In order to
be qualified for a higher rank title the Honda employee must make
the following efforts on his own initiative:

(1) Provide guidance and leadership to subordinates and junior
     colleagues (offer advice and on-the-job training to workers of
     lower rank).

(2) Participate in "trade group" activities (assist in the accumu-
     lation and dissemination of the specialised technology carried
     out by groups of specialists who determine job categories and
     descriptions).

(3) Enter into actual rank-and-file work (every year managers
     directly get involved in production and sales for a fixed
     period - assistant section chiefs participate for at least one
     month and the section chief for a week or more).

(4) Submit problem proposals and solutions (operational and working
     problems are studied with appropriate plans for revision or
     improvement to be submitted to top management, or those in
     charge of the department or workplace to which one is assigned).

(5) Work toward job enrichment and enlargement (attempt to take on
     as many duties and responsibilities of one's higher jobs as
     possible, also make efforts to diversify and build up new
     abilities and skills through voluntary job transfers).

     If a rank title is a classification representing the "level" of
ability, the tool for training and development based upon the "type"
of ability is the typology developed for training purposes. At
Honda it is argued that if there are 20,000 employees, there should
be no less than 20,000 individual training courses. In practice,
however, the qualitative differences in individuals' aptitude and
ability are roughly divided into four groups. Based upon this
each "trade group" has established the basic training course for
each of the four types. The most important purpose here is to
respond to the need to systematically develop abilities through job
rotation in conformity with the personality characteristics of the
individual involved, especially above the specialist staff level.
As for the types there are C (craftsman), M (manager), D (developer)
and R (researcher).

Supplementing the above OJT activities at Honda are off-JT courses. Among them the following three courses are typical of the special features at Honda in that they apply to a wide range of trainees:

(1) Honda fundamental course: a classroom type course stressing team play which is designed essentially to develop the knowledge to be a good company man, culture and background to be a good citizen and contributing member of society, and the creation and development of imagination and innovative powers (44 hours). (Similar courses are given at other companies as well.)

(2) Honda idea creativity course: the level directly before attempting to qualify for one's first rank title. It is team study training designed to teach concrete methods of team creativity management (124 hours).

(3) Honda creativity enrichment course: training designed to enhance team creative powers and efforts. The course is intended for those holding the beginner "rank title".

Finally, idea contests must be recognised for their relative importance in training and development. The idea contest is a creative activity in which employees freely organise groups and compare ideas which will hopefully end up being reflected and integrated into concrete products of their own. The sixth bi-annual idea contest sponsored by Honda was held in 1978. The corporate expense of a single such contest runs as high as $500,000.

Honda is in the process of removing the influence of educational levels, status as blue- and white-collar jobs and seniority considerations from training and development programmes. Instead, possibilities for individual training and development are being promoted by co-operative efforts of individuals, managers and groups of specialists and trainees. The aim is to bolster the over-all power and effectiveness of the organisation. In any case, the Honda example is known to be the most thorough programme in terms of its concepts and aims.

(e) The skill test at
Nissan Motor Co., Ltd.

Among the wide range of training and development activities carried out at Nissan, skill development, particularly skill testing, will be examined. The system of education and training at Nissan had been operative fully ten years before it took the present developed form. The events which particularly strengthened emphasis on skill development were the experiences subsequent to the oil crisis. The aging of the workforce is anticipated in the future as reduced economic growth will curb the number of young workers who can be hired. Under these circumstances there is a pressing requirement to have groups of workers with the highest skill levels attainable.

Programmes at Nissan in the area of skill training and development focus on three areas. They are: (1) company skill competition meets; (2) skill olympics reinforcement training; and (3) Nissan skill tests. The specific programmes of the three functions will be briefly reviewed. There are two factory- and company-wide company skill competition meets held annually. The major purpose is to heighten the interest of the young workers in increasing

their skills.   In 1977 there were 30 different competitive events
in the contest.   A year later they were increased to 42.   The
trades in the competition are actually even more far-reaching than
in the skill testing sponsored by the Ministry of Labour and include
job categories involving conveyors and automated equipment.

Skill olympics reinforcement training consists of training
which is aimed at winning the championship of the regional or nation-
wide meets in which those who placed high in the company skill
competition meets and those who boast of top skill records from
their school days participate.   The champions then enter the International Youth Skill Olympics.   At Nissan Motor Co., Ltd. the
history of entering such international contests is not a long one.
None the less, in 1977 in a meet held in the Netherlands, there were
four prize winners from the company including a champion, a second
and a third place holder.

The Nissan skill tests are programmes which were developed and
realised through the plant-site efforts of the assistant section
managers.   Having substantial responsibilities in the production
process, these managers were a focal point and key to an effective
transmission of skills.   With this in mind, they set up skill
standards committees, and proceeded to designate skill criteria,
draft skill training manuals and design the contents and parameters
of skill tests.

They produced uniform company-wide skill standards.   Skills
are classified by four rankings: elementary, intermediate, advanced
and special.   In making the manual, in addition to the assistant
section managers, there were also participating members from the
section manager and technical specialist class.   The tasks designed
in the skill tests are selected from among the daily operations
performed in the company.   As for their substance the tests examine
aspects of both universal skills and special skills, including the
utilisation of universal machine tools as well as the programming of
specialised equipment and its light maintenance work.   The level of
the examination is somewhat higher than the tests given in the
Ministry of Labour trade skill testing.

5.   Relationship between men
     and jobs

We shall restrict our considerations in this section to the
relationship between individual jobs and the individual workers
performing them.   After first looking at a few of the unique elements
characteristic of the nature of work in the automobile industry, the
problem of finding meaning and sense of satisfaction on the job
("hatarakigai") will be dealt with.   Following that, an example of
efforts to humanise work processes will be presented from this
"hatarakigai" perspective.   Finally, the new development toward
job reorganisation in certain sectors of the automobile industry
in response to the increasing proportions of older workers will be
described.

(a)   Work in the
      automobile industry

Automobile manufacturing is a good example of a complex product
industry requiring a number of different processes.   Seven major production processes can be singled out: foundry, forging, press, machining

heat treatment, assembly and painting.   By further dividing these
basic production steps it is possible to identify an even greater
number of processes.   From the 1960s to the first half of the 1970s
the Japanese automobile industry underwent substantial expansion.
During the period there was an increase in investment for labour
saving equipment in production and a remarkable climb in the operation ratio of fixed capital.   More specifically, a number of major
technological innovations were implemented, including the automation
of work processes, the full utilisation of newly introduced specialised
equipment, complete man-free approach to material handling, and
intensive production and quality control by computer surveillance.

        As was seen from table 2, between 1962 and 1973, the number of
direct man-hours required to produce one compact passenger car was
reduced to approximately one-third.   This table presents the direct
man-hours required for different processes in the production sector
for a finished automobile at the average Japanese automobile
manufacturer.   It is estimated that these man-hours account for
about 40 per cent of the cost composition of the finished automobile.
From 1962 to 1973 total man-hours required decreased by 66 per cent.
Broken down by production process, reductions in the machining function were greatest, being as high as 73 per cent.   The decrease of
man-hours applied to foundry, forging and press was the least at
55 per cent.   For sub-assembly and final assembly the saving in
hours was some 68 per cent.

        As the total number of automobiles produced during this period
grew rapidly, the number of production workers increased even though
there were considerable reductions in the man-hours required to
produce one automobile.   As can be seen from table 7, however, the
span in the percentage increases of workers in the different production processes was great.   For example between 1967 and 1973, the
number of workers in heat treatment and forging functions increased
by only about 1.9 times.   For final assembly, however, the figure
was 3.9 times and for press processes as high as 5 times.   The gap
in these percentage increases was greater than that of percentage
decreases in man-hours broken down by the various production processes.

        An important reason for the large differences in the size of
personnel increases by varying production process was that in the
processes having a comparatively modest increase in personnel there
had been indirect labour or man-hours belonging to supporting functions which had been mixed in together with total required man-hours.
With greater degrees of mechanisation and more complete automation,
these indirect man-hour functions were eliminated and personnel could
be deployed more effectively.   Another explanation would be that for
various manufacturing processes lot production gave way to continuous
work and the use of specialised machinery.   This made it possible
to reduce lost time significantly.   Conversely, in the assembly area
where there were large increases in numbers of production personnel,
work methods had already been quite rationalised and thus any increase in production would tend to immediately require additional
workers.

        To amplify upon this, in terms of job contents, during this
period the largest changes took place not in assembly processes but
in other production areas.   The rationalisation of work methods in
assembly operations had already reached quite a high level and had
become well stabilised.   Other than to reduce output, even adjust-

ment of the assembly line speed was, contrary to popularly held
beliefs, becoming most difficult.   There was almost no room for
"speed up".1

    (b)   <u>"Hatarakigai" - meaning
and sense of purpose and
satisfaction in work</u>

    Over the last ten years "hatarakigai" has been an important
area of concern in the automobile industry.   In the first half of
this period the issue of injecting meaning and fulfilment into work
was very important to corporate management as a countermeasure
against the shortage of labour which then existed.   At the same
time the unions also paid much attention to the question of "hatarakigai".   In 1971, for example, the Toyota Motor Workers' Union made
"the building of a hatarakigai workplace" one of the focal points of
its activity and campaign policy.   That was one year before the
Lordstown, Ohio, strike mentioned earlier.

    In December of 1977 Jidosha Soren conducted an attitude survey
sampling the opinion of some 4 per cent of the union members affiliated with the national body.   The survey was distributed not only
to production workers in the factory but also to a wide range of
union members involved in administrative, technical and sales functions.   There were 16,744 usable responses.   The results of this
survey on "hatarakigai", fatigue and monotony, are partially noted
for reference in figure 8.

    Looking at the situation generally, those who feel a sense of
"hatarakigai" or quality and meaning in their working lives either
"very much" or "fairly much" make up over 60 per cent of the workers
answering the survey.   When it came to the question of fatigue,
"not at all" tired or "not very much" tired comprised about one-fourth
of the respondents.   Almost 20 per cent of the sample answered they
were very much tired.   Over 60 per cent also replied that they find
their work "not at all" monotonous or "not very much" monotonous.
Less than 6 per cent replied that their work was "very much" monotonous.   It is difficult to judge whether or not these responses
should be evaluated as being positive evidence that there is a high
degree of "hatarakigai".   In any case the survey provides us with
some clues.

    That is to say that the same kind of survey was given by
Jidosha Soren in September of 1975 in which identical questions were
asked.   The results of the survey at that time are presented in
parentheses in the horizontal bar marked "total".   If we make a
time comparison between 1975 and 1977, it becomes readily observable
that during this period there is a change for the better in answers
to all three questions.   In other words, those people feeling a
sense of "hatarakigai" increased by 9 per cent, while respondents
experiencing intense tiredness were down by 4 per cent.   Eight
per cent fewer people complained of monotony in their work.   This
may not only be a reflection of the comparative business health of

---

    1 National Institute of Vocational Research: <u>A study of
employment practices in the automobile industry</u> (in Japanese)
(Tokyo, National Institute of Vocational Research, 1976), pp. 19-22.

the automobile industry in the face of over-all economic recession but also probably speaks well for the effectiveness and success brought about through the direct efforts of both labour and management.

A second point worthy of notice on these charts is the difference between the reaction of those engaged in assembly-line work and that of workers in other job functions. The following briefly summarises these differences:

(1) On the "hatarakigai" question, although there is no doubt that the conveyor-line workers do not feel as much meaning and purpose in their work as do the technical personnel, the over-all response pattern of the conveyor-line workers is not much less favourable than the total average.

(2) In terms of fatigue, conveyor-line workers complain of physical exhaustion most loudly along with the sales and service personnel.

(3) When asked about finding work monotonous, the conveyor-line people by far express the strongest awareness of routine drudgery.

This same survey also suggests that "hatarakigai" is highly correlated to the individual's attitude and degree of close association to his job. For example, those seeing their jobs as monotonous sense less "hatarakigai" than those who do not feel that their work is monotonous. Among those employees who view their jobs as either too difficult or too easy, those sensing "hatarakigai"-type meaning and quality in their working lives are few. The survey also makes clear that those enjoying a satisfying sense of "hatarakigai" do so because they "feel a sense of accomplishment in their work", "have the job left up to them" or "sense that they are making the most of their talents and skills".

There is another very interesting observation which can be made from a survey conducted by the National Institute of Vocational Research. The sample involves 280 workers engaged in assembly-line work and 305 people working in non-assembly production functions. It was distributed in three factories of different companies. Rather than the distinction between assembly-line and non-assembly line workers, this survey reveals that the worker's own estimate of how long it takes to become proficient at his job is by far a much more accurate and meaningful indicator of a positive attitude toward work life. It was clear that the workers who held that their jobs required a long period to master also felt that "there are opportunities in my job to express and see my own ideas and proposals materialised", "my work is interesting", "I like my job" and that "if I work hard I will be accordingly promoted".[1]

The results of these studies are in complete agreement with the attitudes of both labour and management in the automobile industry with respect to the "hatarakigai" issue. In trying to enhance the sense of "hatarakigai" among the workforce, both labour and management basically would agree that the following efforts are necessary in addition to the efforts to improve working conditions.

------

[1] National Institute of Vocational Research, op. cit., p. 82.

(1)   Top priority in technological improvements should be placed on
       safety and counter-fatigue measures.   Of next priority will be
       improvement of the environment.   As for the monotony counter-
       measures, improvements should be made whenever practical within
       the framework of the present production system.

(2)   Opportunities for creative participation and chances to utilise
       ability and talent to a maximum will be encouraged by assigning
       the right man for the right job, through group operations, small
       group activities and suggestion systems.

(3)   Long-range measures should include opportunities for training
       and development such as on-the-job training, job rotation,
       skill testing and off-the-job educational programmes so that
       workers can tackle their jobs while looking forward to a
       meaningful future.

(4)   Even in aspects of non-working life every effort should be made
       to make available the facilities and provide the opportunities
       which will assist in experiencing a satisfying sense of
       "hatarakigai" during working life.

   (c)   Programmes designed
          to humanise work

     In designing the production system and work organisation at all
of these companies it is taken for granted that consideration be
given to the aspect of humanising work.   Some of the dimensions of
the policies at Toyota Motor Co., Ltd. will be enumerated which
reflect a clear awareness and recognition of the importance of the
humanisation function in the production process.   To greater or
lesser extents the same kinds of programmes are being carried out
at the other corporations which participated in this study.

   (1)   "Stop button"

     At conveyor-line production positions every worker has his own
stop button.   This serves to ease up at least to some extent the
all-encompassing external control over the worker which is characteristic of assembly-line functions.   It can aid in correcting and
compensating for imbalance in the demands made on the worker.
Namely, when the worker has simply had too much he is provided with
a rescue device.

   (2)   Autonomous line
          operations through
          the use of "kanban"

     Instructions in meeting production schedules and quotas are
passed down only in terms of the number of automobiles assembled at
the final stage with a target established for each model.   Beyond
this, each operational production unit has autonomous control of its
output schedule in terms of the materials, volume and timing.   Each
unit makes its production schedule according to the "order" received
from the immediately succeeding production process.   The information
or operating directions thus passed over from one unit to the preceding
unit or suppliers are marked on specially designed order plates
called "kanban".

(3) Eliminating "islands
     of isolation"

In the machine processing phase of engine factories there is a
tendency for small work units of even a single isolated worker to
develop. Along with causing workers to feel lonely, the accompanying
loss of morale and purpose leads to lost time. Job functions and
assignments are being redesigned into working teams of two to three
personnel.

(4) Co-operation and mutual
     help on the line

There is no fixed concept as to the determination of work
standards for each man on the job. Rather within a given group
there is autonomous regulation and adjustment made for the differing
abilities of individuals. In other words, mutual help and assistance
is encouraged.

(5) Outlook on automation

The basic and widely shared view here is that the tasks and
operations which man feels are unpleasant to perform should be
mechanised or automated. The order of priority here would be to
let machines first handle (1) hazardous work; (2) heavy physical
or manual work or jobs that represent a strain on people; and
(3) simple, repetitive tasks.

As for other important policies to "humanise work" that have
been implemented at the automobile manufacturing companies, study
committee members proposed job rotation and background music.

(d) Job redesign for
     older workers

Along with the postponement of the retirement age as mentioned
in section 2, it has obviously become necessary to design and
establish production functions and workplaces where employees of the
automobile industry can work until the age of 60. In this subsection a description will be given of the job reorganisation and
development programme for older workers carried out by the Nissan
Motor Co., Ltd.

In 1976 at Nissan a survey was made of 5,819 male workers over
40 years of age to determine what jobs were appropriate for them.
Each older worker was assessed as to his suitability for the key
jobs in his own production area. Altogether, there were 14 areas
and 220 key jobs. When it was judged that certain jobs were not
adaptable to the older worker, it was further determined whether the
difficulty was based on an individual human condition or whether it
was due to a specific job requirement.

The survey revealed that on the whole there are needs for the
following countermeasures centred around the worker group over
45 years of age. At present steps are being taken in these
directions because although in 1977 the percentage of employees
over 45 years was 16 per cent in the production worker category,
in another ten years this proportion is expected to increase to
29 per cent.

(1) Through planned job rotation the breadth of job assignment possibilities should be increased. Along with this are added possibilities to reorganise jobs based on the skills thus to be attained.

(2) Skill standards and tests should be fully utilised to promote individual skill development.

(3) In workplaces where mechanisation requiring professional working knowledge is well under way, workers should be taught the accompanying knowledge and skill.

(4) Investment in labour-saving devices should be concentrated on eliminating heavy manual work and jobs which require the taking of unnatural or strenuous physical body positions. (Some 6-7 per cent of all investment in plant and equipment is now being directed to make improvements in this area.)

(5) The physical strength and endurance of older workers should be measured and gauged. With this as a base of reference, physical fitness programmes should be implemented.

(6) Older workers themselves should be encouraged and instructed not to think of themselves as old and useless. On the other hand, young workers should be encouraged to treat older workers with respect.

(7) Efforts should be made to prepare workers psychologically and to provide them with an accumulation of skills to see them through the transition to middle- and older-age.

6. Small group activities
   and self-management

   (a) Small group activities

As in the other industries, most of the automobile manufacturing companies have been actively promoting small group activities under such names as QC (quality control) circle or ZD (zero defects) movement. The small group activities of Toyota Auto Body Co., Ltd. will be described here as one illustrative example.

At Toyota Body small group activities are seen as having four roles to play. The maximum realisation of each is sought through a combination of several group activities. (Examples of activities appear in parentheses.)

(1) The role of allowing workers to take part in planning after the main postulates or purposes of the group have been clearly determined (morning ceremonies, workplace meetings, QC circles).

(2) A place where each member of the group can learn to be more considerate of other group members (prior adjustment of days off, workshop recreation).

(3) Along with making the structure of the group clear, small group activities also perform the role of providing leadership to a few of the members (the subleader system, recreation leader and QC circle leader).

(4) The role of increasing the cohesiveness and bonds of the group as efforts to compete with other groups are encouraged (system of group suggestion, skill contests, company-wide sports olympics).

In addition to the above-mentioned activities, as important systems there are "improvement teams" and "on-the-job college". The improvement team is a system which was started in 1969, and it refers to a team set up in each section. The teams have no direct operational working function. One of their functions is to make recommendations for improving and designing new machinery. Another is to provide assistance when there is someone not in attendance on the line or if there are other hindrances to production. Improvement team members are some 3-4 per cent of total production team members and they are transferred into such units by rotation. The design and production of improved machinery are based upon the suggestions of the workplace and QC circle groups. In 1975 there were as many as 120 cases in which the workers designed such improved equipment.

The on-the-job college is an opportunity to get long-term, intensive specialist training over a one-year period. High school graduates with at least three years of production line experience and an appropriate study theme are eligible. Presently, courses are offered in production equipment, control technology, specialised skills and maintenance. The instructors are all graduate engineers from within the company. When training or study continues beyond working hours, the trainees are paid a training allowance. In some instances the trainees are assigned to the improvement teams, in other cases they will obtain on-the-job training in other areas within the company. "Graduates" are certified on the basis of an examination of their equipment improvement designs, their reports or an evaluation test of their skills. Until the present time there have been some 300 graduates. A great many of those advancing to first-line supervisory positions in recent years are individuals who have come up through the "on-the-job college" system.

(b) Self-management experiments

From the preceding it becomes clear that there is a variety of long- and short-term opportunities to increase skills and make the most of one's abilities even in the assembly-line work. There are also trial experiments being conducted to bring assembly-line work even further under the control of autonomous self-management. Trial efforts in this direction are carried out at the Gunma Factory of Fuji Heavy Industries, Ltd. and at the Honda two-wheeled vehicle assembly plant in Kumamoto.

(1) The Fourth Production Section, Gunma Factory, Fuji Heavy Industries[1]

This section is a workshop of 400 employees assigned to the assembly of two different models of four-wheeled vehicles. The improvements taking place here are worthy of notice because they

[1] This example was provided to the study committee by Mr. Toshimasa Nakano who was invited as a guest from the Gunma Factory of Fuji Heavy Industries.

are the product of the section's own self-sustaining efforts which
are independent from the top management of the factory and from other
operational sections.   One important improvement was the joint
worker effort to make the working environment more pleasant.   This
included the construction of the Subaru (Pleiades) Garden under the
factory roof.   Here, another example of reform, small groups of
workers have autonomously managed the assembly line operations
since 1975.

Conveyor operations had consisted of 63 stations (there were
normally 63 cars on the assembly line at once).   An early reform
was to assign all assembly-line processes to six-man groups except
for the fixed operations which had to be done by a certain specific
worker or number of workers.   One group would follow the movement
of the line and take full responsibility for completely assembling
six cars from start to finish, including any repairs or special
service required.   The assignment of job function and workload
within the group was left up to the group.   It autonomously decided
and adjusted according to the skill levels and physical strength and
abilities of group members.   There were 12 groups and they would
constantly alternate with two of them being able to rest between on-
line cycles.

The application of such working methods was first envisaged in
1973.   After several trial experiments the system was implemented.
Figure 9 shows the results of a questionnaire survey conducted while
still at the experimental stage.   Shortly thereafter the new methods
were put into full practice and there have been no problems with
either quality or volume of output.   Human relations improved between
fellow workers and both satisfying "hatarakigai" and "ikigai" (sense
of fulfilment and meaning in living) were increasingly enjoyed by
workers.

At the beginning of 1977 a second phase developed because of
more demanding production requirements.   Because of this the
12 groups made up of six members each had to be disbanded.   In their
stead a new experimental programme was installed in which the
production process is divided up into eight groups based upon
operational relatedness and proximity.   There is an autonomous
group assigned to each of the eight major functional categories.
Within each group not only work assignment but also inspection and
repairs are carried out independently.   All groups are scheduled
to rotate to a different functional area every three months.

(2)   Kumamoto Factory,
      Honda Motor Co., Ltd.

Honda's Kumamoto Factory is a new facility for manufacturing two-
wheeled vehicles.   From the time the plant was established, autonomous management group activities have been carried out on an
experimental basis.   The purpose of these developments has been to
meet the demands for "hatarakigai", to meet the needs for group
inter-action at work, and also to provide countermeasures against
monotony caused by the introduction of labour-saving devices and
highly automated work processes.

Autonomous activities mean that specific areas of activity are
left up to the group to decide and administer.   This would include
such things as the methods to fulfil production quotas, the
maintenance of quality, position assignment in the workplace,

production process training, equipment improvement, defect control programmes, cost control, improvements of the workplace environment, QC circles, suggestion systems and recreational activities. Although it is felt that the group size should be kept to a few members the formation and organisation of the groups is the independent responsibility of the various sections. In the work-places where autonomous management is practised there is one less supervisory level in the management hierarchy.

The group leader is elected by group members to serve for one year, subject to the approval of the section chief. In the beginning each group met once a week for an hour during working hours with the entire plant stopping. Today, it is totally left to each autonomous group when and how long to take for such meetings. The section chief is theoretically given the authority to reject any of the group's proposals, but he is strongly encouraged to be as widely open to recommendations as possible. When these groups design and implement a training programme it is possible for them to use a special source of "self-development funds".

7. Summary and perspective

When an industry grows at an extremely fast pace it is most difficult to decide which was the main or decisive factor in its development. Certainly, the answer could include any or all of the areas such as evolution of the market, technology, production, labour, management, sales and distribution and subsidiary corporate performance. In most cases, if there are no good, supporting developments in any one of these areas it will probably be difficult to achieve successful growth. Because of this, we probably have to take the rather unexciting but perhaps expected view that all such factors are important. In any case, it is evident that a number of factors linked up to produce the success of the Japanese auto-mobile industry, where in the last 30 years production increased a thousandfold.

Labour and management in the automobile industry during this period obviously worked toward balanced development. This industry had the largest expansion potential. Workers not only enjoyed a substantial rise in economic status, but their social status also increased greatly. The labour unions demonstrated an understanding of the need to lift productivity within the company, and showed a good grasp of international trade problems. In this manner, the unions have co-operated with the companies. The industrial relations practices of the automobile industry have already developed into a model worthy of the attention of the international community.

"The quality of working life" of the individual workers increased at a steady rate. For large numbers of younger workers employment stability, wage increases and shortened hours were achieved. Soon after entering the company they could buy an automobile and live in an air-conditioned dormitory. If they married they could soon own their own home although admittedly on a loan. There is no doubt that the job they were assigned to was not easy but there were ample opportunities for training, personal development and promotion. These merits were greater and fuller than in other industries, especially more prevalent than in stagnant or declining industries. Improvements in job functions and the refreshing physical and mental recharge of job rotation occurred, moreover, at a much brisker clip than in most other industries.

For middle- and older-aged workers there was also a favourable upturn in the quality of working life in the automobile industry. Particularly for those permanent career employees who entered the company early, there were unusually good opportunities for advancement within the company. The extension of the retirement age was also realised ahead of most other industries: now the formal retirement age is linked with the beginning of social security old-age benefits. Various systems of corporate and union employee benefits and services were also developed to blend with and complement the public social welfare schemes. An important realisation particularly reassuring to the older workers is the sense of employment security which results from the knowledge that the compact cars and trucks of the Japanese automobile industry have a firmly established position of strength in terms of international competition.

An important key to understanding the "quality of working life" in the Japanese automobile industry is the training and development factor. Certainly, various improvements occurred in all areas such as production control, work organisation and small group activities. It is agreed, however, that from an international perspective the most unique feature is the fundamental concept that training and development give birth to organisations of uncommon strength and to an equally strong sense of "hatarakigai" or meaning and satisfaction on the job. At first glance, one may be led to judge that there was too much development in the training area or perhaps a tendency toward an excess of education and training activities. In the Japanese context of career development and utilisation of all the workers, however, a criticism of excess training does not apply.

For example, what might a worker learn whose job is to put the wheels on a car as it moves along the assembly line? It may be a somewhat extreme case, but one former personnel director of an automobile manufacturer writes that it is necessary to teach the basic knowledge of such things as the production process at the sub-contracting firms, the technical problems involved there, material quality, rubber production and the future of synthetic rubber.[1] This way of thinking is justifiable even from the perspective of management's strategy to maintain constantly the social organisation of the workplace. This tendency to place a major emphasis on training and development will not slowdown as the workforce in the automobile industry ages or becomes stagnant. On the contrary, such adversity will cause training and development programmes to take on even greater importance.

In considering the issue of quality of working life, there was insistence that this was intrinsically a management problem. In Europe and America the issue of improvement in the quality of working life was really conceived as a means of solving such things as the increase of absenteeism or the growth in defects and poor workmanship. In the Japanese automobile industry, however, even though people have different status and positions within the organisation, there is an awareness and recognition that first of all, all people are the same and have similar desires and needs. From this point of view, then improvements in the quality of working life become the natural and

---

[1] Hajime Okamura: _Dreams, youth and creation - personnel management at Honda_ (in Japanese) (Tokyo, Kaihatsu Sha, 1974), p. 142.

commonly shared good for all to work toward. The first target of labour and management should be the establishment of a democratic and co-operative community where it is possible to run production or business without the occurrence of absenteeism or quality defects. The untiring efforts to improve the "quality of working life" must perhaps be interpreted and appreciated from this context.

The opinion of the study committee, however, was that while the examples of the automobile industry in Japan may be somewhat special and unique to Japan they are by no means isolated from the world. Rather, it was the opinion of this study committee that the change in the needs of workers now enjoying a high "quality of working life" due to the efforts of labour and management in the Japanese automobile industry over the last ten years, was indeed representative of universal change from the international perspective.

The study committee contributed its collective experience and knowledge to this report on the Japanese automobile industry. It is hoped that it may provide some meaningful and useful research hints to both labour and management in other countries. We believe that the Japanese industry can provide some useful technical suggestions and perhaps more importantly may offer some insights into the intrinsic characteristics of co-operative relations in industry. For our part, we here in Japan have become all the more determined to make every effort toward quickly and satisfactorily answering the future needs of our workers. We would like to exchange these results, particularly the successes, with labour and management of other automobile manufacturers in order to build a better industry for all.

Table 1: Productivity indicators of automobile industry (1968-77)

Year	A. No. of cars produced	B. No. of cars exported	C. Total production (trillion yen)	D. Total employment	E. Per capita physical productivity (B÷D)	F. Per capita value productivity (C÷D) (thousand yen)	G. Labour-equipment ratio (thousand yen)
1968	4 198 429	684 369	3.7	538 280	7.80	6 874	2 624
1969	4 850 151	887 033	4.5	560 725	8.65	8 025	2 853
1970	5 454 524	1 223 944	5.3	579 974	9.40	9 138	3 317
1971	5 883 562	1 921 618	5.8	574 818	10.24	10 090	3 723
1972	6 533 572	1 961 706	6.5	607 173	10.76	10 705	3 770
1973	6 994 515	2 168 948	7.6	634 447	11.02	11 979	3 999
1974	6 504 667	2 575 387	9.1	614 774	10.58	14 802	4 627
1975	7 130 999	2 994 169	10.1	601 156	11.86	16 801	4 995
1976	8 050 643	3 820 422	12.0	-	-	-	5 024
1977	8 777 279	4 620 994	-	-	-	-	-

Sources:
A. Automobile Statistical Yearbook (1977, Japan Automobile Manufacturers Association).
B. Automobile Statistical Yearbook (1977, Japan Automobile Manufacturers Association).
C. Automobile Industry of Japan, 1978 (Toyota Motor Company).
D. Ministry of International Trade and Industry, Census of manufacturing firms.
G. Ministry of International Trade and Industry, Business statistics of Japanese firms.

Note: The 1977 car production and export figures are computed on the basis of fiscal year 1977.

Table 2: Direct man-hours required for different production processes (per compact car)

Year	Total (hours)		Foundry, forging and press (hours)		Machining (hours)		Sub-assembly (hours)		Final assembly (hours)	
1962	82.46	(100.0)	19.13	(100.0)	16.37	(100.0)	8.35	(100.0)	38.61	(100.0)
1963	76.22	(92.4)	17.62	(92.1)	14.44	(88.2)	9.53	(114.1)	34.63	(89.7)
1964	73.68	(89.4)	15.31	(80.0)	15.07	(92.1)	8.38	(100.4)	34.92	(90.4)
1965	67.99	(82.5)	14.42	(75.4)	12.32	(75.3)	7.75	(92.8)	33.50	(86.8)
1966	57.82	(70.1)	13.74	(71.8)	11.76	(71.8)	5.78	(69.2)	26.54	(68.7)
1967	58.94	(71.5)	15.52	(81.1)	10.69	(65.3)	4.71	(56.4)	28.02	(72.6)
1968	48.43	(58.7)	17.73	(92.7)	9.81	(59.9)	3.97	(47.5)	16.92	(43.8)
1969	41.41	(50.2)	14.14	(73.9)	7.72	(47.2)	3.30	(39.5)	16.25	(42.1)
1970	37.12	(45.0)	12.32	(64.4)	6.58	(40.2)	3.24	(38.8)	14.98	(38.8)
1971	33.22	(40.3)	10.67	(55.8)	6.02	(36.8)	2.79	(33.4)	13.74	(35.6)
1972	30.09	(36.5)	9.65	(50.4)	5.07	(31.0)	2.98	(35.7)	12.39	(32.1)
1973	28.12	(34.1)	8.61	(45.0)	4.33	(26.5)	2.70	(32.3)	12.48	(32.3)

Source: National Institute of Vocational Research: A study of employment practices in the automobile industry (in Japanese) (Tokyo, National Institute of Vocational Research, 1976). Original data adopted from the Labour Productivity Statistics Research Report.

Note: Index numbers (1962 = 100.0) are entered in parentheses.

Table 3: Union-management consultation at Nissan Motor Company

Type	Subjects for Consultation	Major Participants
Industry Level		
Industry Labor-Management Conference (Confederation of Japan Automobile Workers' Unions (JAW))	*Industry-wide problems in automobile industry (Set up separately for manufacturing, sales, parts and transport).	Union: Three top officers of JAW and presidents of member unions Company: Officers of Japan Automobile Manufacturers Association and presidents of member companies
Divisonal Labor-Management Conference (Federation of Japan Automobile Workers' Unions)	*Division-wide problems (manufacturing, sales and parts) within Nissan group (sales liaison conference held monthly; others less frequently).	Union: Officers of Federation and of member unions Company: Vice president in charge and other officers and managers
Corporate Level		
Central Union-Management Consultation Council	*Basic policies in corporate management *Changes in organizational structure and key personnel *Policies and plans for production, sales and equipment *Policies and plans for employee benfits and services	Union: All the union officers including those serving JAW and Federation Company: President, all the other board members and relevant managers
(Central Consultation Council) Branch Meetings Specialized Committees	*Specialized subjects to be dealt with in CUMCC *Subjects delegated from CUMCC *Other items as judged necessary by either union or management	Union: Officers of Federation and of Nissan Union Company: Vice president in charge, relevant officers and managers
Production Liaison Conference	*Immediate records and plans related to production, sales and exports *Records and plans related to manning, shift-work and overtime	Union: Top officer in charge and relevant directors of Nissan Union Company: Director in charge and relevant managers
Plant Level		
Production Business Contacts	*Plant-level business, production, manning and work-hour schedule *Plant-level employee benefits and services	Union: All the local union officers including local president Company: Plant manager and relevant managers
Special Business Contacts	*Overall management policies at plant level *Urgent consultation items at plant level	Same as above
Workplace Level		
Divisional Conference	*Problems related to work methods, human relations, work environment, etc. For example: Is work environment satisfactory? Is there room for improvement in work methods? Are creative abilities of workers being put to use? Is the human relations cooperative and congenial?	Union: Full-time executive committee member in charge and shop stewards Company: Division and department managers
Departmental Conference		Union: Shop stewards Company: Department manager

Source: Federation of Japan Automobile Workers' Unions

Table 4: Average monthly wages of automobile workers (1967-77)

Year	Yen	Nominal wages		Real wages		Consumer price	
		Index	Rate of change	Index	Rate of change	Index	Rate of change
1967	36 433	100.0	-	100.0	-	83.8	4.0
1968	39 735	109.1	9.1	102.7	2.7	89.0	4.9
1969	44 772	122.9	9.4	108.7	5.8	74.9	6.4
1970	53 397	146.6	19.3	121.2	11.5	101.4	7.3
1971	61 497	168.8	15.2	132.0	8.9	107.2	5.7
1972	70 727	194.1	15.0	144.2	9.2	112.8	5.2
1973	84 047	230.7	18.8	147.6	2.4	131.0	16.1
1974	107 782	295.8	28.2	155.3	5.2	159.6	21.8
1975	121 917	334.6	13.1	159.2	2.5	176.1	10.3
1976	132 487	363.6	8.7	158.1	0.7	192.7	9.4
1977	146 820	403.0	10.8	162.9	3.0	207.3	7.6

Source: Confederation of Japan Automobile Workers' Unions.

Note: Shift work, overtime, holiday work premiums and other variable payments are not included.

Table 5: Lump-sum retirement payments (1977)

Length of service	Payment (Yen)
5	226 500
10	731 100
15	1 665 300
20	3 176 400
25	5 222 900
30	7 534 700
35	9 481 700

Source: Confederation of Japan Automobile Workers' Unions.

Table 6: Monthly costs of employee services in the automobile industry

Year	Per capita monthly cash wages (A)	Legally required benefits and services	Voluntary benefits and services						Total (B)	A/B (%)
			Housing assistance	Sub-sistence services	Cultural, athletic and rec-reational services	Medical services	Others	Subtotal		
1967	54 967	3 240	1 593	1 936	193	765	18	4 505	7 745	14.1
1968	63 235	3 669	2 112	2 039	220	786	15	5 172	8 841	14.0
1969	72 259	4 354	2 222	2 094	258	804	18	5 396	9 750	13.5
1970	84 024	5 142	3 207	2 206	339	916	53	6 721	11 863	14.1
1971	98 031	5 995	3 558	2 630	423	903	82	7 596	13 591	13.9
1972	114 333	7 026	3 813	2 776	462	1 095	65	8 211	15 237	13.3
1973	140 060	9 146	4 128	3 536	512	1 191	186	9 553	18 699	13.4
1974	172 606	11 808	5 031	3 385	612	1 299	214	10 541	22 349	12.9
1975	194 302	13 676	5 749	3 021	747	1 815	335	11 667	25 343	13.0
1976	224 316	16 556	5 860	4 700	985	1 622	616	13 783	30 339	13.5
1976/1967	4.08	5.11	3.68	2.43	5.10	2.12	34.2	3.06	3.92	
1966/1957	1.54	1.74	4.73	3.10	1.51	2.25	0.89	2.98	2.31	

Source: Compiled from Japan Federation of Employers' Associations, Annual survey of costs of employee services.

Table 7: Deployment of production workers

Year	Number of workers (%)						
	Total production workers	Foundry	Forging	Press	Machining	Heat treatment	Final assembly
1962	42 258 (100)	3 283 (7.8)	702 (1.7)	4 334 (10.3)	8 250 (19.5)	1 006 (2.4)	12 013 (28.4)
1963	53 258 (100)	4 012 (7.5)	941 (1.8)	6 666 (12.5)	9 457 (17.8)	1 124 (2.1)	15 226 (28.6)
1964	79 902 (100)	4 097 (5.1)	1 021 (1.3)	10 543 (13.2)	13 764 (17.2)	1 487 (1.9)	27 803 (34.8)
1965	67 535 (100)	4 197 (6.2)	838 (1.2)	7 552 (11.2)	10 561 (15.6)	1 377 (2.0)	21 478 (31.8)
1966	78 123 (100)	4 660 (6.0)	1 150 (1.5)	8 531 (10.9)	12 583 (16.1)	1 468 (1.9)	27 292 (34.9)
1967	92 282 (100)	5 973 (6.1)	1 195 (1.2)	12 235 (12.4)	15 659 (15.9)	1 768 (1.8)	34 049 (34.6)
1968	128 293 (100)	7 371 (5.7)	1 270 (1.0)	21 152 (16.5)	18 283 (14.3)	1 869 (1.5)	39 677 (30.9)
1969	138 360 (100)	7 861 (5.7)	1 300 (0.9)	23 025 (16.6)	19 148 (13.8)	1 864 (1.3)	42 501 (30.7)
1970	142 475 (100)	8 144 (5.7)	1 344 (0.9)	23 851 (16.7)	20 060 (14.1)	1 858 (1.3)	42 243 (29.6)
1971	145 436 (100)	7 816 (5.4)	1 318 (0.9)	24 240 (16.7)	19 826 (13.6)	1 920 (1.3)	43 025 (29.6)
1972	130 525 (100)	7 253 (5.6)	1 230 (0.9)	19 223 (14.7)	18 583 (14.2)	1 631 (1.2)	40 338 (30.9)
1973	145 471 (100)	7 626 (5.2)	1 320 (0.9)	21 480 (14.8)	20 692 (14.2)	1 868 (1.3)	46 578 (32.0)
1973/1962	3.44	2.32	1.88	4.96	2.51	1.86	3.88

Source: National Institute of Vocational Research, A study of employment practices in the automobile industry (in Japanese) (Tokyo, National Institute of Vocational Research, 1976). Original data adopted from Labour Productivity Statistics Research Report.

Note: The last row was added by the writer of this report.

Figure 1: Per-plant production capacity in
the automobile industry

thousand cars/ year

(thousand cars/
month in parentheses)

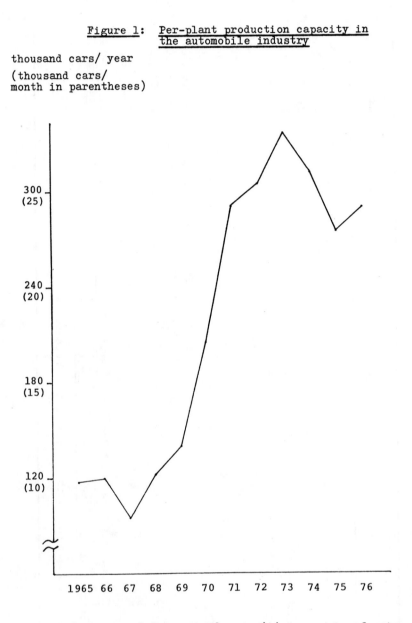

Note: 1. Prepared from annual securities reports of automobile manufacturers.

2. Production combines passenger cars, trucks and buses.

Source: Economic Planning Agency, Economic White Paper, 1977
(in Japanese) (Tokyo: Government Printing Office, 1977),
p.124.

Figure 3: The Life Cycle and Welfare Services at Toyota

Life Cycle at Toyota (life stages): Bachelor · Newly Wedded · Family Building · Towards Maturity · Preparing for Older Age · Enjoying Older Age

Age: 18 · 20 · 25 · 30 · 35 · 40 · 45 · 50 · 55 · 60 · 65 · 70 · 75

Toyota Benefits and Services (key events): Leisure: Self-Development; Marriage: Child Birth; Home Ownership; Education of Children; Preparation for Later Stages; Marriage of Children

'Quality of Family Life'

Toward a healthy and full life:

- SHELTER — Dormitories and corporate housing: Bachelors' dormitories; Corporate housing and rented houses; Toyota apartments
- Home ownership: Housing installment savings; Housing loans: Toyota housing loans; Housing Friends Society; Referral service (company, HOUSING COOP)
- HEALTH — Medical expenses: Health Insurance (Medical care benefits; non-work allowance; child-birth benefits; child allowance/funeral expenses)
- Health care: Employee: Periodical check-up; Inoculation; Overweight countermeasures; Special diseases; Geriatric diseases; Aftercare
- Health care: Family: Toyota Hospital, Health Insurance Center (general treatment, infants, children, breast and uterine cancer, geriatric diseases, counseling); First aid kit
- CONSUMER LIFE — Consumer facilities: Cooperative (group purchase, general stores, credit card service, family group purchase plan, mediation); UNION MEDIATION OF CONSUMER GOODS; Coop (maintenance and service stations)
- Car expenses: Direct purchase plan; Direct purchase loans; Trade-in referral; Used car concession stores; Coop (maintenance and service stations)
- Commuting and work: Commuting expense subsidy; Work clothes and safety shoes subsidy; Lunch subsidy
- STOCK — Property accumulation: Property accumulation savings; Employee savings; Stock ownership association; WORKERS' CREDIT UNION
- After-retirement life: Retirement Allowance; Welfare Annuity Funds
- Education of children: BOOKS FOR NEW SCHOOL CHILDREN

Security against the unexpected:

- Employment security: Authorized leaves
- Income security: Supplementary commuting accident benefits; Toyota Happy Life Insurance; Cancer Insurance; Scholarships for surviving children; Happy Life Insurance
- Financial assistance and mutual aid: Company presents: MUTUAL AID LOANS AND BENEFITS; MUTUAL AID FIRE; MUTUAL AID FIRE INSURANCE; Car insurance; Parking insurance; Blood donation
- Counseling services: GENERAL COUNSELING; LEGAL CONSULTATION; Health Counseling; Traffic accident consultation

[Leisure and Community life]

For relaxation and enjoyment:

- Time away from work: Two-day weekends; long holidays in summer and winter; Paid vacations; Union-management overtime agreements
- Opportunity and place: YOUTH ENCOUNTER: ALL TOYOTA JAMBOREE; PAINTING AND CALLIGRAPHY; OVERSEAS TRIPS; Overseas trips for long-timers; HOHJ SENIORS' ASSOCIATION; LOCAL REC ACTIVITIES; Company programs; Sports events; Clubs and groups; Workplace recreation; Health insurance events; Sports facilities (plants, dormitories); library/Sports Center; Welfare Center; UNION HALL; Sporting goods rental; Resort Health Hostels; Resort Health Hostels
- Information service: TOYOTA WEEKLY; Toyota Newspaper; All Toyota News; Health Insurance Society News; Referral services (courses, books, tape library); English conversation classes; Hobby classes; Sports classes; Cooking, knitting and sewing classes (women's dormitories)

National and Local Government Benefits and Services

- Home Ownership: Housing Loan Corporation; National Annuity; City housing for building private rooms for senior citizens; City housing loans for working people
- Medical Expenses: National Health Insurance; Medicare for infants and senior citizens
- Health Care: Citizen's health check-up; Citizen's health care classes; Home visits to senior citizens
- Older Life: Welfare Annuity (old age and survivor's benefits); National annuity for disabled; Old age interim benefits; Employment insurance
- Education of Children: National and City Scholarships; Child care allowance for children; Subsidy for kindergarten children; Subsidy for private high school students
- Workmen's Compensation: Welfare Annuity (Disability benefits); Child care benefits; surviving children's benefits; Mother and children welfare; "Sunflower" funds; City volunteer service assistance; inter-city traffic accident mutual aid; Citizen's sports accident liability insurance
- Aichi Prefectural Conservation Forest; Forest Park; Youth Park; Aichi Children's land; Kurayoshie Park

Source: Toyota Motor Workers' Union.

Note: Program in capital letters are provided by the Union.

Figure 4: Training and education at Isuzu Motors: administrative and technical employees

Job Function \ Course	Job-related Knowledge	Organizational Development	Specialized Programs	Correspondence Courses	Languages	Special Training (Domestic)	Special Training (Abroad)	OJT
Division Manager						Advanced Financial Management; Division and department managers' conference		"Family" Training; Study meetings; outside seminars; Organization Development
Department Manager	Personnel Management; Finance and Cost Control; Performance Appraisal Training	Management Development			Intensified English Training	Top Management Course (For managers to be loaned out); Instructor's Training		
Unit Supervisor		Leadership Development		Self-Development Course	Preparation for additional, advanced study (domestic or abroad)	Unit supervisors' conference	General Motors Institute	
Intermediate Employee	Electronic Data Processing; Organizatioanl Practices	Women's Leader Training; Teamwork Training						
New Employee	Production Traineeship; Introduction to Organization; Basic Work methods; Team Building	Follow-up (Women)			General English Conversation			
	Required Courses		Elective Courses			Special Courses		On-the-job Training
	Depending on his job function, each employee is required to take prescribed training courses.		Each employee may volunteer to take these courses for his self-development.			Designated individuals are required to take selected, specific courses.		Each department is responsible for OJT programs, which are sometimes subsidized by company.

Figure 5: Training and education at Isuzu Motors: production employees

	Required Courses	Semi-required Courses	Elective Courses
Supervisor	Foreman Conference New Foreman Training 1. Basic training course 2. Residential follow-up Group Leader Conference New Group Leader Training 1. Basic training course 2. Residential follow-up 3. TWI courses	Open Lectures Open Business Courses 1. Quality control 2. Industrial engineering 3. Q.C. Circle 4. Value analysis; value engineering 5. TKJ method 6. Plant visits 7. Lectures Trainer Training (including TWI) Voluntary participation	OJT
Intermediate Leader	Intermediate Leader Training 1. Basic training course 2. Residential follow-up 3. Industrial engineering course	Shop Leader Training 1. Basic Training course 2. TWI course 3. Follow-up	OJT within Department Job related Seminars Skills Proficiency Tests; Skills Olympics
Young Employee	Young Leader Training Workmanship Training Course	Recreation Leader Training Follow-up for Technical College Graduates	"Family" Training Activities Car Maintenance Training Self-development Course; Correspondence Courses Open Lectures English Conversation
New Employee	Middle School Graduates Training (I) Basic Orientation Course for New Employees	Upgraded Full-timer Training Mid-career Probationer Training Follow-up for High School Graduates	Career Orientation Guidance High School Graduates Training (II) Basic Skills Training
Group	Required Courses	Semi-required Courses	Elective Courses
Course	Depending on his job function, each employee is required to take prescribed training courses.	Company provides selected groups of employees with prescribed courses.	In principle, these courses are made available to each employee for his self-development.

On-the-Job Training — Each production unit is responsible for OJT programs, which are sometimes assisted by training staff.

Continuing Education

- 153 -

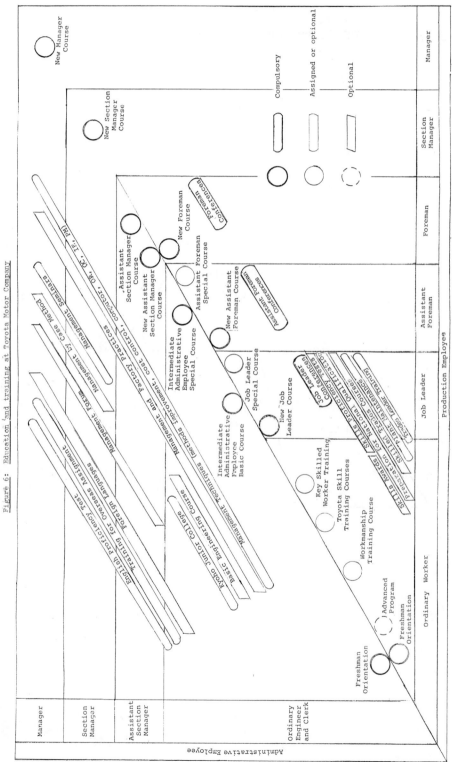

Figure 6: Education and training at Toyota Motor Company

Figure 7: Toyota's environment for employee development

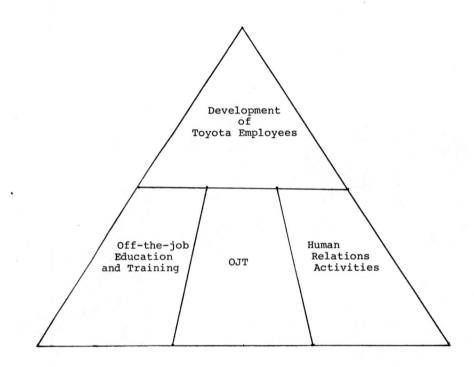

Figure 8: Job satisfaction, fatigue and monotony among automobile union members (1977)

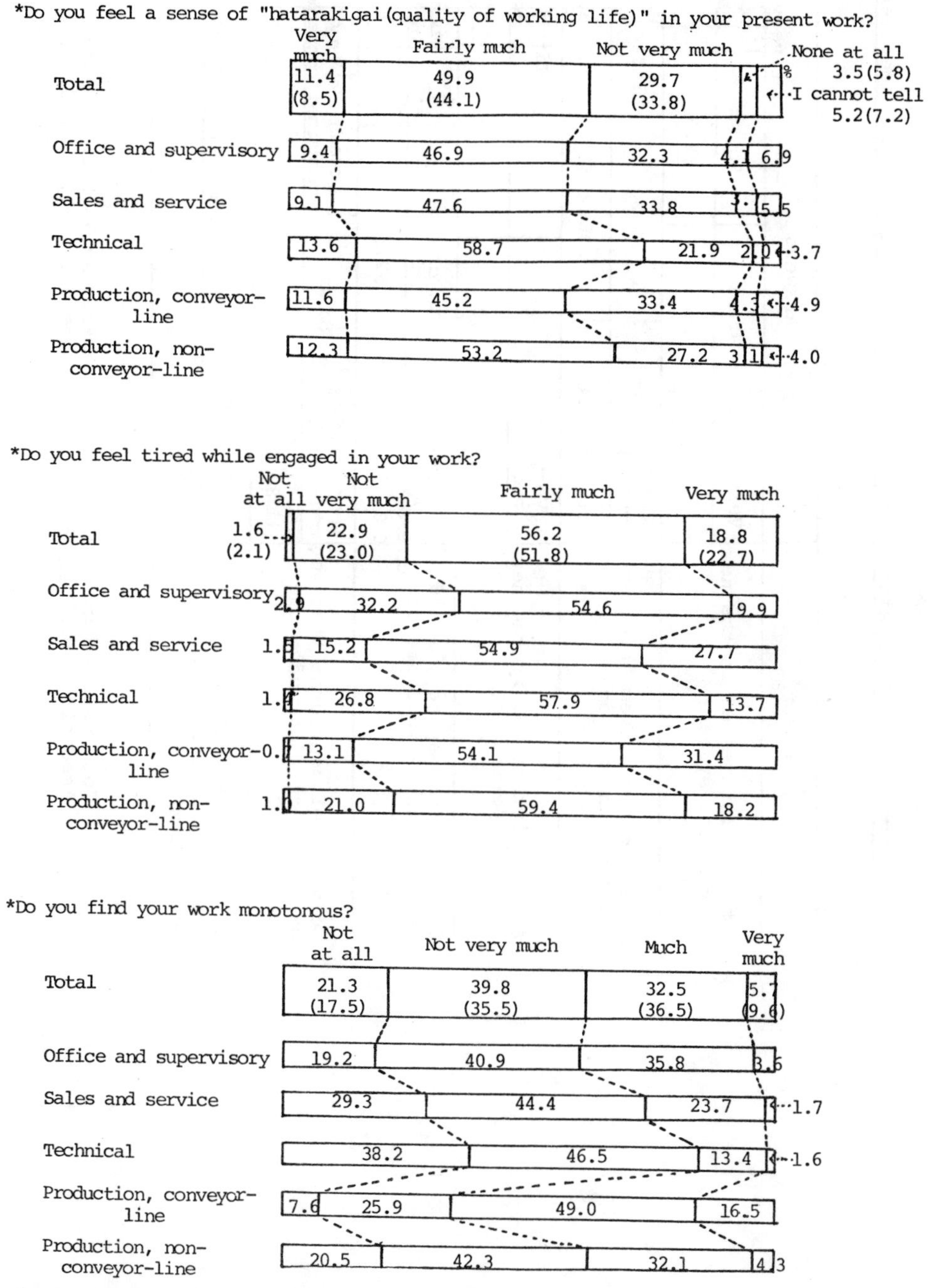

*Do you feel a sense of "hatarakigai(quality of working life)" in your present work?

	Very much	Fairly much	Not very much	None at all
Total	11.4 (8.5)	49.9 (44.1)	29.7 (33.8)	3.5(5.8) / I cannot tell 5.2(7.2)
Office and supervisory	9.4	46.9	32.3	4.1 6.9
Sales and service	9.1	47.6	33.8	5.5
Technical	13.6	58.7	21.9	2.0 3.7
Production, conveyor-line	11.6	45.2	33.4	4.3 4.9
Production, non-conveyor-line	12.3	53.2	27.2	3.1 4.0

*Do you feel tired while engaged in your work?

	Not at all	Not very much	Fairly much	Very much
Total	1.6 (2.1)	22.9 (23.0)	56.2 (51.8)	18.8 (22.7)
Office and supervisory	2.9	32.2	54.6	9.9
Sales and service	1.8	15.2	54.9	27.7
Technical	1.6	26.8	57.9	13.7
Production, conveyor-line	0.8	13.1	54.1	31.4
Production, non-conveyor-line	1.0	21.0	59.4	18.2

*Do you find your work monotonous?

	Not at all	Not very much	Much	Very much
Total	21.3 (17.5)	39.8 (35.5)	32.5 (36.5)	5.7 (9.6)
Office and supervisory	19.2	40.9	35.8	3.5
Sales and service	29.3	44.4	23.7	1.7
Technical	38.2	46.5	13.4	1.6
Production, conveyor-line	7.6	25.9	49.0	16.5
Production, non-conveyor-line	20.5	42.3	32.1	4.3

Source: Confederation of Japanese Automobile Workers' Unions
Note: The figures in parentheses are the results of the 1975 (September) survey.

Figure 9: Worker attitudes toward continuous production experiments

Question	Answers				
Are you interested in the new production system?	Very much 27.8	Much 31.3	So so 32.3	not very much 4.9	Not at all 3.8
Does the new system have merits over the old one?	Very much 16.3	Much 24.7	So so 38.2	Little 17.7	Not at all 3.1
Are you interested in the new system experiments?	Very much 22.4	Much 34.0	So so 35.8	Little 5.2	Not at all 2.8
Under the new system, would safety hazards increase or decrease?	Much decrease 6.0	Some decrease 18.7	No change 52.5	Some increase 14.7	Much increase 8.1
Do you feel confident that you can learn the job under the new system?	Very confident 11.8	Fairly confident 15.6	So so 33.3	Somewhat concerned 26.1	Very concerned 13.2
Do you think quality consciousness will increase under the new system?	Much increase 50.9	Some increase 23.3	No change 23.3		

Source: Toshimasa Nakano, "Measures for Humanizing Work in an Automobile Assembly Plant," IE Review (in Japanese), Vol.17, No.5, 1976.

CHAPTER V

SUMMARY AND CONCLUSIONS

This final chapter seeks primarily to respond to the following two questions. What do the three preceding reports on the quality of working life developments in Japan's shipbuilding, electrical machinery and automobile industries tell us? What do they offer to the labour and management in industrially developed or developing nations as food for thought and action in their search for a better quality of working life?

In response to these questions, this chapter begins with some general comments on the nature of quality of working life issues as coped with by the labour and management in the three Japanese industries. Next, major trends uncovered by the study in various facets of the working life will be reviewed and commented on. When appropriate, more recent developments will be discussed as additional references. The final section of this chapter will then discuss policy implications of the findings from the study.

1. Quality of working life in the
   Japanese perspective

An examination of the three reports reveals that several points stand out as significant features of the way in which the issue of quality of working life was conceived in Japan. In the deliberation of each committee, the form of work organisation, for example, was not perceived to be the most essential issue, although it was accepted as an integral element in the over-all improvement of the quality of working life. As used in the preceding chapters, the quality of working life seems to be understood by labour and management representatives in the following ways:

(1) The "working life" referred to both on-the-job and off-the-job lives of all employees with their lifetime perspectives taken into account. Its "quality", hence, meant the total "values" an individual would derive from his or her association with the enterprise both in material and in non-material ways.

(2) Improvements in the quality of working life were considered to be matters of mutual interest by both union and management representatives, both of whom accepted their relationships as involving elements of "confrontation and harmony". The quality of working life was apparently a significant concern also to management alone.

(3) Initiatives for improving the quality of working life came from both unions and management freely. There was no suspicion on the union side that it was merely a management-initiated "gimmick". Regular consultations and joint efforts by both parties seemed also very common.

(4) There was a clear recognition that the working life continuously expanded the scope of "labour problems". As workers' aspirations rose, new problem facets came to the fore. Also, older

problem areas demanded an increasingly greater degree of
attention and resource allocation.   Thus, both "basic" and
"higher" problem dimensions constituted the quality of working
life issues.

(5) Both the union and management representatives participating in
the study duly admitted that substantial improvements had been
made in their respective industries during the decade covered
by the study.   These improvements, made in such a short time,
may have few parallels in the history of industrial relations.

During the past three decades there has grown a deep-rooted
awareness in Japan that corporations are public institutions
entrusted with a series of social responsibilities.   A recent survey
revealed that 64 of the 100 presidents of major corporations studied
subscribed to the view that "a corporation 'belongs' not only to
stockholders but also to management and employees".   Only 18 per cent
maintained that it "belonged" to stockholders, a legally "correct"
interpretation.   As to the objectives of management, 86 per cent of
the presidents surveyed listed "the welfare of employees and returns
to consumers" in addition to "making profits".[1]   These data clearly
support the commonly held view that Japanese management must work in
a socio-economic environment that strongly favours a balance among
different interest groups.

Particularly, the "interest group" most important to management
is invariably those who do the work, or permanent employees, across
job categories, organisational levels, and often age and sex
boundaries.   In most major corporations where unions are involved,
this management recognition became firmly rooted in the early 1950s
after major upheavals of radical unionism.   As discussed in
Chapter I, a collateral of this management change was often a union
reorganisation pursuing the "confrontation and harmony" principle.
The potential power of labour unions as an adversary, however, has
never since left the mind of management in major companies.

It was in this context that both unions and management began to
accept, first suspiciously at least, the need to simultaneously
improve the corporate productivity and employee welfare in the latter
1950s.   By the time of the present study, both sides had already
experienced working together on this premise nearly two decades in
each of the participating enterprises.   Accordingly, improvements in
the quality of working life became easily accepted by both parti es
as shared common goals, without any contradictions with corporate
objectives or with values of working people both as individuals and
as a collective body.

One incident occurred during the discussions of one of the study
committees which showed clearly where the union and management
representatives stood vis-à-vis an all-out conflict view of labour
management and individual organisation relations.   Some time prior
to the time of study, a book was published which dealt with the

---

[1] _Nihan Keizai Shimbun_, morning, Thursday, 6 Aug. 1981, p. 1.

author's own experiences on the automobile assembly line.[1]   The
author, a freelance reporter, disguised his background and worked
five months for one of the companies represented, and described the
"alienated life" of factory workers, taking a clear "class struggle"
line.   When the book was brought up for discussion, it was totally
dismissed as being "exaggerated, distorted and erroneous" by the
union and management representatives concerned.

In general, it is beyond doubt that for most workers their
quality of working life improved during the period.   From their
viewpoint, such improvements meant sharing the gains from the
increased productivity.   Although the "direct" reason for the
rapid productivity increase in Japan's manufacturing industries may
well have been her accelerated investment in "hardware" as expressed
by the world's highest capital-labour ratio, the improved quality of
working life apparently paved the way towards a greater co-operation
of workers to corporate investment and technological change.   Thus,
an upward spiral effect was taking place between productivity and the
quality of working life, making the three export-oriented industries
some of the major pattern-setters in the field of working life
throughout the country.

With such background in mind, let us now review major findings
from the three industry reports.   The highlights of new developments
are summarised across industries for each subject category, and are
supplemented, when necessary, by reference to additional materials.
Findings are divided into the following major sections: decision-
making mechanism in industrial relations;   basic employment and
security issues;   wages and hours;   employee benefits and services;
personnel development programmes;   and organisation and job improvements.   At the very end of the chapter, a separate section is
provided to discuss the over-all policy implications of these
findings.

2.   Decision-making mechanism in
     industrial relations

Although worker participation in management did not arouse as
much legal discussion in Japan as in Europe, in reality substantial
changes took place during the decade covered by the study in the
decision-making process in the field of industrial relations.
Although some changes were conspicuous and others were subtle, a

---

[1] Satoshi, Kamata: The Despair Auto-Factory (in Japanese)
(Tokyo: Gendaishi Shuppan Kai, 1973), 260 pp.   The book was
brought to the attention of committee members because it was the
only book available in translation on the subject of work alienation
in Japan.   Kamata Satoshi: Toyota, l'usine du désespoir (Paris,
Les Editions ouvrières, 1976), 255 pp., is its French version.   The
views advocated by the author are very close to those held by left-
wing unionists in West European countries.

general trend was to allow a greater voice of wage and salary earners,
as both groups and individuals, in decisions affecting their quality
of working life.   This increasingly interactive trend in decision
making was also coupled with an awareness of greater shared goals on
both labour and management sides, resulting with a relaxation of
aggressiveness and defensiveness and a growing mutual confidence in the
other as a partner.

(a) Negotiation and consultation
     at the enterprise level

In all three industries, collective bargaining carried out at
the enterprise level was increasingly supplemented, if not superseded,
by union-management consultation schemes, which intensified the
union's involvement in decisions and information sharing on a
co-operative basis.   This is in line with a report by the Japan
Productivity Centre that union-management consultation organs were
installed at 90 per cent of the 482 responding firms in 1980.[1]   At
the time of the committee study, a strong interest was expressed by
Denki Roren in further promoting union participation in management.
In 1978, an agreement was reached between the union and management
at Matsushita Electric on a new scheme of union participation in
management.   One of its features was the installation of a management committee which meets at least monthly.   Its membership consists of the president and other designated representatives of
management and the president, vice-president and secretary of the
union.   The objective of the management committee is to enable the
union to voice its opinions on important management policies prior
to final decisions and to make recommendations on major management
policy matters on time.

(b) Worker participation in
     daily decisions

Also at the shop-floor level, communications greatly improved
between unions and management, and supervisors and workers, in both
directions.   One net result was a greater impact of the opinions
and sentiments of employees on final organisational decisions.
Such influence penetrated into different areas of decisions, sometimes without invitations but always without causing major disturbances.   Some of the formalised programmes, such as QC circles and
suggestion systems, may be considered the tip of an iceberg.
Robert E. Cole wrote in 1978, "In Japanese firms ... workers are
given much greater opportunity (than in US firms) for career
development, skill acquisition, and an opportunity to design the
job itself."[2]   The repeated reference to opinion polls by both
management and unions in the preceding chapters is another indication of the increasing "other directedness" in the Japanese
industrial scene, where "others" are really "insiders", whose
opinions count in management or union policy formulation.

---

[1] Japan Productivity Centre: Japanese Labour-Management Relations: Merits and Problems (in Japanese) (Tokyo, Japan Productivity
Centre, 1981), p. 220.

[2] Robert E. Cole: "The future of worker participation in Japan",
in Japan Productivity Centre, Labour-Management Relations in a Matu-
ring Economy (in Japanese) (Tokyo, Japan Productivity Centre, 1978),
p. 192.   Quotations adopted from his original English text.

(c)   Increased influence of
      private industry unions

     All the three industrial unions, Denki Roren (electrical
machinery), Zosen Juki Roren (shipbuilding) and Jidosha Soren
(automobile), play an important role in the IMF-JC (International
Metalworkers Federation - Japan Council).   Since its formation in
1964, the Council has growingly assumed a central co-ordinating
function for major industrial unions in manufacturing crossing the
traditional barriers between Sohyo, Domei, Churitsu Roren, and
Shinsanbetsu, the four national centres of Japan's trade unionism.
All of the three industrial unions, in turn, play a leadership role
for member enterprise unions in respective industries, performing
research, education, surveillance and co-ordination functions.   In
shipbuilding and automobile industries, unions hold regular
conferences with each industry's leaders for information exchange
at the utmost top level on issues having long-term effects on technology, market and human resources.

(d)   Industrial Labour Round-
      Table Conference

     One important development must be mentioned here, which is not
covered by the industry reports but is vital to a proper understanding
of the nature of change in industrial relations at a higher national
level.   In January 1970, the Industrial Labour Round-Table Conference
(Sangyo Rodo Konwakai or Sanrokon) was organised as a "private"
consulting organ of the Minister of Labour.   Since then, it has been
meeting once every month.   This "wise men's" conference is a forum
on top leaders from the national government, labour unions, industry
and learned circles, to communicate freely on labour-related national
issues as "individuals".   At times, the Prime Minister and other
cabinet members have also participated, making the Conference a de
facto top national consensus-building committee on major economic
and social policies affecting labour.   The significant role played
by the Conference in the formulation of a national consensus at the
second oil shock of 1980 is a well-known fact.   This further testi-
fies that labour has indeed established its place firmly in the total
society of Japan.

3.   Basic employment and
     security issues

     Basic security issues, including employment stability, did not
diminish in importance during the period covered by the industry
reports.   On the contrary, reflecting members' increasingly diversified aspirations had to strive earnestly to fill in the gaps that had
grown as new security issues in workers' eyes.   As discussed in
Chapter I , an employment crisis hit Japan in the latter part of the
1970s, but unemployment had not yet posed a serious problem when the
industry reports were being prepared.   In fact, casual ties of the
participating corporations were not too great, with the possible
exception of those in the shipbuilding industry.   Therefore, what
follows as a summary of development in this area seems largely
applicable to all the industries concerned.

- 162 -

(a) Lifetime employment
security

Throughout the period, employment security was assured for all
the permanent workforce in the three industries. Labour market
conditions remained extremely favourable to jobseekers, and many manufacturing industries even experienced labour shortages. It was
during this period that lifetime employment became widely recognised
as one of the "three pillars of Japanese industrial relations".[1]
"Temporary" workers virtually disappeared from industries, including
shipbuilding and automobile. Instead, the shipbuilding industry
nowadays relies on subcontractors and the automobile industry depends
on seasonal workers, who migrate to work on the assembly line during
winter - away from their farms. When redundancy became a crucial
issue, employment insurance schemes were revised (1974), and employment stabilisation funds were created (1977) by the Government to
meet contingencies. Unemployment figures, however, have never
exceeded 2.2 per cent over the last decade.

(b) Extension of working careers

During the period, all the unions involved successfully negotiated a postponement of compulsory retirement from the traditional
55 years of age. It was one of the major union goals since there
had existed a vacuum period without income guarantee between 55 and 60,
when welfare pension old-age annuity payments were to begin. Retirement age was postponed from 55 to 58 in shipbuilding (1975), from
55 to 60 in electrical machinery (1962-72), and from 55 to 60 in
automobile (1965-73). The establishment of subsidiaries to re-employ
retiring workers became also widespread during the period as exemplified by the efforts of Nippon Electric Co. Ltd. This phase of
employment relations seems still in a process of change, since most
employed people desire to continue work until 60 years of age at
least, and many even until 65.

(c) Safety in the workplace

Active efforts were made during the period to improve the safety
environment, particularly in the industries known for less
enviable safety records. The Nippon Kokan's examples of improving
equipment and "human system" and of union participation in safety
administration are very typical. The continuous declines of
accident frequency and severity rates reported for the shipbuilding
industry and for Hitachi Ltd. are highly illustrative of the national
trends. National safety records in manufacturing firms (100 employees
or over) show that between 1970 and 1979 accident frequency rates
dropped from 9.20 to 3.65, and severity rates dwindled from 0.88 to
0.36. The enactment of the Industrial Safety and Health Law (1972)
was an important step to promote safety in the light of new technological requirements and changing social values.

---

[1] See, for example, OECD: Reviews of Manpower and Social
Policies: Manpower Policy in Japan (Paris, OECD, 1972); OECD: The
Development of Industrial Relations Systems: Some Implications of
Japanese Experience (Paris, OECD, 1977).

(d) Health maintenance and care

In addition to the national health insurance scheme, which primarily covers the medical care of the sick and diseased, a number of new measures were installed during the period for prevention of diseases and for promoting physical fitness. In the preceding reports, cases are cited for Mitsui Shipbuilding and Engineering, Nippon Kokan, and Hitachi Ltd., which again seem to exemplify the general trends in the industries concerned. Emphases have shifted from simple medicare to early identification of diseases, to maintenance of physical fitness, and finally to encouragement of active sports for promoting physical strength. Hitachi Ltd. also reports improvements in health records between 1967 and 1976 which were attained through the efforts of a joint labour and management committee.

(e) Security measures in case of misfortunes

Also during the period, new resources, both capital and human, were increasingly made available to ease unforeseen misfortunes that may fall upon any employees and their families. Additional reparations for death while on duty were institutionalised in the shipbuilding industry on top of payments from the Workmen's Accident Compensation Insurance. Surviving children's scholarship annuity is another common item in the shipbuilding industry as the case of Mitsui Shipbuilding and Engineering exemplifies, and so is a "home helper" system. Rehabilitation training is still another helpful programme at Nippon Kokan. Employment of handicapped persons is also an area where progress was made. The examples from Oki Electric and Matsushita Electric, while still small in scale, will probably serve as important models in the future. The Matsushita Volunteers' Club is an example of the union's independent initiative to help any member of the worker's family suffering from a chronic illness or a mental or physical handicap.

4. Wages and hours

Wages and hours, the traditional hard core of conditions of work, were neither neglected during the period. To use the term "wages" may be somewhat misleading in Japan where most "blue collars", another taboo word in recent years, are monthly salaried. No distinctions are made between them and "white collars" in other conditions as well, including work hours. With this in the background, this section tries to summarise significant changes in the area of "wages and hours". It is in fact where the top priority was placed by unions during most of the period, until a more basic issue of unemployment came to the front.

(a) Wages, bonuses and retirement allowances

For all the years after the Second World War, wages, bonuses and lump-sum retirement allowances constituted the "three pillars" of compensation over the collective bargaining table. All three items increased in amount substantially during the decade. Then a major reorganisation began in retirement allowance plans toward its end, reflecting revisions in public pension schemes and the compulsory

retirement age.   Cash wages (excluding variable payments such as
holiday and overtime premiums) multiplied 1.7 times in shipbuilding
(1966-76), 1.7 times in electric machinery (1968-77), and 1.6 times
in the auto industry (1967-77).   Bonuses, which generally amount to
five months' wages per annum, increased almost in parallel.   Retirement allowances, however, did not grow proportionately.   Both
unions and management agree that the significance of lump-sum retirement allowances has declined as the national pension plans have
become increasingly dependable as a source of income after retirement.
Some companies have already begun to pay part of lump-sum allowances
as annuities on retirees' option.

(b)   Determinants of general wage
        differences

     One basic issue over which labour and management fought conti-
nuously since the end of the Second World War in Japan is the relative
weights of "livelihood" and "contribution" as "determinants" of over-
all wage differences among total wage and salary earners.   Both
sides, though far apart at the outset, have gradually come closer to
each other, and a fair equilibrium seems now to prevail between the
two factors.   The three-way split of "personal wages, job wages and
ability pay" at the ratio of 4:5:1 at Toyota Auto Body may be
considered a representative case for most union members.   However,
minor adjustments in "power relationships" among components are still
called for every year, as exemplified by the appeal of the Toyota
Auto Body Union and the changes in the wage structure and payment
schemes in the electric machinery industry.   An over-all trend seems
to be a squeeze of compensation differences, an indication of the
victory of "egalitarianism", while a penetration of "meritocracy"
seems salient for the members of top and middle management groups.

(c)   Toward a single-status
        workforce

     The period covered by industry reports witnessed a decisive
move toward a single-status workforce in manufacturing companies.
The shipbuilding industry finally eliminated the distinction between
blue- and white-collar workers during the period;   the industry was
the only one left behind among the three industries studied.   Incentive wages, which had remained in part of the auto industry, became practically extinct, too.[1]   The mesh of the formerly two
separate categories of workers has resulted in a further squeeze of
income differences.   Although the industry reports do not touch the
subject, available statistics clearly show that blue- and white-
collar distinctions are no longer meaningful indicators of income
disparities.   For example, a new university graduate engineer
(age 22, with 16 years of formal education) earned a median salary
of 114,800 yen in Japan's manufacturing industries in June 1979.
During the same month, a production worker with 8 years of schooling
and 35 years of service, 50 years of age, earned 226,500 yen.   An
average "career income" of a high school graduate production worker
is roughly estimated nowadays to be about 70 per cent of that of a
university graduate.

---

[1] The use of individual incentive wages dwindled from 20.9 per
cent of the firms studied in 1958 to 5.6 per cent in 1974.   That of
group incentive schemes also dropped from 23.3 per cent (1958) to
7.5 per cent (1974).   Nikkeiren: The Current State of Personnel
Management, Fourth Survey (in Japanese) (Tokyo, Nikkeiren, 1975), p.14.

(d) Reduction of working hours

It was during the decade that a nation-wide campaign prompted the introduction of a five-day work week throughout large-scale companies in Japan under the guiding hand of the Ministry of Labour. At yearly negotiations, unions and management agreed to reduce working hours and working days for the succeeding year. Thus, the total working hours per year were reduced from 2,072 hours (1966) to 1,968 hours (1975) in shipbuilding, and from 2,078 (1967) to 1,996 hours (1977) in the automobile industry. The electrical machinery industry, the pace-setter in shortening work hours, reduced from 2,312 hours in 1955 to 1,955 hours in 1975. Working days were reduced from 296 to 246 days during the same period in shipbuilding, and from 293 days to 249.5 days in the auto industry on an annual basis. The current working hours in the electrical machinery industry range from 2,000 to 2,032 hours per year. Flexitime arrangements did not take root, with the only exception of Sumitomo Shipbuilding and Machinery Company during the period.

5. Employee benefits and services

In the early postwar years, employee benefits and services were reorganised in two important ways. One development was the elimination of distinctions between different categories of workers. Nowadays, all the programmes, voluntary or otherwise, apply equally to all the employees including managerial personnel. The other change was in the way decisions were made on employee benefits and services. At the beginning, union participation took the form of sheer protests and aggressive demands. Nowadays, practically all the programmes are the results of business-like union-management negotiation or consultation. It is not uncommon to find a joint organ such as the Central Employee Benefits and Services Committee at Hitachi Ltd. Several new trends took place during the period in this general area.

(a) Growth of social security
     programmes

While the total costs of employee benefits and services increased sharply during the period, including those of voluntary programmes, the most significant change in the area seems to have occurred outside each company. It was the nation's all-out effort to strengthen and improve social security programmes that began in 1973. The direct costs of employee benefits and services in manufacturing industry averaged, in 1979, 18.6 per cent of the yearly payroll including wages and bonuses. The costs increased more or less in parallel with the payroll, quadrupling in nominal terms during the 1970s. In its latter half, however, legally required payments began to occupy a majority share in the total "fringe" expenditure at each firm, whereas previously voluntary programmes used to cost more than social security programmes in all large firms. There are two implications. First, national programmes will increase in importance as contingency measures more than corporation-operated programmes. Secondly, workers in smaller firms will benefit from this development more than workers in larger firms who may have been already covered by some voluntary programmes.

(b) Housing - the focus of
    voluntary programmes

    During the period, housing assistance was the central focus of
employee benefits and services at most firms.   Particularly,
assistance for home ownership was a central concern of both management and unions.   The introduction of Property Accumulation Savings
System through a special legislation in 1974 gave a further impetus
to the zeal for making savings for future home ownership.   Hitachi
offers a variety of assistance programmes.   In the case of Toyota
Motor Co. Ltd., 33 per cent of the voluntary programme budget went
to housing assistance.   In the automobile industry, however, it was
found that investments in housing already began to fall off.   This
is, in the long run, likely to spread to other industries, as the
housing needs of workers are met.

(c) Meeting newly surfacing needs

    New programmes were added during the period to the list of
employee benefits and services, partly because new needs became
activated, and partly because more money became available than
before.   Thus, Mitsui Shipbuilding created new subsidiaries to
provide employee services in real estate, insurance, sightseeing and
drivers' education.   The company also introduced optional insurance
programmes for life, cancer, fire, automobile, traffic accidents
and travel.   Club activities enjoyed most by shipyard workers became
very similar to those favoured by university students.   NEC likewise
provided a host of programmes under the "Green Communication Movement",
geared primarily to the needs of young workers.   Particularly, the
Industrial Safety and Health Law of 1972 provided a legal backing to
company-sponsored recreational activities.   Its article 70 reads,
"The entrepreneur must make an effort to take necessary steps,
including provision of convenience for physical training, recreation
and other activities, in order to maintain and further promote the
health of workers."   Meeting individually different needs is still
another new priority in the area of employee services as at Toyota
Motor Co.

(d) Co-ordinating programmes
    for a life cycle

    Interest rose in the early 1970s in formulating labour policies
based on varying needs of workers at different life stages.[1]   Prime
Minister Miki proposed a comprehensive set of policies called the
Life Cycle Programme in 1975.   It was in this context that Toyota
Motor Workers' Union examined available benefits and services
provided by the union, company and governmental agencies against the
life stage needs of its members in an attempt to identify the
necessity for further improvements.   Although not as explicitly,
most unions and management likewise carefully scrutinised employee
benefits and services around that time.   As a result, some unions
began to agree with management even on the need to reduce or
curtail obsolete programmes which were no longer in great demand.
In the earlier time, unions always insisted on retaining "vested
interests" when management proposed a surgery on such programmes.

    [1] Shin-ichi Takezawa: "Changing workers' values and implications
of policy in Japan", in Louis E. Davis and Albert B. Cherns, eds.,
The Quality of Working Life, Volume One (New York, The Free Press,
1975), pp. 327-346.

6. Personnel development programmes

Personnel development is an integral subsystem of the present-day employment system in Japan. It is not the only means whereby the employer imprints in the worker necessary skills and knowledge to do a job. The shipbuilding report makes only a short reference to "education, training and development" dismissing it only as a regular, routine responsibility of management, too common and obvious to bring up in particular. Apparently a similar psychology worked in the case of the electric machinery industry; its report makes no special reference to the subject. In contrast, the auto industry report devotes a large space to a detailed description of the philosophy, organisation and programmes relevant to personnel development. In the author's view, the auto industry's experience in this field is certainly outstanding but not necessarily exceptional. It should, therefore, be appropriate to summarise the findings assuming that such qualifications are equally applicable to the other industries.

(a) Maximisation of opportunities for every member

"A satisfactory long-range integration between the needs of workers and corporate requirements" was a professed goal of education and training in the automobile industry. This goal was being approached by companies through provision of "opportunities for continuing education and further growth of skill capacity". The underlying assumption here is that every human being wants to make a continuous advancement in his/her life. There are important conditions for this assumption to be realistic: (1) differences before hiring which are beyond one's control, e.g., race or nationality, do not lead to discriminatory actions; (2) formal schooling before hiring does not separate worker groups sharply in terms of career paths; (3) there is an ample opportunity to prove one's performance and ability; (4) promotion of some sort (in pay, position, work, classification, etc.) is abundantly available for those who demonstrate initiative; (5) surpassing peers and seniors on a merit basis is possible but is practised only prudently; (6) there is a genuine respect among members for outstanding achievement made in and outside the workplace; (7) there is a continuous encouragement and coaching by higher standing members of the work group; and (8) there is a systematic attention given to the growth potential of each individual. When all the personnel practices are meshed together and seen as an integral whole, well-managed companies in Japan seem to satisfy most of these conditions for their permanent members. One group, however, is usually excluded: those women workers whose work careers are categorically cut short.

(b) Education and training programmes

Education and training programmes must, therefore, be viewed only as part of the total system of personnel development. Japanese programmes are not necessarily "training programmes" that are designed to impart the knowledge and skills immediately required on the job. The programmes provided by Isuzu Motors Ltd. and Toyota Motor Co. Ltd. seem quite typical of the formal classroom education and training activities maintained by large manufacturing concerns.

Combining worker categories, however, seems more complete at Toyota
than at Isuzu. Honda's education and training concepts and
practices are among the most outstanding throughout the Japanese
industry and may be the closest to the "ideal type" attainable in
the present Japanese context. Honda's relatively short history
makes this deviation from the "traditional wisdom" possible.
Nissan's skill test is an excellent example of a heavy involvement
of lower-level line management in personnel development of production
employees.

(c) Appointment of key management personnel

A decade and a half from the late 1960s was a period when two
seemingly contradictory moves were observed simultaneously in
personnel administration. One was the move toward greater egalitarianism as referred to earlier. The other was the move toward
greater meritocracy in personnel actions. When both moves occurred
together, an important new development emerged: promotional decisions to key management positions increasingly tended to disregard
differences in formal schooling background. This was a blow to less
able university graduates, but a welcome change to able and ambitious
workers with a less favourable background. Since this is a
sensitive subject, only two references are given in the automobile
report, but the trend seems universal. Isuzu reports on the re-
classification of 30 to 50 employees a year from production to
administrative or technical categories. At Toyota Motor, 33 out of
84 section managers in the manufacturing area were found to be
originally from production ranks. A section manager in production
divisions may have up to 500 employees under him with two or more
echelons of supervision in between. This combination of egalitarianism and meritocracy is not confined to the automobile industry
and is probably the most important source of dynamism in the private
sector throughout the country.

(d) Problems of older workers

Toward the end of the 1970s both unions and management, particularly those of large firms, had to face a new challenge of ageing
workforce. The three industries studied were relatively "young"
industries, but their reports already described signs of problem
awareness as well as attempts at solutions. Problems were faced
because all the personnel subsystems were formerly built on the
assumption that workers would retire at 55, and then were
challenged by the extension of retirement age. Furthermore,
ageing was expected to escalate because the anticipated slowdown
of the economy would bring in fewer young workers into organisations.
The preceding chapters not only report on explicit concerns with
the issue in some industries (shipbuilding and electrical machinery),
but describe specific countermeasures: withholding seniority wage
increases and cutting wages for workers employed beyond the previous
formal retirement age (electrical machinery), establishment of
subsidiaries to absorb the older workers who are to leave the
original employer (Nippon Electric), work restructuring for
older workers (Hitachi Shipbuilding and Engineering), and job redesign and employment promotion for older workers (Nissan Motor).
While many of these policies are common to all industries, not all
of them are fully congruent with the present personnel system of
younger employees. Apparently, this is an area where accommodations
and readjustments are further called for.

7.   <u>Organisation and job improvements</u>

    The quality of working life in its narrowest sense refers to
reforms in work organisation and job content.   This concern itself
is a historical product in the western socio-cultural context.   But
it also has universal elements since workers anywhere may suffer
from repetitive work, job monotony, isolated work, dead-end jobs,
dirty work, and a lack of autonomy on the job.   Workers in Japan,
too, experienced dissatisfactions with some of these aspects of
working life, even though no management crises were reported as a
result of such dissatisfactions.   In all probability, timely management actions, taken together with all other measures related to the
over-all quality of working life, may have been adequate to prevent
a further deterioration of this situation.

    (a)   <u>Magnitude of work</u>
          <u>dissatisfaction</u>

    Throughout the three reports, there exists a recognition that
dissatisfactions with work contents constituted an important concern
to both management and unions.   Each report, however, gives the
impression that the situation was well under control.   The electrical
machinery report specifically states that discontent with monotonous
work "was not something that posed a critical threat to the workers'
basic life goals".   None the less, it was found that a considerable
investment was made by unions and management in each industry to
carefully investigate this new problem area.   At Ishikawajima-Harima
Heavy Industries, a joint labour-management team was sent to Europe
to study "industrial democracy" and "humanisation of work".   Apparently Honda and Matsushita likewise dispatched a similar labour-
management team.   Surveys on job satisfaction were conducted several
times by Denki Roren and also by Jidosha Soren, Nippon Kokan, Oki
Electric and Toyota Auto Body, to name only known ones.   Denki Roren
appointed a special committee to study "humanisation of work" in 1976.
All in all, there is no doubt that the <u>hatarakigai</u> issue became an
important concern to unions and management when industry faced a
crucial labour shortage during the high economic growth of the late
1960s and the early 1970s.

    (b)   <u>Job enlargement and</u>
          <u>job enrichment</u>

    It is obvious that the three industry papers include only a few
cases which might be called "pure" examples of job redesign or work
restructuring undertaken for the explicit purpose of improving that
aspect of the quality of working life.   In fact, the JEL method at
Mitsubishi Electric may be the only genuine case of "job enlargement
or job enrichment" that can meet the rigorous "scientific standards
of job redesign" of the West.   The series of "experiments" at
Mitsubishi Electric were inspired and promoted by one of the
corporation's top management, who himself was an outstanding
industrial engineer thoroughly acquainted with the American developments in the field.   The "job integration" at Hitachi Shipbuilding
and Engineering, on the other hand, is a case of multi-purpose work
restructuring of an indigenous origin.   In either case, diffusion
to the plants or shipyards other than the sites of initial breakthroughs was limited.   However, both examples became known as
pioneering models and were intensively studied by industrial
engineers and personnel managers.

This limited appeal of job reform as a means to improve the
quality of working life has several reasons.   To start with, job
structure itself is not as rigid in Japan as in the West.   Changes
in work methods and work assignments are daily occurrences, and
job redesign is a routine responsibility of line management.   (This
partly accounts for the fact that the drastic change made at Fuji
Heavy Industries was initiated by a line manager.)   This is possible
because wages are linked with job contents only very remotely.   In
fact, this last point was even intensified during the period.
Then, as implied by the questions raised by Mitsubishi Electric's
management itself, there exists a strong scepticism as to the
ultimate value of the job reform approach.   Stated differently,
the quality of working life is perceived to be a problem area
requiring a more comprehensive, multidimensional strategy for its
improvement.

(c) Small group activities

Instead of going all out to job restructuring, which is
basically an individual-oriented approach, the management strategy
most widely adopted in Japan during the period happened to be the
one that stressed group participation.   Because small group
activities were so widespread among all the companies involved in
the study, it was necessary to limit only one company from each
industry to make major reporting.   Thus we had cases presented by
Mitsubishi Heavy Industries, Hitachi and Toyota Auto Body on their
respective small group movements.

Small groups such as QC circles and ZD groups primarily perform
three functions.   First, they identify production problems and
analyse the causes.   Secondly, the same groups formulate concrete
action plans to solve the problems.   Finally, the groups implement
solutions and review the results obtained.   Thus, the group
activities constitute a self-contained, perpetual process in which
production workers participate for the sake of improving organisational work performance.   Group members are provided with the
training necessary for this part of work, such as basic statistics,
use of analytical tools, knowledge on products and work methods,
and other relevant information and skills required for creative
problem-solving and work improvement on the spot.

The significance of small group activities as a means to
improve the "quality" aspect of working life was revealed by a
unique study conducted by the union of Ishikawajima-Harima Heavy
Industries Co. Ltd. on its "jishukanri" movement.   The study
showed clearly that workers themselves supported the movement
enthusiastically.   But small group activities are not a panacea
against all evils.   Some of the problems involved were pointed
out in the report of the electrical machinery industry.   Its
unions were found "quite reluctant to grant that small group
activities ... are in themselves an example of an improvement in
the quality of working life".

(d) Experiments on autonomous
     management

     There were several isolated cases of autonomous management
or self-management in the preceding three reports. The most
salient examples come from Mitsubishi Electric's Nakatsugawa Works
and its branch factory at Iida. The case of an automobile assembly
line at Gunma Factory, Fuji Heavy Industries, was a successful
application of the concept to a car plant, but larger manufacturers
did not find the method applicable. The successful experience at
Honda's Kumamoto Factory has found only limited applications in
other factories of the same company. All these cases made use of
the concept "jishukanri", translated as self-management or
autonomous management. The same word was used by Ishikawajima-
Harima to refer to its small group activities as in the case of the
steel and iron industry where the word is abbreviated as JK movement.[1]

     This situation seems to suggest that these examples remained
primarily as experiments. Since the work organisation is already
flexible, the introduction of self-management as a way of delegating
authority on a fixed basis is not the direction in which industry
seems to be moving. Instead, it is highly probable that small
group activities are already functioning with a considerable
degree of autonomy, filling the gap between the technological
demands of hardware and the human needs of production workers.
The accelerated use of robots to replace dehumanising tasks is
still another new development which has an implication to the
humanisation of work.[2] This trend is again not likely to inspire
a further interest in self-management.

8.   Some policy implications

     In this report recent developments in three major Japanese
industries are summarised with a focus on those features which
the respective study committees considered major improvements in
the quality of working life in the late 1960s and the 1970s. Just
like any other cases of industrial relations, these developments
must be viewed in a proper socio-historical perspective before
their applicability can be duly appraised. To say the least, they
will not serve as "good models" for other countries, unless con-
texts match that in Japan during the period. Neither can they be
dismissed as isolated, irrelevant examples, unless other countries
prove not to share any aspects of the context in common. This
final section gives some over-all remarks that hopefully facilitate
the interpretation of policy implications of the Japanese experience
in a broader perspective.

---

[1] In 1980, Nippon Kokan alone recorded 109,446 employee
suggestions on work methods improvements through the efforts of
some 3,500 JK groups, participated in by 23,000 workers, resulting
in an estimated saving of 64 billion yen.

[2] Early in 1981, it was estimated that 38 per cent of some
57,000 robots in use in Japan were employed in the automobile
industry, performing tasks such as welding, painting and loading
and unloading plastic moulds and pressed metals.

(a) Multiplication of
    workers' needs

The Japanese developments clearly show that the developments
in the area of quality of working life are a multi-layer phenomenon.
The growth of the wealth generated during the period made it both
possible and inevitable to increasingly accommodate the changing
needs of workers.   However, changes in workers' needs did not
follow a simple course of development.   New types of needs,
particularly so-called "higher-level" needs, which remained
latent and dormant before, came to the surface.   As elsewhere,
for example, alienation resulting from work began to attract widespread attention also in Japan, and allocation of human and capital
resources to this new area was made as ikigai ("quality of life")
and hatarakigai ("quality of working life") became important public
issues.

But improvements in other aspects of working life were likewise necessary in order to meet the changing aspirations of the
workforce.   Although no cost calculations are available, those
aspects which required the greatest expenditure increases seem
to be the traditionally important areas of working conditions.
The central targets of unions' bargaining efforts during the period
no doubt lay in wage increases, reduction of work hours and work
days, accident prevention, and security in old age.   However,
improvements sought and realised in these traditional areas of
working conditions were not only confined to further "quantitative"
gains in long-standing benefits and prerogatives.   Important
improvements also included "qualitative" changes in work environment and working conditions that were necessary in the light of
changing patterns of workers' aspirations.

It is worth noting, too, that so-called "activation of
higher-level needs" occurred primarily when the more "basic needs"
became relatively satisfied, such as those for job security,
safety and health, and adequate housing.   When economic conditions
deteriorated after the first oil crisis, concerns of both unions and
management grew rapidly with respect to the financial capability of
corporations to maintain the "lifetime employment" practices.   This
concern was expressed in the concluding sections of the reports
for the shipbuilding and electrical machinery industries respectively.   In fact, shortly after the study, the shipbuilding
companies involved decided to introduce measures to encourage
voluntary early retirement as part of their "weight reduction"
programmes.   Unions approved these plans and a number of older
employees left employment.   By 1981, however, all the three
industries seem to have regained sound financial conditions.

(b) Interest representation in
    the quality of working life

The Japanese experience suggests that the continuous inter-
play of management and unions at the enterprise, plant and
department levels is a key factor to the development of well-
balanced programmes to improve the quality of working life.   In
the Japanese context, the enterprise-based unions must, by
definition, seek to reconcile the immediate and long-range interests of employees within the framework of respective companies.

Management also has the dual task of ensuring the corporation's survival and growth and maintaining a healthy and motivated work-force at the same time. As a result, there is a mutual interest in developing a quality of working-life programme which is meaning-ful to individual employees' welfare and is financially sound. This communality of interest in the quality of working life firmly underlies the developments discussed in the preceding chapters.

Stated another way, the quality of working life in Japan has no connotation of unilateral management initiative to undermine unions.   The assumption of both parties is that in that particular area common interests are greater than conflicting interests.   In this respect, the Japanese experience differs greatly from many of North American and West European experiences in the quality of working life.   Likewise, another underlying assumption of the Japanese case may be brought to the open regarding the relationship between individuals and their workplace.   Since this relationship is accepted to be not conflict-ridden, threatening or restrictive as in some other cultures, Japanese workers regard participation more as an opportunity for self-expression, imagination and creativity than as a means for them to control their environment in self-defence.

It may be worth noting that this acceptance of communality rather than conflict of interests as a more important variable in work relations is a relatively new development.   It was not the case 30 years ago, when the conflict view prevailed overwhelmingly throughout the nation.   Most experienced managers would agree that even the QC circles began to take firm root only a decade and a half ago.   The improvement in the general climate of industrial relations has been made possible by the economic growth, but it has provided only one of the necessary conditions.   Most of the credit seems due to management and unions who have performed their respec-tive roles, particularly in search for ways to ensure the maximi-sation of immediate and long-term interests of employees in their enterprises.

(c) Pursuit of universalistic values

At this point, the most crucial question to ask is whether or not the Japanese experience in the quality of working life has any relevance to the rest of the world.   If the Japanese developments consist of solely particularistic elements, they have little practical significance to labour and management in other nations. The best way to answer this question may be to examine whether or not the goals sought and achieved through the new developments, together with pre-existing programmes, have any inherent elements of universalistic appeals to the labour force.

The answer to this question seems affirmative in most ways. Three interest areas of the working people will be discussed: security, rewards and development.

(1) Security

Job security of the total workforce is pursued to a maximum
degree through career employment practices.   Job transfers with
in-house retraining and without pay fluctuations further assure
employment and income security.   The extension of retirement
age helps to reduce the anxiety over old age, although not sufficiently.   Introduction of contractual benefits as emergency
measures, coupled with optional programmes, help to ease the burden
of contingencies.   New safety and health measures are important
improvements to meet the basic needs of physical security.   Home
ownership is assured for practically everybody.   Work hours and
work days have been reduced, which may also add to a secure and
wholesome life.

(2) Rewards

Status differences have been substantially reduced among
different types of workers.   New entrants start from production
jobs, and this also applies to engineers.   In turn, many production
workers do climb the management hierarchy when their merits are
demonstrated.   Virtually all the managerial appointments are made
through promotion from within, and no parachuting from outside is
accepted.   Although wages increase with age, young workers' wage
disadvantages have been considerably reduced.   A modest degree
of wage differences has been brought in to reflect individual performance and ability and differences in job contents and work
environment.   Above all, most employees with a long service record
belive that they, as individuals, have been well rewarded through
their "membership" in the enterprise and the union.

(3) Development

The Japanese system has a number of built-in features for
career progression and development for individuals.   At the
beginning, fewer and less critical distinctions seem to be made
in Japan on the basis of pre-entry background of schooling than in
the West.   Wages rise for everybody as family responsibilities
increase with age.   In the place of work, due respect is given in
social relations as one gains age.   Training is provided at
regular intervals to all workers.   Abundant opportunities are
available for making creative contributions through suggestion
systems, small group movement, and in the case of staff workers,
ringi system (small meetings).   Career growth is given recognition
through upgrading and promotions in job contents, workers' classification system and managerial responsibilities.

(d) Problems left for future
resolution

There seem to be still problems left unresolved in the quality
of working life in Japan.   In spite of the achievements in which
union and management representatives who participated in the study
apparently take pride, the Japanese system of working life has areas
where future improvements seem apparently called for.   Here, some

of the immediate problems will be pointed out which may be resolved
within the present structural framework of management and union
practices.   They also represent some of the areas where Japan may
fall behind in the pursuit of universalistic values in the working
life, despite a number of achievements made in that direction as
just discussed.

(1)   Working hours and working days may have to be further reduced,
       as Japanese workers will ask for their share of the nation's
       still growing productivity.   Unions are likely to push this
       line as indicated in the electrical machinery industry report.
       But changes will be slow because a majority of Japanese
       workers who work in small- and medium-sized sectors cannot
       easily catch up even with the present level achieved by the
       companies reported in this monograph.   Also, throughout the
       nation there is still a respect for long hours of hard work,
       practised more commonly at the top level of management than at
       the shop-floor level.

(2)   In spite of the relatively high level of fulfilment of
       values sought after universally by people at work, particularly
       at the macro- or long-range level, micro-level problems of job
       monotony and dirty work will still remain unresolved, and may
       even worsen in the future.   This point was again pointed out
       in the electrical machinery industry report.   The industry has
       this problem because long-term measures for the enhancement
       of quality of working life do not apply to its female workers
       who comprise a majority in many of the home appliance and
       electronics manufacturers.

(3)   Although there is no reference in any of the reports, which
       primarily discuss the world of male workers, the quality of
       working life of women seems to be a growingly important issue,
       too, in the Japanese scene.   One focus of the problem is the
       participation of high-level womanpower in large-scale industries
       as managerial and technical employees.   Large companies have
       so far made only a slow progress in integrating women into their
       traditionally all-men team of middle and higher management.
       Women are also divided as to their choice of majors in
       universities and career preferences and consequently do not
       represent a strong pressure group.   Some legal protections
       afforded women are also not compatible with the way Japanese
       technical and managerial employees work.

(4)   Perhaps the greatest cause of uncertainty lies in the possible
       international consequences of the relatively high level of
       quality of working life jointly achieved by labour and manage-
       ment in Japanese industries.   It is obvious that the resulting
       high motivation of employees to seek common goals through the
       growth of their enterprises is behind the Japanese economic
       success.   The success in turn further accelerates the chain
       reaction by making the union management relations less
       conflict prone and more co-operation minded.   But is this
       spiral to be stopped, even though it is at the root of
       increasing trade frictions between Japan and older industria-
       lised nations?

certain consumer product areas. With these prospects in mind, both labour and management of the electrical machinery industry face an inevitable restructuring of the industry. New policy plans and concepts in the area of labour relations are also being formulated based upon this outlook.

(b) Industrial relations in the electrical machinery industry

The Japanese labour union movement in earlier days was characterised by repeated and explosive strikes in an impoverished economy and under a radical left wing leadership. From about 1956 things gradually began to come under control, having passed through a "red purge" (weeding out of extreme communist leaders) era brought about in a climate of corporate reconditioning, against a background of national deflation policies, and also through the instructions and encouragement of the occupation forces. At this time the electrical machinery industry was on the road to recovery, being supported by expansion in demand for heavy electrical equipment needed for plant and equipment investments in growing basic industries. Within a short period of time, the industry would also profit from the strong home appliance boom. In these surroundings and forces, Denki Roren (All-Japan Federation of Electric Machine Workers' Union) was founded in 1953.

Denki Roren is an industrial union affiliated with Churitsu Roren. Denki Roren is the largest single industrial union in Churitsu Roren. Its 550,000 members comprise 40 per cent of the workers in the 1,350,000 affiliated membership of Churitsu Roren. It should be noted that Churitsu Roren itself has considerable influence as it is often the deciding power factor among the other three national centres - Sohyo, Domei, Shinsanbetsu. Since 1959, Churitsu Roren has been a member of the Shunto Joint Struggle Committee, and to this extent co-operates with Sohyo in pursuing wage and other demands.

Denki Roren also has an important role due to the high growth and internationalisation of the electrical machinery industry. That began when she participated with other major industrial unions of steel, shipbuilding and automobile in forming the IMF-JC (International Metalworkers Federation - Japan Council) in 1964. Denki Roren has since been part of the leadership in this movement to unify the labour front in the metal and machinery workers' unions; an organisation which has transcended the boundaries of the four national centres.

The labour movement in the electrical machinery industry is fundamentally based on the single enterprise unit. This is no different from the pattern observable in other private industrial sectors. The workers are organised with the other workers of the same firm, and most belong to a union operating a union shop type system. The individual worker is not directly affiliated to Denki Roren. Rather it is the enterprise union that joins the industrial union's upper body. Collective bargaining is carried out at the enterprise level, and labour agreements are negotiated and signed between labour and management at company level.

The leadership and guidance given by Denki Roren to its affiliated unions come from two different sources. One is that in deciding the course of policy actions within the federation, the 14 major labour unions of the large-scale firms such as Hitachi, Toshiba, Mitsubishi and Matsushita have an unusually strong influence.

In 1975, production of the electrical machinery industry was valued at 10,800 billion yen (at 300 yen per dollar this is about 36 billion dollars). This corresponds to 8.5 per cent of the total manufactured output for that year, and represents an increase of 145 times over the 1950 figure. In 1950, the electrical machinery industry only comprised 3.1 per cent of total manufacturing industry production. In the following quarter century the number of manufacturing establishments in the electrical machinery industry had increased by 6.3 times while the number of people engaged in the industry rose by 7.3 times. In comparison, the figures for the manufacturing industry as a whole during this same period were limited to a 2.1 times increase in establishments and a 2.7 times growth in workforce.

The application of new technology and well organised and equipped systems of automated mass production were among the major factors underlying the high rate of productivity which brought about the rapid growth of the electrical machinery industry. As domestic market factors, the surges in demand for durable consumer goods and investment in plant and equipment tended to stimulate production. In foreign markets as well, the increase in imports of durable consumer goods by developed industrialised nations, and the expansion of imported equipment and machinery by developing countries also contributed to the rapid growth. Government assistance policies for research and development, export promotion and financing contributed substantially to the growth. Finally, the real key to growth can be said to be the ingenuity and efforts of management and workers which tied all the factors together, making the most of them for maximum productivity.

It is estimated that there are presently about 1,250,000 workers in the electrical machinery industry. According to the Census of Manufacturing Firms of MITI (Ministry of International Trade and Industry), in 1955 there were 230,000 in this industry. By 1970, as many as 1,340,000 were employed. Presently, the workforce has fallen below the peak figure. The percentage of female employees among the total workforce is about 35 per cent for the electrical machinery industry as a whole. It is as high as 60 per cent in electronic parts and acoustical instruments and equipment. In contrast, in heavy electrical machinery and computers, where male employees are predominant, the proportion of females is around 30 per cent.

According to the forecast of the Industrial Structure Council, production growth in the electrical machinery industry until the year 1985 is expected to be maintained at about an 8.5 per cent level. This is about 2.5 percentage points above the macro-economic growth forecast for the economy in general, and is the largest growth expected among all machinery and tool industries. The decline from the high growth era into a period of considerably lower over-all growth seems unavoidable.

In order to cope with changed conditions, the companies of the electrical machinery industry are promoting technology intensification and expansion into international markets. Concomitantly, an even greater strengthening of efforts to reform the financial and manpower structure is also taking place. Probably these efforts to cope with the low growth era will be complicated by movements toward import restrictions and tariff barriers in the markets of industrially advanced nations and by rapidly growing less developed countries who are catching up and moving into and many keystrokes. Multiple copying of the codes and full stop (by making copies of copies) will save you considerable time and effort.

7.2 EMPLOYING A TYPIST

Some universities will require the students to produce their own reports as part of their training. Elsewhere, many students will not have access to the typewriters and word processors necessary for them to produce their own reports. Others may be slow or inaccurate typists. If the regulations specify a typewritten report, then these students will have to employ a typist to type the report for them.

It is important that you and your typist can function as a team. If you try to carry out the task on the basis of a benevolent master and a dutiful slave it will be doomed to failure. A good typist can contribute greatly to the final appearance of your project and smooth the whole production process for you. At the other end of the scale, an incompetent or antagonized typist can seriously impede your efforts to produce a good report.

The first problem is finding and engaging a good typist. There are several sources of typists who could be employed to type your project report. The best source will undoubtedly be the departmental secretaries. They are conversant with the material they will be asked to type, and with the conventions and house style required for the project reports. However, the departmental secretaries are very perceptive and have had the opportunity to observe you for several years. They will be well aware of your foibles and those of your supervisor. Certain students and certain groups may find that the departmental secretaries are strangely unavailable to type their reports.

If the departmental secretaries are unable to type the report themselves, they may be able to put you in touch with a retired departmental secretary who undertakes typing at home. This is a very good second choice for you. The retired staff should still remember the departmental requirements and the correct way to type chemical and scientific terms. They may not have access to the latest office technology, but if they wish to continue typing project reports in the future they will produce the very best work they can.

Next on the list are the typists who advertise on the notice boards in the department or your hall of residence. These typists can be of very variable standard. While they may be able to type an English Literature PhD thesis superbly, they may be completely baffled by a simple chemical formula. Ask more senior students if they can recommend any of them before approaching the typist or agency.

Some students may be tempted to employ one of their parent's secretaries to type their report. This is not a good idea. They may be very good secretaries, but can they type moderately difficult chemical text and set out tables correctly? Additionally they may live far away, impeding your teamwork and making last-minute corrections very difficult. Furthermore, it is unfair to them, as any difficulties you encounter may sour the working relationship between your parent and the secretary.

Similar strictures apply to inviting a relative to type your project report. Post-graduate students will be able to regale you with tales of how marriages have nearly reached the divorce courts when one partner types, or rather mistypes, the other's thesis.

As a last resort you will have to search the classified advertisements in the local newspaper or telephone directory to find a typist. Once again the relative complexity of the chemical manuscript you produce will eliminate many possible typists. If you are very lucky you will stumble upon an excellent typist who will make an excellent job of your project report. Unfortunately it is more likely that it will be a case of the blind leading the blind towards a second rate report.

Regardless of how you find your typist it is essential to engage one in good time. Remember the best typists will usually be snapped up first. Typists, unlike galley slaves, are not chained to their typewriters and are allowed holidays and other free time. If you engage the typist at the start of your project you will be able to specify the approximate size of your project report and reach agreement on deadlines. Such agreements allow the typists to plan their workloads and organize their lives.

It is important that your typist be reliable, since you will be held responsible for the mistakes and shortcomings of those you employ. The best safeguard against unreliability is the recommendation of others. Lone typists are very vulnerable to having their work disrupted by illness. Young, recently retired typists may well become indisposed at any time in the near future.

When engaging your typist ask to see copies of similar work that has been typed in the past. This request may gratuitously insult the departmental secretaries. In this case go to the library and look at examples of their typing. Do not be surprised if, in return, you are asked to produce a sample of your handwriting. If the typist cannot read your handwriting the partnership is doomed from the start.

You have additional reasons for requesting to see similar work. Can the facilities available to your typist produce the specialized text that a chemistry report requires? Can they cope with subscripts, superscripts, bold and italic type? Is the typeface itself suitable? Are Greek letters available or will they have to be improvised? How will your tables appear?

No typist will type a project report for a box of chocolates or a bunch of flowers. This is not to say that these are not suitable gratuities to acknowledge a job well done, but for your typist your report is a strictly commercial transaction. Three systems of payment are in force. In one the typist charges a rate per hour. In the second a rate per page is charged, possibly with a premium for tables. The last is a flat fee for the project.

The first system always seem to have great rip-off potential. You may engage a typist who types at the author's rate of 10 words per minute who would charge you three times as much as a moderately competent typist typing at 30 words per minute.

A rate per page seems to be the most equitable method. Typists with pressing debts or extravagant tastes may charge the full rate for a page containing five lines of text. Those who wish to be engaged by other students in the future will usually amalgamate short pages when calculating payment. Very few typists enjoy typing tables, even with the power of modern word processing systems at their command. You will frequently be asked to pay a premium (often 50% of the page charge) for tables.

It would seem sensible to take a specimen, completed project report with you when meeting your typist to agree a fee. The report will allow the typist to make a better estimate of the labour involved.

Whatever system of charges you agree to, make sure that you are in agreement about what is included in the charge. Many typists who charge by the page make an additional charge for the time it takes to make **your** alterations and corrections. All typists should correct **their** errors free of charge.

You should also determine at an early stage of your negotiations the charge that will be made for copies. Normally you will be supplied with a working copy, upon which corrections can be made, as the typing progresses. Once this working copy has been agreed to be in its final form, then no further corrections can be made and a master copy is produced.

If multiple copies of your project report are required, you will then need to decide if these are to be produced by the typist or by photocopying. If there are many diagrams, structures and display equations in your report then photocopying may be the best solution irrespective of cost. If you are to pay for the production of photocopies, ask your typist about charges. The typist may have negotiated a favourable rate with a local copy centre.

It will not set your working relationship with your typist off to a bad start if a written agreement covering all the above points is drawn up at the outset. Both of you will then know exactly where you stand and it could save much acrimony later. Indeed, many typists actually welcome such an agreement but are hesitant to suggest one themselves lest they be thought to be totally financially orientated.

Once you have engaged a typist keep in touch with them; reassure the typist that you will still require the project report. At all costs do not let your typist think that you have dropped off the edge of the world. You will find that your typist will be pleased to give you advice about constructing tables so that these will fit onto the page. Your typist should also be able to help you with other aspects of producing your report. The advice you receive from this source may save you much fruitless labour and wasted time. An experienced secretary can often transform a poor quality manuscript into a good report. Nevertheless, you cannot rely on finding such a paragon and it is always your responsibility to produce the best possible manuscript.

Not all business partnerships are successful. If things are going badly between you and your typist then the partnership should be dissolved in both your interests. However, you should take care that you do not initiate the breakdown by providing poor quality, late or illegible copy, and then demanding that a perfect typescript be completed at two hours notice. On the other hand, you may have engaged a typist who can neither spell nor operate the word processor's spell-check program. Neither may you have the time to teach an inexperienced typist the intricacies of producing chemical text. In both these cases you may need to seek another source of help in producing your typescript.

Do not waste too much of the typist's time by trivial enquiries. You have not employed the typist to make polite conversation or cups of coffee when you deliver batches of manuscript. Do not neglect the common courtesies of life, but remember that time is money to typists just as it is to millionaires. In particular avoid contacting your typist at work during normal working hours if you are not the typist's sole employer. This could jeopardize the typist's main job.

The teamwork will really start once you start to produce manuscript copy for the typist. Then you will need to agree on the style of presentation and many other minor matters. The greatest help you can give to your typist will be to know exactly what you require, and to make the style and appearance of your manuscript as close as possible to those of the actual report.

7.3 THE TEXT

You should ascertain the style of presentation since this will influence the layout of the typescript. For example, if the report is to be bound, you should leave a margin of at least 30 mm on the left hand side of each page. Do not make the lines of text too long by using a small typeface or leaving a narrow right-hand margin. About 70 characters per line will be found to be suitable. A typical, double spaced page of text will then contain about 250 words.

Double spacing is to be preferred for chemical reports since single spacing causes sub- and superscripts to become entangled with those on adjacent lines. You should also consider whether to improve the appearance of the text by making it fully justified (like the text of this book). Some word processing systems are driven crazy by long chemical words and you may be unable to use this feature. Make some tests before insisting on full justification.

Normally your report will be written on one side of the paper only. If, for economy, your report will be written on both sides of the paper, you must ensure that the larger margin is on the right-hand-side of even-numbered pages. This implies that odd numbered pages will be the right hand pages of the bound report.

If you are employing a typist to type your report it is as well to discuss the style of presentation required. Always ascertain that the technology in use can cope with the special requirements of producing chemical text. It may be a good idea to make a list of your requirements to give to your typist. A list of agreed requirements delivered with the manuscript could also save arguments later. The requirements might include:

- Leave a left-hand margin of . . . mm
- All pages to be right-hand pages/odd numbered pages to be right-hand pages*
- Top, bottom and right-hand margin . . . mm minimum
- Maximum line length 70 characters
- Number each page at bottom centre/top right*
- Fully/left hand* justify
- Double/single* space the text
- Indent paragraphs
- Do not break chemical formulae at ends of lines
- Avoid widow and orphan lines
- Unless longer than one page do not break tables between pages
- Centre equations, but place number in parentheses at right-hand margin
- Leave suitable spaces (or pages) where indicated for art work.
* Delete where inapplicable.

7.3.1 Mathematical material

Système International (SI) units should be used throughout your report. However, while physical chemists should refer to temperatures in Kelvins, lesser mortals are permitted to use degrees Celsius for mere melting points. Always leave a space between the quantity and the unit, but beware of bad line breaks that leave a number hanging at the end of a line. Avoid very large or very small numbers either by qualifying the SI units with multiplying prefices or by using scientific notation. The latter is recommended since it is more simple to give values the desired degree of accuracy.

Abbreviate the unit when associated with a number but write it in full in the text. Thus '. . . yield 1.2 kg . . .' but 'The same method was used to prepare urea on the kilogram scale'.

Whole numbers up to ten are normally written in full. Other numbers are typed out as, for example, 123. You must never begin a sentence with such a number. '123 samples were analysed' is incorrect. Change the sentence around to 'All 123 samples analysed gave satisfactory results' or provide some further information to avoid starting with a number.

Fractions are difficult to type and it is better to convert all fractions to their decimal equivalents before including them in your report. For example, it is generally better to write 'The electron rest mass is 5.5×10^{-4} of the proton mass' or even 'The electron rest mass is 0.00055 of the proton mass' than 'The electron rest mass is 1/1836 of the proton mass'. Even this last form is still better than splitting the fraction on two single spaced lines thus:

$$\text{line 1} \qquad \frac{1}{}$$
$$\text{line 2} \qquad 1836$$

which in turn will present many less problems than writing it on a single line thus:

$$\frac{1}{1836}$$

Both the bar fraction representations are inelegant, since the numerator is not centred over the denominator. Additionally they require you to be very conversant with the capabilities of your word processing system and the characteristics of your printer. They will undoubtedly take longer to type than to calculate as decimals and the last form will not print successfully on anything but the most advanced laser printer. It is customary to type decimal fractions with a leading zero as in 0.123 rather than .123. This also applies to table entries.

Any mathematical equations in your report should be numbered. You should use a different numbering system (which also looks different) for these to the one you used for chemical equations.

7.3.2 Fonts

Printed scientific works use different fonts, either through long-standing custom or as a means of clarifying the text. The most commonly used fonts are *italic*, **bold**, superscripts and subscripts.

Representing these correctly in your manuscript or typescript may cause you and your typist some problems. Italics are denoted in both manuscript and typescript by single underlining, and bold type by wavy underlining (Figure 7.1(a)). Most typists are not conversant with proof marking systems used in publishing houses. It is better, for example, to place sub- and superscripts carefully in their correct places in the manuscript than to

The complex $\underline{cis}$-$[Pd\,Me_2\,(PPh_3)_2]$ eliminates ethane intramolecularly $\underset{\lambda}{under}$ these conditions. The ligand $\underset{\sim}{7}$ forms a $\underline{trans}$-complex which ~~does~~ cannot eliminate ethane on heating.[43]

(a)

The complex $\underline{cis}$-$\left[PdMe_2(PPh_3)_2\right]$ eliminates ethane intramolecularly under these conditions.   The ligand $\underset{\sim}{7}$ forms a $\underline{trans}$-complex which cannot eliminate ethane on heating.[43]

(b)

The complex cis-$[PdMe_2(PPh_3)_2]$ eliminates ethane intramolecularly under these conditions. The ligand 7 forms a $trans$-complex which cannot eliminate ethane on heating.[43]

(c)

The complex cis- $[PdMe_2(PPh_3)_2]$ eliminates ethane intramolecularly under these conditions. The ligand **7** forms a $trans$-complex which cannot eliminate ethane on heating.[43]

(d)

Figure 7.1 Appearance of: (a) manuscript; (b) typewritten text; (c) dot matrix printer output; (d) laser printer output.

use a circumflex over subscripts and a small vee underneath superscripts.

If you or your typist are using a simple, manual typewriter, then the best attempt, within the limitations of the machine, may look something like that in Figure 7.1(b). The limited keyboard of the typewriter had no square brackets so these have had to be added by hand. They can be drawn in freehand, but a neater result is achieved by using a stencil and a 0.35 mm drawing pen as shown here. This pen has also been used to underline the italics and bold type in the text. A cheaper solution would be to use a fine, black, ball point pen. The text must be double spaced when using a manual typewriter's full sized numbers or the sub- and superscripts of adjacent lines will become entangled. The super- and subscripts have been obtained by moving the typewriter carriage one notch backwards and forwards, respectively. It is usually quicker to leave spaces for subscripts in long chemical formulae or in equations, and then notch the carriage forward before inserting all the subscripts on the current line.

Laser or dot matrix printers usually handle these problems much better. However, this versatility is achieved at the expense of cluttering up the text with printer control codes. Their inclusion slows down the rate of typing the text since each control code usually requires several key-strokes. Further, fonts not only have to be turned on, they also have to be turned off, which requires still more key-strokes. Failure to turn off a font means the text continues to be printed in the unwanted font until the next change of font is ordered. Time and keystrokes can be saved by incorporating font changes in macros.

One problem that can arise with some dot matrix printers is that they advance the paper by one dot (0.12 mm) each time a subscript or superscript is turned off. A long ionic formula with many sub- and superscripts can cause a line of text to droop alarmingly (Figure 7.1(c)).

Another problem that occurs when you wish to print sub- or superscripts in italics is the order of requesting the fonts. Thus when wishing to print the final character of the point group C_{3v} do you request subscript or italics first? The order will depend upon the font hierarchy adopted by your word processing system or printer. Finding out this information means searching through the badly written, obscure sections of your instruction manuals, so it is usually quicker to carry out a few trials. Some printers merely become confused by the double instruction and print the point group as $C_{3\underline{v}}$.

Besides using different fonts, scientific papers also use different alphabets. Greek letters are widely used in chemistry to denote geometrical isomers such as γ-lactam, or stereochemistry {e.g. $\Delta(-)_{589}[\text{Co}\{(\text{R})-(-)\text{pn}\}_3\lambda\lambda\lambda]^{3+}$}. They are also used in spectroscopy (e.g. $\pi \rightarrow \pi^*$), crystallography (e.g. 2θ scan), mechanistic studies (e.g. β-hydride elimination), thermodynamics (e.g. ΔH^o) and radiochemistry.

Since many word processing systems and their associated printers cannot cope with Greek letters, it is as well to be prepared to draw them in by hand. A few preliminary tests will enable you to make suitable provision in your manuscript. If you change to a higher quality printer for your final printout, do take care to ensure that it can also cope with unusual characters. Greater cost, speed or print quality do not necessarily imply that a wider range of characters will be available.

If you do have to draw the Greek characters in by hand, ensure that you leave space for their insertion. Word processing systems always ignore spaces at the beginning of a line, so if the first word on a line was 'β-ray' merely leaving a space will mean the new line begins '-ray'. When this happens you will have to break the left hand margin when you insert the character β by hand. To avoid such untidiness you can substitute dummy Roman letters for the Greek characters. You should be able to alter these letters unobtrusively to the required character. For example 'n' can easily be converted to π. Often italic characters are more useful. A single stroke coverts 0 to θ, while beta can be drawn by adding an extra loop to p. Similarly, the addition of tails to u or n converts them to μ and η, respectively. Even symbols can be pressed into service; $\setminus$ is a good starting point for λ, as is _ for Δ.

Always alert your typist to the presence of Greek characters by making a note in the margin of your manuscript. These notes should follow the style 'Gk beta', 'uc Gk delta' and so on.

Symbols may also have to be drawn in. The most common are long reaction-arrows or the reversible reaction sign. Neither does the London Transport logo superscript (e.g. $\Delta H^{\ominus}$) so beloved of thermodynamicists appear on any keyboard, extended or otherwise.

When typing out mathematical material you should remember that variables should be italicized. However, functions (for example cos, $\log_{10}$, ln or sin) are normally printed in Roman type.

7.4 TABLES

Tables are a powerful way of organizing numerical data. They are capable of greater accuracy than the equivalent graphical presentation (Section 7.5). Furthermore, you can use tables where graphical presentations are impossible, as is the case with tables of analytical data.

Each Table should be numbered sequentially in the text and have a brief, descriptive heading as shown in Figure 7.2. Each column should have

Table 8. Physical properties of complexes containing two tertiary alkyl-phosphine or -arsine ligands

Complex	Conductivity /Siemens[a]	Anion peaks /cm^{-1}[b]	Anion symmetry
$[Cu\{P(C_5H_9)_2Ph\}_2][BF_4]$	28.7	1100	T_d
$[Cu\{P(C_5H_9)_2Ph\}_2][ClO_4]$	28.0	1105	T_d
$[Cu(FBF_3)(PCy_2Ph)_2]$	20.6	1080, 1035	C_{3v}
$[Cu(PCy_2Ph)_2][ClO_4]$	27.0	1100, 600	T_d
$[Cu(OClO_3)\{As(C_5H_9)_3\}_2]$	24.7	1130, 1030	C_{3v}

[a] Determined on mM nitrobenzene solutions.
[b] Nujol mull spectra.

Figure 7.2 Appearance of a typical table.

a heading that shows the property which is the subject of the column. Where appropriate this property should be divided by the unit of measurement so that mere numbers appear in the body of the table. These column headings should be ruled off from the table heading and the body of the table. Do not use a page-wide series of underscores to construct these rules, as the underscores do not make a continuous line. If you draw in the rules by hand, triple spacing the text at the point they occur will give your tables a neater appearance.

Tables should be constructed so that they lie vertically on the page. Vertical tables can often be obtained merely by transposing the columns and rows of a horizontal table. Only in extreme circumstances should horizontal tables be included. If your report is to be preserved on microfiche, your readers will have to lie along the bench to read horizontal tables!

Remember that your standard line length will be about 70 characters. Tables that require more characters per line than this will have to be revised or printed horizontally. Horizontal tables can accommodate a maximum of about 120 characters per line (including spaces).

One cause of excessive table width is the presence of invariant or near invariant columns. The former should never appear in any table. The information can be conveyed in either the title or a footnote. Near invariant columns can be avoided by using footnotes. Suppose you have a series of reaction rates measured by 298 K except for one entry where the temperature was 293 K. Instead of having a column for temperature you could entitle the Table 'Rates of esterification reactions at 298 K' and place a superscript italic letter after the rate obtained at 293 K. In the footnotes to the Table 'f at 293 K' might then appear.

Footnotes can also be used to convey additional information whose inclusion would make either the title or column headings too unwieldy. Figure 7.2 shows how footnotes can be used in this way. Because table entries are usually numeric you should normally use letters to denote footnotes. The footnotes appear after the page-wide rule drawn below the last row of the table.

If you are typing a table yourself you will find it needs careful planning to achieve a neat layout. You should leave a minimum of three spaces between columns and have the columns evenly spaced across the page by increasing the intercolumnar spacing equally where this is possible. Numerical entries in a column should be aligned on the decimal point.

Tables are difficult and time-consuming to plan and type. Once you have tried to construct a successful table you will see why typists usually charge a premium to type them. The labour involved may tend to influence the number of tables you wish to include, particularly if you are typing the report yourself.

When drawing up the structure of a table try to ensure that the rows and columns are placed in some kind of logical order. If a column depends upon the data contained in another column place it to the right of the latter. Arrange the entries in the table either in decreasing or increasing order of a key property. If there is no trend amongst the properties then arrange the entries in alphabetical order. Another valid system might be to place your entries in order of increasing relative molar mass for organic compounds or in order of increasing atomic number of inorganic species.

Tables should be placed on a single page. If the table is too long to fit on one page then the second page should have the column headings repeated at the top. These headings should be ruled off as they were at the start of the table.

7.5 GRAPHS

If the trend shown by the data is more important than their precise values, you should consider presenting the data in graphical form. It is not good practice to present the same data in both graphical and tabular form.

Graphs are becoming more popular as many word processing systems can now cope with their inclusion in the text. However, the golden rule is 'If you can tell it was drawn by a computer, it isn't good enough'. That is, a 45° line should be represented as a line and not as a staircase. More or less steeply inclined lines drawn by inferior computer systems show even more obvious breaks of slope. Another feature that mars many computer-drawn graphs is the inappropriate scale of the axes' labels. Further, the range of characters available for these labels is often insufficient for chemical needs.

One sure way of achieving a poor-quality diagram with current technology is to scan a diagram in a journal and then incorporate this in your text. If you want a really bad quality diagram try enlarging your scanned diagram for inclusion in your project report.

You may think that the only alternative to computer generated diagrams is to equip yourself with a drawing board and a full set of draughtsman's instruments and pens. A decade or more ago this was the only way you could have drawn neat diagrams. Fortunately a felicitous combination of both methods can be used to prepare eminently acceptable diagrams.

A laser printer can be used to prepare axis labels and even the scales' numerals. These can be rendered in the correct size using a variable magnification photocopier. The bald body of the graph can be drawn either by a computer and printer giving high resolution graphics or by yourself using a drawing pen and tracing paper. The variable magnification photocopier can be used to reduce the pasted-up original to its final size. Reduction to final size is preferable to enlargement to final size since any minor imperfections are also reduced.

If you are fortunate enough to own a drawing board and tee-square, or can borrow them, then use them when you draw your graphs on tracing paper. If you have no access to them, there is no need to stand in front of a graphics supplier's window calculating how many meals you will have to forego to own them. You can make an adequate drawing surface by obtaining a large, smooth cardboard box from a supermarket and taping several sheets of this cardboard together to give a stiff, smooth surface about 500 × 500 mm. Tape an A3 size piece of graph paper, ruled in millimetre squares, to the top surface to complete your drawing board. The graph paper allows a transparent ruler to replace an expensive tee-square. Drawing board owners should also fix a similar sheet of graph paper to their boards before starting drawing.

For special purposes other types of graph paper can be used as a base. Phase rule investigators may wish to use triangular graph paper. Logarithmic paper may be more suitable for kineticists or radiochemists.

Unfortunately there is no alternative to buying a drawing pen. These are available at many stationers as well as graphic suppliers. Several makes are available, and for the small use you will make of a pen there is no reason not to buy the cheapest. The pens come in many sizes and a nib width of 0.5 mm is recommended. The slightly stepped nibs of stencil pens are to be preferred since they make it more difficult to smudge lines drawn against a straight edge.

Tracing paper should always be used. Not only can you trace the graphs from rough copies but it gives cleaner reproductions than typing paper. The latter, being softer, less smooth and more absorbent than tracing paper, tends to pick up as the drawing pen moves across its surface and gives a feathered edge to any lines drawn.

More pronounced feathered edges can be produced by allowing the ink from the drawing pen to be drawn by capillary action underneath the ruler and related drawing guides. This can be prevented by modifying drawing guides intended for pencils or ball-point pens. If you place small pieces of sticking plaster underneath rulers, set squares, protractors, or other drawing guides that would otherwise lie directly upon the drawing's surface you will prevent the ink from seeping underneath them, even when you incorrectly hold the drawing pen at an angle to the guides. The sticking plaster will also help to prevent the guides from sliding over the surface of your drawing while being used. Take care not to smudge your diagrams by moving drawing implements across new lines that are still wet. Drawing ink takes a long time to dry on tracing paper when the humidity is high.

Another advantage of tracing paper is that guide lines may be made on its surface in pencil before or during drawing with ink. Once the ink is thoroughly dry, the pencil lines can be erased using a soft rubber eraser. It is even possible to erase ink lines that have been misdrawn or smudged on the tracing paper by using a special ink eraser which is available quite cheaply from graphic suppliers. You will find that small mistakes and minor smudges can be removed more conveniently by gently scraping the tracing with the corner of an old razor blade. Smooth over the scratched surface with a pencil eraser before reinking the offending portion. Burnishing with a pencil eraser after using an ink eraser is also beneficial. The pencil eraser can also be used to generally clean up any drawing once the ink has dried thoroughly.

Tracing paper is available in several weights. The $90\,g\,m^{-2}$ weight is the most suitable. Lighter papers are too flimsy and do not withstand rough usage. Heavier papers are a waste of money. You can protect your drawings by storing and transporting them rolled up in tubes. Do not buy storage tubes from your graphic supplier. The discarded centres of kitchen rolls take A4 diagrams and the centres from 300 mm wide rolls of kitchen foil are a perfect fit for 298 mm wide A3 diagrams.

Axis labels can be prepared not only from computer print out but by the 'poison pen method'. This method consists of cutting out the relevant words and figures from the photocopied text of a chemical journal or catalogue and sticking them on the bald diagram photocopy. If all the above strategies fail, you will have to draw the axis labels using a stencil. If you will also need to draw structural diagrams or display equations (Section 7.6) one of the very specialized chemistry stencils will serve to label axes as well. Advanced chemistry stencils also contain a set of numerals in a smaller font. You will find these invaluable for drawing correctly proportioned sub- and superscripts. Otherwise buy the cheapest 5 mm alphanumeric stencil you can. This should be compatible with your 0.5 mm pen.

Fill your pen with black drawing ink and cap it firmly when not in use to prevent the nib drying and clogging. Try to use if frequently to prevent this. If it should clog, shake it horizontally (away from important work!) to dislodge the blockage. In severe cases soak the nib unit overnight in luke warm water. Never use boiling water or organic solvents on the nib unit.

Straight lines can be drawn against a straight edge. Curved lines can be drawn against a flexible curve or by using french curves. To stencil, firmly fix a long ruler to your board (or use the tee-square, locked in position where possible) to support your stencil. Slide the stencil along this edge and use the pen vertically in its letters to write out the numerals and labels. It is as well to practise using the stencil upon typing paper before using it upon your prize diagrams. You can make this practice pay by drawing the axis labels or display formulae. Save these attempts and measure them so that you can evenly space your final copy on tracing paper.

In all cases try and draw your diagram in the correct proportions to fit the space available. As with tables try to make the graphs fit the vertical rather than the horizontal format. Graphs can be spoilt not only by inappropriately scaled labels but also by inappropriately sized points. A good size to aim for is about 5% of the longest axis, but if many points are drawn they will need to be smaller. Very large points, drawn to encompass

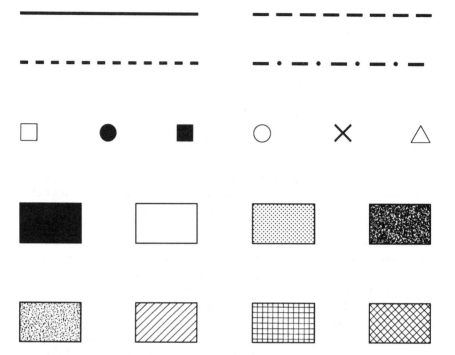

Figure 7.3 Types of lines, points and shading used to distinguish different experiments.

experimental errors, should be avoided. The errors should be indicated by bars extending from the points.

If you are including several curves or lines on one graph these should be clearly distinguished from each other. Different points (Figure 7.3) can be used for each set of results. Invert your stencil and use the vee to draw triangles, or use the sides of capital ens to draw squares, filling in the vacant side(s) in either case using a ruler. Better still (or in addition) label each curve with a capital letter. Use the figure legend to explain which curve is which by referring to the letter.

The master diagram can be prepared from the tracing by photocopying. Remember to place the diagram face-downwards in the photocopier or you will need to issue all your readers with a mirror. Also place a sheet of clean, white paper behind the transparent diagram or you will obtain an interesting photocopy showing the interior of the machine as well. Any labels can be stuck on the master photocopy with an office glue stick. Store the master diagram is a dry place to avoid these labels peeling off.

Some of the numerous ways of presenting graphical information are shown in Figure 7.4. Bar or column charts (Fig. 7.4(a)) are not widely used in chemical publications. If you are including several different columns or

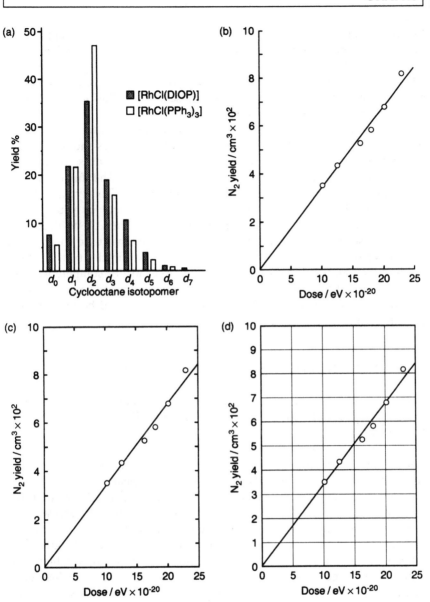

Figure 7.4 Presentation of graphical information: (a) column chart; (b) open graph; (c) boxed graph; (d) boxed graph with grid.

bars upon your chart these can be distinguished by different shadings. To save time leave the largest total area unshaded. The smallest total area can be a full black. Very large full black areas can cause problems for photocopiers having a bad day. The stippled and scribbled areas shown in

Figure 7.3 can be drawn quickly without recourse to expensive apparatus. Successful, regular cross-hatching is difficult to achieve even when using top quality technical drawing equipment and should not be attempted when using a cardboard drawing board. Another advantage of stippled or scribbled shading is that they cannot cause optical illusions which may make the bars or columns appear curved.

Line graphs (Figure 7.4(b–d)) are more common and differ mainly in the way the axes are shown. The simplest merely has two axes and is known as the 'open' type. The next stage is to complete the axes around the remaining two sides to form the 'boxed' version. The final stage of development is to include the scale grid within the box. This type, although common in the *Financial Times*, is not recommended for your project report. Like the box type it requires additional lines to be drawn. It requires a second pen with a nib half the width of that used to draw the remainder of the graph to draw the scale lines within the box. Further, upon reduction, the thinner lines are often either lost or compete with the more important lines. If the exact values of the points are so important as to require an internal scale then the information should be presented in tabular form.

7.6 REACTION SCHEMES AND OTHER FIGURES

You can generate inorganic reaction schemes in a similar way to graphs by using a laser printer and the poison pen method. Reaction schemes show the conversion of starting material A to product B by several steps or routes, or show the sequence of steps in a mechanistic pathway. By tradition the starting material, isolable intermediates and products are shown 1.4 times larger than the reagents which appear above the arrows. All that is required is to make an additional 70% reduction of those reagents and conditions that will appear above or below the arrows. The reaction schemes should be numbered sequentially, i.e. 'Scheme 1', 'Scheme 2' and so on, throughout your report. It is usual to give each scheme or figure a concise, descriptive caption. Brevity can be achieved by omitting verbiage of the form 'A scheme showing . . .', or 'A histogram of . . .', since it should be clear that the art work is either a scheme or a histogram, respectively.

A similar type of illustration but which is classed as a figure is the 'Reactions of . . . ' diagram. An example, prepared by the poison pen method from laser printer output, is shown in Figure 7.5. In these figures there is no clear pathway as there is in a scheme. Note the economic method of dealing with the reagents normally shown upon the reaction arrows. This uses lower case Roman numerals on the arrows and gives the reagents and conditions used in the figure's caption. The arrows have been

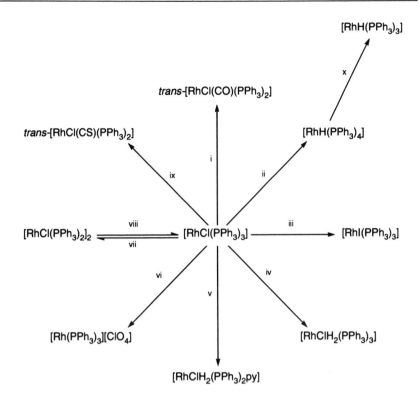

Figure 17. Reactions of [RhCl(PPh₃)₃]: (i) RCHO, C₆H₆/EtOH; (ii) NaBH₄, PPh₃, EtOH; (iii) SiMe₃I, 25°C; (iv) H₂, PPh₃, C₆H₆; (v) H₂, py; (vi)TlClO₄, Me₂CO; (vii) C₇H₈, 109°C; (viii) PPh₃, C₇H₈, 25°C; (ix) CS₂, MeOH; (x) -PPh₃, EtOH.

Figure 7.5 A typical figure produced by the 'poison pen' method.

drawn in with a drawing pen; solid heads to the reaction arrows disguise small imperfections when they are drawn by hand. Some stencils have arrow heads included in their symbols. These are difficult to position accurately and filling them in with ink again disguises small placement errors.

Organic schemes and figures present more problems, since you will normally wish to convey structural information. Advanced, specialized, computer graphics programs are beginning to cope with this problem. However, many of the best systems are not yet compatible with all the word processing packages in common use. Lesser packages do not yet produce acceptable results (Section 7.3). Using them will seriously reduce the quality and appearance of your report. The main disadvantage of all

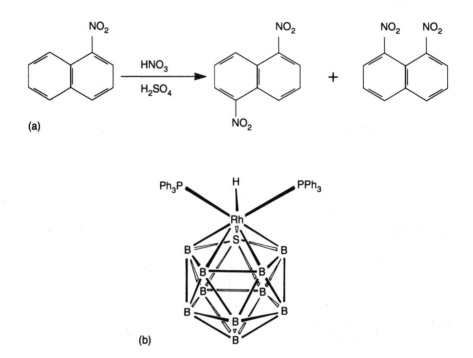

Figure 7.6 (a) Display equation; (b) structure.

computer packages is the length of time it takes to become proficient in their use.

Display equations (Figure 7.6a) can be regarded as small figures. Ensure that when they are reduced they will fit between the margins of the page. Do not be tempted to reduce the length of the arrow to achieve this, as you may wish to include reactants or conditions above and below this. If necessary draw them on two lines, breaking the equation after the arrow. Inset the products from the left hand margin. Ideally all your display equations should be reproduced at the same magnification. This is also the cheapest solution since several originals can be placed in the reducing photocopier at once.

Alternatively, you can use one of the relatively expensive, specialized stencils referred to above. These are usually produced for the 0.5 mm drawing pens, although smaller versions are also available which are compatible with narrower-nibbed pens. If you are hoping for a future career in research or teaching, they may prove to a worthwhile investment (although they may be overtaken by advances in computer graphics).

Possibly your department may have a stencil for student use, or it may be possible for a group of you to buy a communal stencil. It may be the most economic course for you to have a few diagrams drawn professionally. Ask the technical staff of the department or the university's visual aids service if there is anybody who offers this service.

Rub-down lettering may seem an alternative to physically drawing diagrams but this is also an expensive solution. Rub-down sheets of chemical structures are available and these can be supplemented by the more familiar alphanumeric sheets. However, workers in zinc chemistry will run out of zeds long before they run out of ens since the distribution of letters on the sheets reflects their occurrence in written English.

If none of these solutions is appropriate, a little improvisation will enable you to produce adequate structural formulae for your report. You can adopt the poison pen method with structural formulae culled from the chemical literature or the Aldrich catalogue. You could also trace enlarged copies of these using a drawing pen, ruler and tracing paper. Reaction arrows can be drawn with a pen and lettering added to the master diagram in any of the ways described above.

Inorganic structures, which are less common in the literature, may need to be traced from your own drawn masters. If you are not typing your own report, you must discover well in advance if the system your typist will use can cope with your requirements. If it cannot, you will then have time to make alternative arrangements for the more specialized components of your report. What you must do is to show the location and size of any diagrams you wish to include on your manuscript so that the typist can leave the correct spaces for them.

7.7 PHOTOGRAPHS

For reasons of cost the publication of photographs in scientific journals is strongly discouraged. This attitude spills over into reports and you must normally have a very good reason to include any photographs in your project report. Photographs of apparatus, for example, are not sanctioned because it can be adequately specified in the text or shown in a line diagram.

Some of the only cases where photographs might be permissible include photomicrographs of catalytic surfaces or a series of photographs illustrating corrosion studies. Photographs of space-filling molecular models are at the bottom limit of acceptability. Nearly all these subjects can be photographed successfully in monochrome and it is unlikely that you will wish to include colour photographs in your report.

Unfortunately most commercial photographic establishments seem geared to producing colour photographs. It is becoming increasingly difficult to obtain good quality black and white prints of the type required for your report. Before deciding to include any photographs you should make sure that you can obtain good quality prints in which the range of tones varies smoothly from clear white to full black.

The finished prints should be either of A4 size with the same width white margins as the text (see Section 2 above), or be no wider than the text so that they can be mounted on a normal page of your report. This page must be typed or printed before the photograph is affixed since photographs cannot pass through laser printers or around rollers.

The larger A4 size prints can be bound into your report along with the other pages. Smaller prints can be fixed to an ordinary page with a photographic spray mountant or, if the facilities are available, fixed to the page with dry mounting tissue. Excess dry mounting tissue can be trimmed from the edge of the prints with a sharp blade. Excess spray mountant can be removed by a swab dampened with 40–60° petroleum ether.

Ideally the prints should be made on glossy surfaced, fibre based photographic paper. This gives better quality, more durable prints than can be obtained from resin coated paper.

In most cases the photographs will be taken and processed for you by the department's technical staff who will do their best to meet your requirements. Photomicrographs, particularly those taken with a scanning electron microscope, are usually of low contrast and require skilled printing. It is worth discussing methods of showing scale on photomicrographs with the technical staff. It is the author's belief that the scale should be shown on the original negative so that any subsequent enlargement or reduction is shown automatically and does not require calculating afresh each time.

If you are taking your own photographs they should be in sharp focus and clearly defined. The subject should fill the picture. You will probably be able to meet these conditions more easily by using a 35 mm SLR camera than with a compact camera. The former has a better viewfinder system and can accept medium focal length lenses (90–135 mm) which allow you to fill the frame with the subject from a greater distance. This greater camera to subject distance gives a more natural perspective. If you do use a compact camera, use the tele lens setting to achieve this effect.

For the best quality results use a slow black and white film (25 to 100 ISO) and avoid overdevelopment. It is a good idea to take several photographs of each subject, varying the exposure settings on your camera if this is possible.

Avoid cluttered backgrounds. Small objects can usefully be photographed on a sheet of graph paper to give a better idea of scale. Otherwise use a sheet of medium grey paper as a background. This colour avoids misleading through-the-lens exposure meters as would a black or white background. Further, these background colours blend with the black carbon or white hydrogen atoms of a space-filling molecular model.

Lay the subject near the front of the grey paper and curve the remaining paper up behind it. This avoids the sharp angle between the bench and the background from appearing as a confusing black line in the final print.

If you use flash as your source of illumination it should be diffused to avoid harsh shadows. Either bounce the flash onto the subject from a large white sheet of paper, which acts as a reflector, or place a piece of tissue over the flash window. In both cases make increases in the exposure to compensate for the weaker light that results. Use another large white sheet of paper on the far side of your subject to reflect light back into the shadows as a further means of reducing their otherwise inky blackness.

Photographic quality is usually destroyed by photocopying. If more than one copy of your report is to be produced, have the required number of photographic prints made and affix them to duplicate pages.

7.8 INSTRUMENT OUTPUT

The output from many instruments, particularly spectrometers, is often a graph. Unfortunately the chart paper used on many instruments is singularly unsuitable for inclusion in your report by direct photocopying. Attempts to reproduce it in your report may look nearly as bad as the infrared spectrum shown in Figure 7.7(a).

This figure deliberately shows many faults. First, the whole spectrum is reproduced when only part may be required to elucidate the point you are trying to make. Secondly, the standard panel for sample details has been retained instead of including any relevant details in the figure's caption. Most importantly, the reprographic process has shown the over numerous chart divisions almost as strongly in some places as it has the spectrum itself which was drawn in the traditional red ink. Elsewhere the chart divisions are weak or absent on the photocopy. There is no excuse for reproducing a spectrum overlaid with the diagonal stripe indicating that the end of the chart paper is imminent.

For reproduction in your report you should select the portion of the spectrum you require and draw it with black ink in the instrument's pen upon a plain, white roll of chart paper. Using your drawing pen you can then add suitable calibration marks upon the paper. You can add axis labels using any of the methods detailed in Section 7.5. The master diagram can then be reduced to the required size for inclusion in your report (Fig. 7.7(b)).

The digital output from modern spectrometers can be recorded and saved upon a computer disk for later manipulation or reproduction. Properly used, these instruments allow you the luxury of 20/20 hindsight. If you are using an earlier generation of instrument you must be prepared to change to a plain chart paper and a black inked pen whenever you think

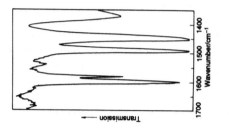

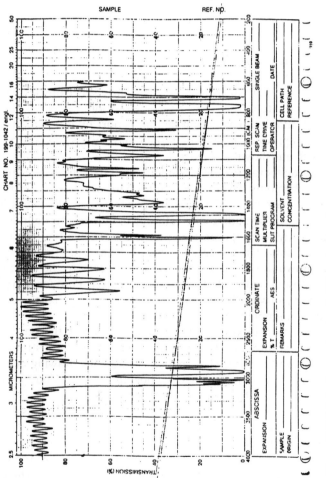

Figure 7.7 (a) Instrument output; (b) report version.

you have captured a spectrum worthy of reproduction in your report. It is better to record a few, eventually unwanted, fair copies of spectra than to have to repeat a reaction or whole preparation merely to record a spectrum of reproduction quality. If you should have to repeat your work for this purpose your only consolation must be that you are inadvertently checking the reproducibility of your work.

7.9 PROOF READING

It was noted above that the manuscript you supply to your typist should be as close to the final version of your report as possible. If you are typing the report yourself this is also a worthy objective since you will make fewer mistakes typing from an accurate manuscript.

In the main this accuracy can be achieved by carefully reading through the manuscript to eliminate the errors it contains. The process is known as proof reading and it is a skill you can soon learn. You will realize that you are becoming a skilled proof reader once you regularly find typographic errors in everything from newspapers to novels.

The reason you find these typographic errors is because you are reading the work of others. When reading your own work you have the fatal tendency to read what you wish to be there rather than what is actually there. It is very beneficial to have your text proof read by somebody outside the subject. The author's wife, a bacteriologist, finds innumerable errors in his chemical manuscripts simply by reading what is written and by not ignoring errors that a chemist, more immersed in the topic, would overlook. It may be possible for you to proof read the work of a student from another discipline in return for help with proof reading your own project report. Biologists call this process symbiosis!

Some word processing systems incorporate a program to check spellings. These are very useful but have their limitations. Some typographic errors give rise to valid words thus 'dread' becomes 'drear' by hitting 'r' on the line above for 'd'. Most importantly the programs' vocabularies, although large, do not include many chemical words. Although some programs make provision for additions to the master vocabulary, many chemical words are so similar that they can be mistyped and creep through if total reliance is placed upon the machine. Other programs allow through American spellings. Thus both words in the following pairs may be equally valid, litre (liter), colour (color) and behaviour (behavior).

It can be seen that there is, as yet, no substitute for human proof reading, although the programs do pick up many of the mistakes. However, proof reading is not solely concerned with the correction of spelling mistakes. While the programs can often tell if a word has been typed twice in succession, they cannot tell you which word has been omitted, nor can they point out that sentences begin with a capital letter. All these things are left to the vigilance of the human proof reader.

Even then there are other tasks for the proof reader who must ensure that cross references are correct. If the statement 'The reduction potential of aqueous bromine to the bromide ion ($E° = 1.065$ V) is greater than that for the reduction of ferric ion (see Section 4.7.3) occurs, then the proof reader must check that the value for the reduction of Fe^{3+} to Fe^{2+} does indeed appear in Section 4.7.3.

Other duties of the proof reader that merge with those of the sub-editor include checking that all chapters, references, equations, figures, tables and structures are numbered in their correct sequences. There are so many tasks to be accomplished that it is better to approach them methodically and use the following list.

Check-list for proof reading the manuscript

- Are all pages present, numbered and in the correct order?
- Are all spellings (particularly chemical words) correct?
- Are all formulae correct?
- Do all headings agree with the contents list in style, number and position?
- Do balanced equations actually balance?
- Are all alterations clear and unambiguous?
- Are all symbols clearly marked?
- Are all requests for different fonts clearly shown or implied?
- Is the punctuation correct?
- Are all tables, figures, schemes and structures mentioned in the text?
- Are all cross-references correct? (Always refer to sections, never to pages.)
- Have the spaces for artwork been indicated?
- Are all the sections and subsections numbered sequentially?
- Are all references numbered correctly?
- Are all names in the reference section spelt correctly?
- Are all equations numbered sequentially?
- Are all tables numbered sequentially?
- Are all columns and rows present in the table?
- Are all columns of the table correctly aligned?
- Are all figures numbered sequentially?
- Are all structures numbered sequentially?

Once the manuscript has been converted into typescript the whole process must begin again. It is to be hoped that you detected most of the errors in the manuscript because you will pay to have any residual errors corrected in the typescript. However good your typist is some additional minor errors will have crept in while the manuscript was being typed. These will also have to be detected. Again, it is as well to be methodical about the whole process and go through the following check-list.

Check-list for proof reading the typescript

- Is the typescript legible? Is it black (not grey)? Has it become damaged in the printer? Are copies smudged?
- Are all words spelt correctly? Check particularly all chemical, foreign and proper names which may be outside the typist's or spelling check program's experience.
- Are words correctly capitalized?
- Are all chemical formulae correct? Check all subscripts, ionic charges and nesting of brackets.
- Has any passage or word been omitted?
- Has any passage or word been included twice?
- Are all special terms and symbols in the correct font?
- Are all headings in a correct and consistent style?
- Is the report in the correct order?
- Are the pages numbered correctly?
- Has space been left for any characters or symbols you must insert yourself?
- Have the correct spaces been left in appropriate places for artwork to be included?
- Are there any bad line or page breaks that require correction?
- Are the margins correct?
- Are all lines correctly spaced?
- Are the paragraphs inset?
- Is the punctuation correct?
- Are all the sections and subsections numbered sequentially?
- Are all references numbered correctly?
- Are all equations numbered sequentially?
- Are all tables numbered sequentially?
- Are all figures numbered sequentially?
- Are all structures numbered sequentially?
- Are tables correctly presented? Do columns of figures align on the decimal point? Has any column or row been omitted?
- Is all the text in the correct font? (Pay special attention where the font has been changed legitimately.)

Graphic supplies

Most university towns have graphic supplier's shops where you can buy drawing pens, ink and tracing paper. In case of difficulty, drawing requisites can be obtained from Oram and Robinson, Cadmore Lane, Cheshunt, Waltham Cross, Hertfordshire, EN8 9SG.

Specialized chemistry stencils can be obtained from the Aldrich Chemical Co. Ltd, The Old Brickyard, Gillingham, Dorset, SP8 4BR.

The project talk | 8

In later life you will almost certainly be required to talk about your work before a formal gathering of your peers. The lecture on your project work may well be your initial experience of doing this. In many ways this is unfortunate, since you will be performing before a knowledgeable audience who earn their daily bread by giving lectures themselves. When examination stress is added to these factors, it is not surprising that many students regard a lecture on their project as a baptism of fire.

This chapter will show you how to increase your confidence by improving your performance. The improvement can be made by considering the lecture's content, the style of delivery and the use of visual aids.

8.1 BUILDING YOUR CONFIDENCE

The main thing you have to fear when talking about your project is fear itself. If you are over-anxious about lecturing to the assembled staff and your fellow students then your performance will suffer, and an autocatalytic cycle will be initiated to the detriment of your presentation. It is, therefore, very important to prevent your anxieties from feeding upon themselves. Anxieties are cowards and can often be vanquished merely by confronting them. Some of the more common sources of anxiety are listed below.

- Looking a fool
- Making a mistake
- Omitting something of importance
- Being unable to answer questions.

It is of little comfort to realize that many of these anxieties are both irrational and unlikely to occur. However, if you spend your lecture waiting in dread for a calamity to happen, then it is likely that it or another less common blunder will occur.

If the sources of each anxiety are investigated it is possible to take countermeasures against the anxiety and banish it. By far the most common anxiety is 'looking a fool' which is a blanket term for several associated anxieties. These stem from a lack of self-confidence and include 'I look a mess', 'I have a funny accent', 'I gabble when under stress', 'I will talk too loud/too softly' and 'I will suddenly be lost for words'. Some of these fears are not totally irrational except that the most beautiful or handsome students frequently believe that the audience will home in on the one minor flaw in their appearance.

You will gain confidence by appearing at your best when presenting your lecture. This is not to say that you should be done up like a dog's dinner to the detriment of your comfort. However, there is no need to gratuitously insult your audience by appearing in ragged or unwashed clothing. Similarly, males sporting designer stubble or females with the latest spiky, green hairdo will alienate some of the more fuddy-duddy senior academic staff.

A neat, clean and not overly flamboyant appearance should be the aim. If you feel comfortable and know that you have avoided the wilder excesses of dress and appearance, then there is little reason to believe that others will think you look foolish.

Another way of looking a fool is to have to dash to the toilet in the middle of your lecture. Always visit the toilet immediately before you give your lecture, because anxiety can speed up some physiological processes. Never encourage visits to the toilet by partaking of alcoholic drinks to 'steady your nerves' before your lecture. If you read the final chapters of Kingley Amis's *Lucky Jim* you will see how alcohol, far from improving your performance, can seriously detract from it.

Avoid irritating your audience by some persistent mannerism or phrase. Good examples of the latter can be heard when sportsmen are interviewed. Never put your hands to your face, or commit such breaches of accepted manners as indulging in a scratching session when you are speaking. Do not pace about while speaking. This distracts the audience from the content of your lecture.

A suitable lectern is of valuable assistance when delivering a lecture. Placing your notes upon it stops you from looking down onto the table when reading them. Holding onto its sides anchors you in place and stops you worrying about what to do with your hands. Additionally this posture helps you project your voice to the back of the room. However, avoid clutching it rigidly throughout your lecture or you will look as if you have been welded in place. It may be necessary to move slightly to present your visual aids. Site your projector near the lectern otherwise your lecture will degenerate into a series of route marches between the two accessories.

Many students mistakenly believe that a pronounced regional or national accent will be a handicap when they are talking about their project. This is quite untrue but an attempt to overlay it with standard

English will leave you paying less attention to what you say than to how you are saying it. This is a sure recipe for disaster. While many find accents attractive, regional colloquialisms are not usually suited to conveying advanced scientific thoughts and should be avoided.

The remaining anxieties can be countered by careful preparation. It is always good practice to prepare the text of your lecture in advance and read it to a tape recorder. As you listen to the playback you should be able to identify those parts of the text that could be improved. Try to speak at an even pace throughout like the newsreaders of radio and television. It will seem measured, or even slow, but that is better than an incomprehensible gabble. The duration of the taped performance will tell you if the script of your lecture needs pruning or if you have time to go into more detail.

Do not forget to allow time for the audience to assimilate your slides or demonstrations. Every slide needs a minute's talk, so it is better to present a few good quality slides than many bad ones. Demonstrations will absorb much more time and are even more accident prone. They are correspondingly impressive if carried out faultlessly and with aplomb. Practice is **essential**.

A few performances of your lecture, first to yourself via the tape recorder and later to your friends, will increase your experience and boost your confidence. Small groups of students make good trial audiences for each others' lectures.

A script for your lecture is a great help when you are first speaking to an audience. The most important thing to remember is that your lecture is not a public reading of your project report. Your script should be in a different style to your report and allow more interaction with your audience.

If you are using slides these also serve as an outline script. You can use the slides as reminders and time markers while you are speaking. Although scripts destroy spontaneity, they do act as a safeguard against omissions and mistakes.

It is very simple to avoid talking too loudly or too softly during your lecture. An earlier visit with your fellow students to the lecture theatre or room where the talk is to be given will allow you all to practise your delivery. You will find that even large lecture theatres do not require you to shout at the volume normally reserved for abusing referees. Provided you speak with your head thrown slightly back, your projection will allow you to be heard at the back. Your audibility will be improved by stressing the last syllable of each word slightly more that you would in ordinary conversation. Never hang your head down and mumble into your lecture notes. This will ensure that you are inaudible to anyone beyond the third row. Always face your audience when speaking. Never mutter incantations to the blackboard when talking about the writing on it.

Arrange a system of hand signals for too loud/too quiet with a friend.

Ask your friend to sit at the back when you give your lecture and act as your volume control. If your friend can also smile at you occasionally during your lecture this will improve your self-confidence.

Being unable to answer questions is a frequent anxiety. It does have some foundation, but usually the only person in your audience who knows more about your project and its subject will be your supervisor. If you have remained on good terms with your supervisor you should have nothing to fear from this quarter. The most likely source of questions will be any errors in your presentation. Members of staff who are used to proof reading and marking examination scripts are very adept at locating these errors, particularly when they occur on slides or transparencies. In Section 8.3 you will be advised how to detect errors in your visual aids before projection.

Students would be less worried about the questions after their lecture if they knew how difficult it can be to devise intelligent and relevant questions following even a competent lecture on a well constructed project. This is why the staff have to resort to drawing your attention to the minor blemishes mentioned above. If, from the corner of your eye, you see the chairman scribbling away furiously during your delivery do not be alarmed. It is more likely that a possible question is being noted than that you have made a serious blunder.

That is not to say that perceptive questions cannot arise from most unlikely sources. The author recalls an inorganic chemist, whose wife was a haematologist, severely testing a student's knowledge of the relationship between blood-iron levels and obscure medical conditions.

To create a better impression, and to guard against such eventualities, you should read around your topic thoroughly. Obviously you cannot be expected to know everything and it is permissible to reply 'I am sorry, I don't know about that aspect' on one or two occasions during question time. Repeating this formula more frequently will certainly damage your marks, but probably not so severely as digging a huge pit for yourself under astute cross-questioning.

The wider knowledge you have gained from reading around the subject can often be used to parry questions by showing you are aware of a related aspect of the subject. Although it is unethical, you could always plant one or two questions amongst your colleagues in the audience. These favours can be returned when it is their turn to speak on their projects.

The most difficult questions to answer are not the intelligent ones but the stupid ones. However lucid your presentation has been there will always be one member of your audience who has totally misunderstood it. Unfortunately these people often feel compelled to demonstrate this fact to the others present by asking a stupid question. Faced with such a question you not only have to look at your whole project from a totally different angle, but simultaneously devise a civil and rational answer. Perhaps the best tactic is to ask for clarification of one part of the question. Then you will gain time to think and the questioner instead may become confused.

Answering questions is a valuable part of your training. It should not be looked on as an ordeal but as an opportunity to demonstrate your knowledge of your project.

8.2 WRITING THE SCRIPT

It is vital to remember that your project lecture is not a public reading of your project report. One of the most important differences between the two is the combination of the experimental and results sections in the lecture. The audience will wish to know how you obtained each result before you discuss its significance. However, both your project report and lecture will benefit from having an authoritative and concise introduction. These may not differ too greatly in style, although only the most important features of your introduction can usually be included in your lecture because of the limited time you have available.

Nevertheless it is important that you do not present facts too rapidly for them to be assimilated by your audience. You can dilute the flow of facts by including more detail than is customary in a written report. One example that springs to mind is a more detailed description of what happened during a reaction. In your report you normally only give the initial and final colours of your solutions, in your lecture you can describe the rate and sequence of colour changes observed. You can also tell your audience more about the difficulties you encountered and how you overcame them.

This latter feature illustrates another essential difference between a report and a lecture. Reports are read to retrieve the facts, but lectures can only convey these facts successfully if you gain a rapport with your audience. Involving the audience in your own difficulties and excitements makes them more receptive to the ideas you are trying to convey. Some lecturers are able to use humour to win their audience over to their side. Be careful of this tactic: it is easy to misjudge the mood of your audience. If you consider yourself an amateur comedian then strictly ration your jokes. A pun usually avoids giving offence and both bad and good puns seem to be equally memorable.

Although you should have developed your arguments logically in your report, it is even more important that you do so in your lecture. Your audience cannot refer back to an earlier page to help them follow your arguments. Concentrate on one theme at a time and keep the argument lucid and simple.

Try and avoid hypotheses based purely upon numbers even if you are dealing with numerical material. Numbers are very difficult for the audience to remember while they are listening to you talk. Rely on trends if you can. State that a bond is shorter in one compound than another, rather than giving the exact bond length in each case. This would require your audience to remember both values and carry out mental arithmetic during your lecture! If the exact numerical values of the property are very important state them on a slide or transparency and keep this in view while you discuss the significance of the values. In this way members of the audience do not have to rely upon their memories. Similarly, structures are difficult to carry in the memory when listening to a continuing theme. If structural features, which are often difficult to describe, are important, show the structure on a slide while talking about it.

Above all, try and sound committed and enthusiastic about your project. Audiences detect a lack of commitment before they detect a lack of ability. If you sound half hearted about your project then the staff may be subconsciously half hearted about awarding you marks for your lecture. Always accentuate the positive aspects of your work. Say how pure your intermediate was to disguise the miserable yield (or *vice versa*!). Play down the mundane aspects of your results and concentrate upon the novel features you have unearthed.

Continue this positive attitude into your conclusion. Do not be afraid to state boldly what you consider you have achieved. Ending on a defeatist note leaves the way open for a sadistic questioner to turn it into rout. By ending on a positive note you make it much more difficult for a damning question to be asked.

8.3 VISUAL AIDS

Visual aids enliven any lecture provided that they are relevant and legible to the back row of the audience. The simplest visual aid is the chalk mark on the blackboard. When writing on the blackboard make sure that you write boldly enough for those in the back row to read what you have written. Do not write large sections of your lecture on the blackboard. You are not talking to a primary school class too young to take their own notes. Long periods spent in silence with your back to your audience is not a good style to adopt. Involved diagrams must be prepared in advance. This requires more advanced visual aids whose images can be projected upon a screen.

These images may either be on 35 mm film (slides), or on overhead projector transparencies. The latter are easier to produce, more versatile, and can be seen by your audience in an undarkened room. Flip-charts may be used for small audiences, but assessments are usually carried out before larger groups where this type of presentation is unsuitable. However, the type of visual aid you select will probably be dictated by the facilities available in your department. You should ascertain well in advance of the lecture what visual aids can be used.

You should also find out if the method you intend to use will be appropriate to the room that it will be used in. Slides normally require a blacked out room. The smaller magnification of overhead transparencies allows them to be shown in ordinary illumination. However, a bright, sunlit room will result in degraded images and will only be suitable for the boldest and most simple transparencies. If the room is equipped with curtains make one of your friends responsible for drawing them when you show transparencies.

Whatever method of projection you use, your original artwork should be of the highest quality since any imperfections will be greatly enlarged upon the screen. Laser printers are ideal for preparing text or the labels for graphs' axes. However, many computer graphics packages and structural formulae programs are still too crude to give acceptable images. You may still need to draw out these parts by hand using a drawing pen.

Transparencies for overhead projectors are easily made by photocopying A4 originals onto transparent film. Photographic slides cannot be prepared so simply since most cameras cannot focus closely enough to fill the frame with an A4 original. You will probably find it best to photograph A3 originals to obtain 35 mm slides. Since most typewriters and graphic aids are geared to the A4 size this adds to the difficulty of producing the original artwork. Very few students have the photographic skill or equipment to produce acceptable 35 mm slides. However, anybody who can operate a copying machine can produce an overhead transparency from original artwork.

The full and accurate range of colours obtainable is the principal advantage of 35 mm slides. Most overhead transparencies are reproduced as black on clear, although coloured bases are available. Colour can be added by hand to overhead transparencies using coloured pens. Few departments have the facility to produce coloured overhead transparencies although these can be made commercially at fabulous expense in most cities.

The most common mistake you can make is to try to include too much information on each slide. A trip to the back row of the lecture theatre will soon show you that complicated reaction schemes or large tables are unsuitable subjects for slides. You can avoid this common mistake by taking a sheet of A4 paper and, using a thick felt tip pen, writing out your text. The maximum quantity of information per transparency is all you can write on the A4 sheet in this way.

Avoid detail and concentrate the main points. Do not add verbiage to the transparency's text. Say 'First-order kinetics' instead of 'Let us next consider first order kinetics'. Never use transparencies showing normal size typescript: this will look like the type size newspapers use to report the croquet results when it appears on the screen. Always enlarge typescript to at least 7 mm high on the transparency to ensure legibility. Ten or twenty millimetre high lettering is even better.

Tables can usefully be replaced by graphs, since not only are too many data in a table confusing, but your audience will not have time to assimilate them. Tables, with their greater precision, may play an important part in your written account where your readers can examine and compare the information presented at their own speed. However, in your lecture you will be dictating the rate of information presentation.

Reaction schemes are best broken down into a few steps per slide. After all, you can only talk about one step at a time.

The greater versatility of the overhead transparency arises from your ability to add to or subtract from the information it presents at will. Information can be subtracted simply by blanking off the appropriate portion of the transparency with an opaque sheet. This is very difficult to do with a 35 mm slide.

Do not allow your audience to read the entire transparency while you search for a piece of opaque paper, and avoid knocking the transparency askew when blanking off part of it. Instead, improve your presentation by pre-positioning the opaque paper. This paper can be fixed to one side of the transparency mount with a piece of adhesive or masking tape as shown in Figure 8.1(a). If you have a choice, the latter is better because it does not weep adhesive on heating and literally gum up the works. Alternatively, use an overlay by making the second point on a second piece of transparent base which can be fixed to the side of the master transparency's mount in the same way (Fig. 8.1(b)).

Transparent overlays are very useful for making sequential points (e.g. steps in a reaction mechanism). You should not attempt to use more than three overlays on a transparency lest you commit the cardinal sin of placing too much information on one transparency. You will find it is easier to manipulate the overlays if you fix tabs (to help lift them) on the opposite side from the hinge. In the hot, dry atmosphere above the projector platen, static electricity causes the original transparency to adhere to overlays. Take care that your overlays, which hang down from the projector platen when not in use, do not obstruct the flow of cooling air to the projector's powerful bulb.

The overlays should be drawn on a sheet of tracing paper that has been fixed over a copy of the main transparency. Used intelligently this method should ensure the correct register of any overlay. Where very accurate register of an overlay is required draw a cross with a fine pen in the same corner of each tracing and make sure these are in exact register before starting on each overlay.

Always provide yourself with several blank acetate sheets and marker

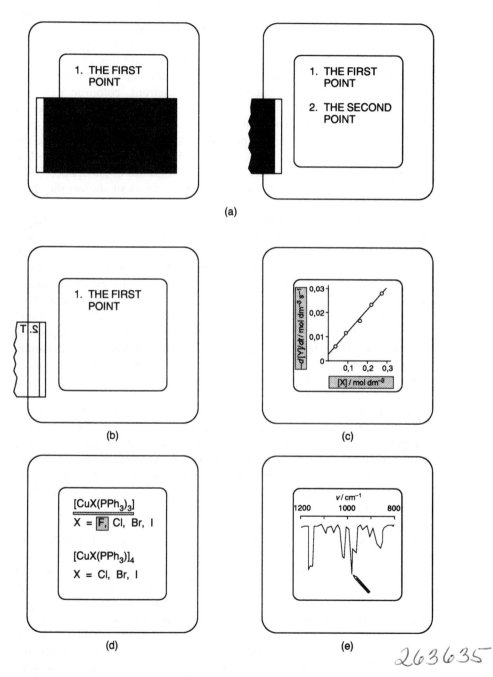

263635

Figure 8.1 Increasing the versatility of transparencies for the overhead projector.

pens for them before giving your lecture. You can then make additional points, possibly in response to questions, upon these spare sheets without defacing your original transparencies which they overlay.

You can increase the impact of monochrome transparencies by highlighting the main points with colour. You can add this with a suitable felt tip pen. However, you may only wish to highlight your current point. You can do this by placing a piece of transparent, coloured Perspex® (polymethylmethacrylate) over the item. Small pieces of fluorescent red or green acrylic sheet about 3 mm thick can be obtained as cheap offcuts from the manufacturers of shop signs and fascias. You can cut these pieces to the desired shapes with a hacksaw. The rough sawn edges are smoothed successively with a file and decreasingly coarse grades of glasspaper. Take care that you do not scratch the soft facing surfaces of the acrylic sheet when working with the material.

A group of you could easily make up a communal set of acrylic shapes for your lectures. Your kit of prettily coloured pieces of acrylic sheet should include a variety of squares and rectangles. Long rectangles of contrasting colours can be laid over the axes' labels on graphs to emphasize them (Fig. 8.1(c)). A 15 mm square can be used to overlay a single character on the transparency. Thus it can be used to highlight the number of an item in a list. Rectangles can be used to highlight words, and very thin rectangles can be used to underline titles to increase the impact of monochrome transparencies (Fig. 8.1(d)). If you attempt to use very small pieces of acrylic sheet you will encounter problems from static electricity, which will prevent you placing them accurately.

It is very useful to make a pointer from the acrylic sheet. You should make this about 150 mm long and no more than 10 mm wide. Evenly taper one end of the original rectangle to a point. This pointer can be laid on a transparency to indicate the item under discussion, for example a peak in an infrared spectrum (Fig. 8.1(e)). Lay the pointer upon the transparency, do not move it and irritate your audience by waving it about while you are speaking. Thin knitting needles are better pointers than pencils, which in turn are infinitely superior to fat, stubby fingers.

Never forget that you can project the image of any coloured, transparent object on the platen of an overhead projector. The internal reflections of small crystals give rise to black images on the screen, but if you dissolve the crystals in a non-flammable solvent contained in a small Petri dish or beaker then this can be placed on the platen and projected. It is even possible, if you exercise great care, to show colour changes during a reaction by carrying out the reaction in a beaker on the platen. Never spill liquids on the projector unless you wish to bring your lecture to an expensive and spectacular end. Never use corrosive liquids on the projector. In case of disaster switch off the projector immediately and have a kitchen towel to hand to mop up any spillage.

You must carefully proof read the art work before making the final transparency or slide. This is difficult since diagrams do not lend themselves to systematic scrutiny. For example a branch in a mechanistic scheme can lead to part of it being overlooked. If you have stencilled the lettering for the diagram or graph it is very easy to suffer from sign writers' disease and omit letters or add them twice. The worst example the author ever saw was one he prepared for an American undergraduate class. This had 'litre' and 'liter' randomly alternated throughout the slide. Fortunately this was so bad that the mistakes were detected before producing the transparency. It is much more difficult to detect a single mistake. The problems of finding a single mistake in a complicated diagram are a further incentive not to include too much detail.

Check-list for proof reading artwork
- Are all words spelt correctly?
- Are all formulae correct?
- Do equations balance where required to do so?
- Have pieces of display formulae been omitted?
- Is the slide well arranged and balanced?
- Has any extraneous information been included? (Prune your material ruthlessly.)
- Are there any smudges or other blemishes present?
- Are all graph axes labelled and scaled correctly?
- Can overlays be placed in correct register?
- Does each scheme and graph bear a title?

8.4 DELIVERING YOUR LECTURE

If you have followed the advice given in the previous sections you should have written your script, prepared your visual aids and checked the timing of your lecture. On the day of your lecture you should be comfortably dressed and have with you your script, visual aids and other sundry accessories. If you are using slides these should be correctly spotted and placed in the correct order before handing them to the projectionist. If you are using overhead transparencies these should also be placed in their correct order. Do not forget to take spare acetate sheets and pens to write on them, acrylic highlights and any other visual aids you wish to use.

Immediately before your lecture you should check that there is a pointer, a blackboard eraser, sufficient chalk in a variety of colours and that the blackboard is clean. Look at all surfaces of roller boards lest some practical joker has written a derogatory message on a surface you will bring into view during your lecture.

Pay similar attention to projection apparatus. Check that it is in working order and that the optics are clean. An efficient department will have a spare projector standing by.

If you are to operate the projector yourself you should know how to do so. Learn before your lecture, not during it. If you have made preliminary checks on the effectiveness of your visual aids in the same lecture room, you will have learnt how to operate the apparatus, and where the plug points and light switches are. Make sure that the projector is at the correct distance from the screen to give an image of the desired size. If the image is too small, move the projector away from the screen. If it is too large move the projector towards the screen. If you are using both portrait and landscape format slides ensure that both will fit on the screen.

It is also important to ensure that the projector is square on to the screen. If one side of the image is smaller than the other, move the projector towards the other, larger side. Unfortunately many projectors are pointed upwards to throw an image on a screen higher than the projector. This results in a 'keystone'-shaped image. It will not usually be possible for you to raise the projector sufficiently to obtain an orthogonal image.

In severe cases the keystone effect will make it impossible for you to focus sharply on the entire slide simultaneously. The best compromise is to focus the projector sharply for one third of the distance from the top of the image. You may need to alter the focus as you progress down your slide. This is irritating for both you and your audience but it is better than having the audience strain their eyes.

If you are using slides instead of overhead projector transparencies, you may require the services of a projectionist. To help your projectionist, have all your slides in the same type of mount. Glass mounts are better, since the slide will not 'pop' out of focus as the film base changes curvature as it dries out in the heat of the projector's lamp.

Arrange your slides in the correct order before giving them to your projectionist. Have the first slide on top of the stack. Draw a diagonal line with a broad, felt tip pen across the side of the stack once it is in order. This makes it easy to see if a slide has become displaced or is missing.

The slides must also be correctly oriented before projection. You should place a coloured, 5 mm spot on the bottom left hand corner of the mount when the slide appears as you wish it to be seen on the screen. Slides should be placed in the projector with this spot in the top right hand corner facing away from the screen. These spots can be purchased from stationers or photographic suppliers. However, it is cheaper to make them from coloured sticky labels using a standard 80 mm punch.

You must agree on a signal with your projectionist when you are ready for the next slide. It may be simply announcing 'Next slide, please' or tapping your pointer on the floor. To avoid confusion make your slide series sequential. Do not ask the projectionist to return to a slide during the course of your lecture. If you want to show a slide a second time have a copy made and insert this into the sequence at the correct point.

If you are projecting the slides yourself, spare sufficient time to master the remote control device. Make sure that you can refocus smoothly, and know which button to press to move forward through your slide sequence. Remote control projectors benefit more than most from a homogeneous set of thin, glass-mounted slides.

Check-list for your lecture
- Does your material fit the time allowed?
- Have you rehearsed your presentation?
- Can your visual aids be projected/displayed?
- Can your visual aids be seen clearly in the back row of the lecture theatre?
- Do you know how to operate the projector(s)?
- Are the projectors aligned and focused on the screen?
- Are the illumination levels of the room and screen images compatible?
- Is the lectern in the correct position?
- Do you have the following with you?
    Your script
    Visual aids
    Acrylic highlighters
    Pointer
    Coloured chalks
    Board eraser
    Spare acetate sheets and ohp pens
    Watch or clock
    Your project report for reference
- Is your script in the correct order?
- Have you visited the toilet?

Poster presentations

Posters play an increasingly important part at chemical conferences, not least because acceptance of a poster often means a reduction in conference fees for impecunious postgraduates. Nevertheless, posters are a useful way of imparting recent results and making valuable contacts at conferences. Accordingly many chemistry departments ask students to present their project results in poster form. The more enlightened departments even go so far as to imitate the custom of international conferences and offer a bottle of aqueous ethanol as a prize for the best poster.

It is to be hoped that your department will not follow that other custom of international conferences and fail to disclose the size of the display boards for each poster. You should find out the size of your display board as early as you can so that you can design your artwork to fill this area as neatly as possible.

When you prepare your poster you should remember the golden rule that you applied to your slides or overhead transparencies – **don't include too much detail!** All that is required is a clear, brief exposition of what you have achieved. People can read your poster at their own pace in contrast to a project lecture which is given at your pace. Therefore, it is permissible and even desirable to include spectra, tables, reaction schemes or crystal structures, since these enable you to break up the passages of text into small, comprehensible blocks.

Once upon a time producing these blocks of text was a daunting task for all but the most artistically gifted students. Fortunately the development of the laser printer and the enlarging copy machine has made it possible for anyone to produce a visually cohesive poster. Have your text printed out by the best quality laser printer you can find, since any imperfections will be magnified upon enlargement. You can also use the laser printer to prepare captions for figures and to label the axes of graphs.

Depending upon the quality of your word processing system you may also be able to produce diagrams and chemical structures via the laser printer. Again apply the rule 'If you can tell it was done on the computer it isn't good enough', and be prepared to draw these items out by hand. Only the most advanced systems will provide you with coloured diagrams, so you should give some thought to increasing the appeal of your diagrams by making provision at the design stage for later manual application of colour.

Including colour may mean that the diagrams you used in your written report will need modifying before using them in your poster. If you are colouring a diagram with crayons or pens, use regular hatching running in one direction only. If you are using a paint brush, make sure that the ink or paint is sufficiently dilute. An even application of colour is best achieved when **all** the area being coloured remains damp while being painted or colour-washed. Mix sufficient paint or ink. Do not make the elementary mistake of running out of material half-way through colouring.

It is very easy to decrease the visual appeal of your poster by using too many presentational gimmicks. You should aim for a dignified style. A single typeface throughout is much better than using every font on your printer simply because, like Everest, they were there. Audiences are surprisingly critical of style. The author recalls a poster of his which was dubbed the 'UNESCO poster' merely because of an overlavish application of coloured column charts. He was saved from total ignominy by a neighbouring French poster which used aluminium foil hexagons to denote benzene rings. This was named the 'Playschool poster'.

Each poster requires a bold heading stating the title of your project and your name. Find out if it is departmental practice to include your supervisor's name also. If this is the case, place the supervisor's name last and follow it with the asterisk which denotes the senior author. Some departments produce these title boards for each project, in others it is your responsibility to set the scene for your project. If the remainder of your poster is on white paper, have the title printed on coloured paper to emphasize it.

Once you have all your artwork prepared, try to find out how it may be fixed to the display board. If you have mounted the diagrams upon boards make sure that you have enough long pins to fix them in place.

The presentation of your poster to the public gives them an opportunity to ask questions about the work you have described. This should present you with few problems, particularly if you have already delivered your project lecture. Nevertheless, you should have a copy of your project report to hand to answer any very specific queries.

When standing by your poster you should remember that you too are on display. As mentioned in Chapter 8 it is desirable to avoid the wilder flights of fashion on these occasions. Who knows if one of the visitors may wish to employ you on the strength of your project work?

10 | Applying your project skills

There is a sense of anticlimax after you have completed the last part of your project assessment, and it is all too easy to put your slim project report away in a drawer. You may resolve that nobody, not even a doting mother, will read it again. This is a very negative attitude to adopt towards something that has taken up a large slice of your life during the past year. Instead your project report should be regarded as an asset.

Will you be attending any job interviews in the near future, or are you seeking a research post at another university? You should take your report to these interviews since there may be an opportunity to produce it as evidence of your abilities. These opportunities are particularly likely to occur if your interview is informal and your interviewer is able to talk to you alone for any length of time.

Industrialists will welcome evidence that you are able to write a report. They will be grateful that they can teach you more productive things than report writing, even though they set great store by progress reports. Indeed, the experience you have gained may make your reports stand out and bring you to the attention of your new overlords much more rapidly than might otherwise have been the case.

Similarly another university department will look more favourably upon a candidate who can provide evidence of successfully completing an undergraduate project. It is even possible that you have chosen to apply for a research post in the same field as the project which fired your enthusiasm for research. More broadly, your project may have made you decide on a career in research rather than the service industries.

Many Masters degrees now also involve some project work. You will soon realize that the tricks you learnt completing your first project can easily be applied to the next, and that the second project will be much easier than the first. With a little refinement many of the lessons you learnt will also be useful when writing your PhD thesis.

Your report and the few overhead projector transparencies left from your lecture may be your only tangible reminders of your project.

However, you will continue to draw benefit from the intangible aspects of your project for many years to come.

You should have learnt to use the library more effectively after preparing your project report. Your project may also have made you aware of the potential of the primary literature. This will allow you to improve your lecture notes by investigating important topics in more detail and incorporating some recent advances and applications. You will find it is a surprisingly effective method of revision to write out more comprehensive and up-to-date lecture notes. By using suitable original examples to illustrate your examination answers you must improve your standing in the eyes of the examiner. Your better library skills will improve your performance in tutorials and the benefit you gain from them.

It is to be hoped that one of the most important things you learnt while doing your project was how to use your time effectively. Making good use of every little moment will be of paramount importance in the rup up to finals. Later you may have the opportunity to organize your own section in accordance with the organizational skills you first learnt when organizing your project schedule.

When writing your report you learnt how to rank and organize topics. Surely you can do this again when answering questions in your final examinations? If nothing else, the pressure of completing your project on time will have prepared you for the pressure of the final examinations.

While a successful project must increase your self confidence, even a less successful project can provide clues to areas of weakness. When revising for finals, remember that you are not really working if you only revise the things you know. Real progress is made by improving your performance in substandard areas. One word of warning – if you should find an examination question which asks about your project topic do not spend the entire examination writing about it. A perfect answer will only gain the maximum marks for one question. Equally, do not attempt to pervert other questions into questions about your project. This is only marginally less reprehensible than trying to pervert questions to correspond with last night's revision.

It may be some time before you can develop the minor managerial skills you learnt when you employed a typist and worked together as a team. However, you will frequently have occasion to remember and apply what you learnt in that exercise. This may be later in your career or even in your private life when you engage an architect to propose alterations to your mansion.

It will also be a long time before you are likely to address an audience as distinguished as that which attended your project lecture. Public speaking before lesser audiences should now hold no terrors for you. Once you have reached the stage when you cannot truthfully use the opening words 'Unaccustomed as I am . . .' you will become quite blasé about the prospect of speaking in public.

You should be able to look back on your project with pride and find many opportunities to apply the knowledge you have gained. Perhaps one day, far in the future, when you are congratulated on a good performance in some sphere you will be able to reply,

'It was nothing really – I learnt to do that when I was working on my student project in chemistry.'

Index